Privacy and Identity Protection

Privacy and Identity Protection

Information Security: Cyberattacks, Data Breaches and Security Controls
Paul Scholz (Editor)
2019. ISBN: 978-1-53615-880-9 (Hardcover)
2019. ISBN: 978-1-53615-881-6 (eBook)

Consumer Protection: Recalls, Data Security and Congressional Issues
Ralf Schaefer (Editor)
2019. ISBN: 978-1-53615-876-2 (Hardcover)
2019. ISBN: 978-1-53615-877-9 (eBook)

Government Reports on Information Security and Technology for March 2019
Mathias Schweitzer (Editor)
2019. ISBN: 978-1-53615-848-9 (Softcover)
2019. ISBN: 978-1-53615-849-6 (eBook)

Drones in the U.S.: Privacy Issues and Regulatory Considerations
Sophia Barrett (Editor)
2016. ISBN: 978-1-63484-918-0 (Softcover)
2016. ISBN: 978-1-63484-919-7 (eBook)

Federal Cybersecurity: Identification and Mitigation Efforts of Sector-Specific Agencies
Jeffery H. Matthews (Editor)
2016. ISBN: 978-1-63485-310-1 (Softcover)
2016. ISBN: 978-1-63485-311-8 (eBook)

More information about this series can be found at
https://novapublishers.com/product-category/series/privacy-and-identity-protection/

Damon Solis
Editor

Guidelines for Digital Identity Verification

Copyright © 2023 by Nova Science Publishers, Inc.

All rights reserved. No part of this book may be reproduced, stored in a retrieval system or transmitted in any form or by any means: electronic, electrostatic, magnetic, tape, mechanical photocopying, recording or otherwise without the written permission of the Publisher.

We have partnered with Copyright Clearance Center to make it easy for you to obtain permissions to reuse content from this publication. Please visit copyright.com and search by Title, ISBN, or ISSN.

For further questions about using the service on copyright.com, please contact:

	Copyright Clearance Center	
Phone: +1-(978) 750-8400	Fax: +1-(978) 750-4470	E-mail: info@copyright.com

NOTICE TO THE READER

The Publisher has taken reasonable care in the preparation of this book but makes no expressed or implied warranty of any kind and assumes no responsibility for any errors or omissions. No liability is assumed for incidental or consequential damages in connection with or arising out of information contained in this book. The Publisher shall not be liable for any special, consequential, or exemplary damages resulting, in whole or in part, from the readers' use of, or reliance upon, this material. Any parts of this book based on government reports are so indicated and copyright is claimed for those parts to the extent applicable to compilations of such works.

Independent verification should be sought for any data, advice or recommendations contained in this book. In addition, no responsibility is assumed by the Publisher for any injury and/or damage to persons or property arising from any methods, products, instructions, ideas or otherwise contained in this publication.

This publication is designed to provide accurate and authoritative information with regards to the subject matter covered herein. It is sold with the clear understanding that the Publisher is not engaged in rendering legal or any other professional services. If legal or any other expert assistance is required, the services of a competent person should be sought. FROM A DECLARATION OF PARTICIPANTS JOINTLY ADOPTED BY A COMMITTEE OF THE AMERICAN BAR ASSOCIATION AND A COMMITTEE OF PUBLISHERS.

Library of Congress Cataloging-in-Publication Data

ISBN: 979-8-88697-838-4

Published by Nova Science Publishers, Inc. † New York

Contents

Preface vii

Chapter 1   **Derived Personal Identity Verification (PIV) Credentials** 1
William Newhouse, Michael Bartock,
Jeffrey Cichonski, Hildegard Ferraiolo,
Murugiah Souppaya, Christopher Brown,
Spike E. Dog, Susan Prince and Julian Sexton

Chapter 2   **Digital Identity Guidelines: Enrollment and Identity Proofing** 193
Paul A. Grassi, James L. Fenton,
Naomi B. Lefkovitz, Jamie M. Danker,
Yee-Yin Choong, Kristen K. Greene and
Mary F. Theofanos

Index 237

Preface

Misuse of identity, especially through stolen passwords, is a primary source for cyber breaches. Enabling stronger processes to recognize a user's identity is a key component to securing an organization's information systems. Homeland Security Presidential Directive-12 (HSPD-12) mandated deployment of a common identity credential in 2004, which resulted in Personal Identity Verification (PIV) Cards and their supporting infrastructure. The goal was to eliminate wide variations in the quality and security of authentication mechanisms used across federal agencies as reported in Chapter 1. Chapter 2 provides requirements for enrollment and identity proofing of applicants that wish to gain access to resources at each Identity Assurance Level (IAL). The requirements detail the acceptability, validation, and verification of identity evidence that will be presented by a subscriber to support their claim of identity.

Chapter 1

Derived Personal Identity Verification (PIV) Credentials[*]

William Newhouse
Michael Bartock
Jeffrey Cichonski
Hildegard Ferraiolo
Murugiah Souppaya
Christopher Brown
Spike E. Dog
Susan Prince
and Julian Sexton

Volume A: Executive Summary

Executive Summary

- Misuse of identity, especially through stolen passwords, is a primary source for cyber breaches. Enabling stronger processes to recognize a user's identity is a key component to securing an organization's information systems.
- Access to federal information systems relies on strong authentication of the user with a Personal Identity Verification (PIV) Card. This

---

[*] This is an edited, reformatted and augmented version of NIST Special Publication 1800-12, dated August 2019.

In: Guidelines for Digital Identity Verification
Editor: Damon Solis
ISBN: 979-8-88697-838-4
© 2023 Nova Science Publishers, Inc.

"smart card" contains identifying information about the user that enables stronger authentication to federal facilities, information systems, and applications.
- Today, access to information systems is increasingly from mobile phones, tablets, and some laptops that lack an integrated smart card reader found in older, stationary computing devices, forcing organizations to have separate authentication processes for these devices.
- Derived PIV Credentials (DPCs) leverage identity proofing and vetting results of current and valid credentials used in PIV Cards for issuing credentials that are securely stored on devices without PIV Card readers.
- The National Cybersecurity Center of Excellence (NCCoE) at the National Institute of Standards and Technology (NIST) built a laboratory environment to explore development of a security architecture that uses commercially available technology to manage the life cycle of DPCs.
- This NIST Cybersecurity Practice Guide demonstrates how organizations can provide multifactor authentication for users to access PIV-enabled websites from mobile devices that lack PIV Card readers.

Challenge

In accordance with Homeland Security Presidential Directive 12, the PIV standard was created to enhance national security by establishing a set of common authentication mechanisms that provide logical access to federal systems on PIV-Compatible (PIV-C) desktop and laptop computers. With the federal government's increased reliance on mobile computing devices that cannot accommodate PIV Card readers, the mandate to use PIV has created the need to derive credentials for use in mobile devices in a manner that enforces the same security policies established for the life-cycle credentials in a PIV Card.

NIST has published guidance on DPCs, including a proof-of-concept research paper. Expanding upon this work, the NCCoE used common mobile devices available in the market today to demonstrate the use of DPCs in a manner that meets existing security policies. The flexibility of the technologies that support PIV, along with a growing understanding of the value of strong digital authentication practices, has resulted in an ecosystem of vendors able to provide digital authentication solutions with the capacity to adhere to the policies outlined in NIST guidance for DPCs. These mobile PIV standards-based credentials carry the designation of Derived PIV.

With experts from the federal sector and technology collaborators who provided the requisite equipment and services, we developed representative use-case scenarios to describe user authentication security challenges based on normal day-to-day business operations. The use cases include issuance, maintenance, and termination of the DPC.

Solution

The NCCoE has developed two DPC example solutions that demonstrate how DPCs can be added to mobile devices to enable multifactor authentication to information technology (IT) systems while meeting policy guidelines. The NCCoE DPC Project is aimed primarily at the federal sector. Private-sector organizations can leverage these solutions to extend identity proofing and vetting of a primary identity credential to credentials for mobile device users in the commercial sector who use smart-card-based credentials or other means of authenticating identity.

To that end, the example solutions are based on standards and best practices, and derive from a simple scenario that forms the basis of an architecture tailored to the public or private sector or both.

The NCCoE sought existing technologies that provided the following capabilities:

- Authenticate users of mobile devices by using secure cryptographic authentication exchanges
- Provide a feasible security platform based on Federal Digital Identity Guidelines
- Leverage a Public Key Infrastructure (PKI) using mobile devices provisioned with credentials derived from and managed like the credentials on a PIV Card
- Support operations in PIV, PIV-Interoperable, and PIV-C environments

- Provide logical access to remote resources hosted in either a data center or the cloud

While the NCCoE used a suite of commercial products to address this challenge, this guide does not endorse these particular products, nor does it guarantee compliance with any regulatory initiatives. Your organization's information security experts should identify the products that will best integrate with your existing tools and IT system infrastructure. Your organization can adopt this solution or one that adheres to these guidelines in whole, or you can use this guide as a starting point for tailoring and implementing parts of a solution.

Benefits

The NCCoE's practice guide to *Derived Personal Identity Verification (PIV) Credentials* can help your organization:

- Extend authentication measures reliably to devices without having to purchase external smart-card readers
- Allow users to access the information that they need, using the devices that they want to use
- Meet authentication standards requirements for protected websites and information across all devices, both traditional and mobile
- Manage the DPCs centrally through an Enterprise Mobility Management system, reducing integration efforts and associated costs
- Leverage the Federal PKI Shared Service Provider Program, enabling cost savings associated with a contractor-provided service

Volume B: Approach, Architecture, and Security Characteristics

Abstract

Federal Information Processing Standards (FIPS) Publication 201-2, "Personal Identity Verification (PIV) of Federal Employees and Contractors," establishes a standard for a PIV system based on secure and reliable forms of identity credentials issued by the federal government to its employees and contractors. These credentials are intended to authenticate individuals to federally controlled facilities, information systems, and applications as part of access management. In 2005, when FIPS 201 was published, authentication of individuals was geared toward traditional computing devices (i.e., desktop and laptop computers) where the PIV Card provides common multifactor authentication mechanisms through integrated or external smart card readers, where available. With the emergence of computing devices, such as tablets, hybrid computers, and, in particular, mobile devices, the use of PIV Cards has proved to be challenging. Mobile devices lack the integrated smart card readers found in laptop and desktop computers and require separate card readers attached to devices to provide authentication services. To extend the value of PIV systems into mobile devices that do not have PIV Card readers, NIST developed technical guidelines on the implementation and life cycle of identity credentials that are issued by federal departments and agencies to individuals who possess and prove control over a valid PIV Card. These NIST guidelines, published in 2014, describe Derived PIV Credentials (DPCs) that leverage identity proofing and vetting results of current and valid PIV credentials.

To demonstrate the DPC guidelines, the NCCoE at NIST built two security architectures by using commercial technology to enable issuance of a Derived PIV Credential to mobile devices that use Federal Identity Credentialing and Access Management shared services. One option uses a software-only solution while the other leverages hardware built into many computing devices used today.

This project resulted in a freely available NIST Cybersecurity Practice Guide that demonstrates how an organization can continue to provide multifactor authentication for users with a mobile device that leverages the strengths of the PIV standard. Although this project is aimed primarily at the federal sector's needs, it is also relevant to mobile device users with smart card-based credentials in the private sector.

Keywords: cybersecurity, Derived PIV Credential (DPC), Enterprise Mobility Management (EMM), identity, mobile device, mobile threat, multifactor authentication, personal identity verification, PIV Card, smart card

1. Summary

Homeland Security Presidential Directive-12 (HSPD-12) [1] mandated deployment of a common identity credential in 2004, which resulted in

Personal Identity Verification (PIV) Cards and their supporting infrastructure. The goal was to eliminate wide variations in the quality and security of authentication mechanisms used across federal agencies. The mandate called for a common identification standard to promote interoperable authentication mechanisms at graduated levels of security based on the environment and the sensitivity of data. In response, Federal Information Processing Standards (FIPS) 201 specified a common set of credentials in a smart card form factor [2] called a PIV Card. PIV Cards are now used government-wide as a primary credential for federal employees and contractors. PIV Cards enhance security by using a standard issuance process by which agencies perform identity proofing and background checks. PIV Cards provide multifactor authentication as part of both physical and logical access management to government facilities and federal information systems.

When FIPS 201 was published, logical access was geared toward desktop and laptop computers, which enabled multifactor authentication via a PIV Card through integrated or connected card readers. The increased use of mobile phones and tablets as part of logical access makes leveraging the PIV credential challenging. Mobile phones and tablets lack integrated smart card readers and would require the user to attach a separate card reader to authenticate with their PIV Card. To address this challenge, Derived PIV Credentials (DPCs) were introduced to extend the value of the PIV standard into today's mobile environment. The issuance of a DPC is based on a user's proof of possession of a valid PIV Card, thereby leveraging identity proofing and background checks that have already been completed, to issue a new set of credentials for use on a mobile device. A mobile device that contains the user's DPC can authenticate to websites and portals that use verification of PIV credentials for access.

The National Cybersecurity Center of Excellence (NCCoE) Cybersecurity Practice Guide *Derived Personal Identity Verification (PIV) Credentials* demonstrates how Derived PIV Credentials can be issued to PIV Cardholders' mobile devices by using commercial off-the-shelf products and by leveraging the PIV standard for remote authentication to information technology (IT) systems. The NCCoE's Derived PIV Credentials Project is aimed primarily at the federal sector. However, private-sector organizations can leverage these solutions to extend identity proofing and vetting of a primary identity credential to credentials for mobile device users in the commercial sector who use smart card-based credentials or other means of authenticating identity. To that end, the example implementations in this practice guide work from a simple scenario that forms the basis of an architecture tailored to the public and private sectors.

Starting with the National Institute of Standards and Technology (NIST) Cybersecurity Framework [3], the Risk Management Framework (RMF) [4], and security controls from NIST Special Publication (SP) 800-53 [5], this document also references NIST SP 800-157, *Guidelines for Derived Personal Identity Verification (PIV) Credentials* [6]; NIST SP 800-63-3, *Digital Identity Guidelines* [7]; FIPS 201-2, *Personal Identity Verification (PIV) of Federal Employees and Contractors* [2]; Internet Engineering Task Force (IETF) Request for Comments (RFC) 4210; NIST SP 800-181, *National Initiative for Cybersecurity Education (NICE) Cybersecurity Workforce Framework* [8]; and NIST's *Mobile Threat Catalogue* [9].

We designed the example implementations and architectures to incorporate standards-based, commercially available products. The solutions can be used by any organization deploying DPCs and that is willing to perform its own risk assessment and is ready to implement controls based on the organization's risk posture.

Section 1: Summary presents the challenge addressed in this volume (Volume B: *Approach, Architecture, and Security Characteristics*). The example implementations address the challenge and benefits of DPC solutions. The summary also explains how to provide feedback on this guide.

Section 2: How to Use This Guide explains how business decision makers, program managers, IT professionals (e.g., systems administrators), and other stakeholders who will be responsible for procuring, designing, implementing, and managing deployments of DPCs for mobile devices might use each volume of the guide.

Section 3: Approach offers a detailed treatment of the scope of the project, describes the assumptions on which the security platform development was based, explains the risk assessment that informed platform development, and provides an overview of the technologies and components that industry collaborators gave us to enable platform development.

Section 4: Architecture describes the functional architecture of our example solution, including Cybersecurity Framework Functions supported by each component that our collaborators contributed.

Section 5: Security Characteristic Analysis provides details about the tools and techniques we used to perform risk assessments pertaining to DPCs. It also summarizes the test sequences we employed to demonstrate security platform services, the Cybersecurity Framework Functions to which each test sequence is relevant, and NIST SP 800-157 [6] controls that applied to the functions being demonstrated.

Section 6: Future Build Considerations is a brief treatment of other applications that NIST and the NCCoE might explore in the future to further support DPCs.

The appendixes provide a list of acronyms, references, key definitions, and a requirements table derived from NIST Internal Report 8055 [10].

1.1. Challenge

Mobile phones and tablets that lack card readers are being increasingly deployed by federal agencies. Additionally, laptop personal computers without built-in card readers are increasingly being used by PIV users in mobile situations away from their desktop environments. These mobile devices are not able to use the PIV Card directly to leverage the security and control characteristics of the FIPS 201-2 PIV system standard.

Implementing DPCs in mobile phones and tablets is challenging due to the wide array of mobile device models and platforms, which offer different ways to store the credentials and different key stores, including application containers (i.e., software containers) in credential management systems (CMS) and removable storage options (i.e., Universal Serial Bus [USB] and micro Secure Digital [microSD] cards). This is further complicated by the rapid update cycles of proprietary mobile operating systems with which developers must keep pace.

Additionally, the guidelines in NIST SP 800-157 for managing the Derived PIV Authentication certificate throughout its life cycle (issuance and maintenance) and its interactions with the PIV Card life cycle present challenges to the implementer such as managing integration efforts between DPC and PIV Card issuing systems. Further, the DPC implementers must acquire the Derived PIV Authentication certificates from approved public key infrastructure (PKI) service providers, necessitating integration with these service providers.

Enterprise Mobility Management (EMM) solutions, which implement the mobile security policy requirements of an organization, must also be considered when implementing DPCs. Many federal agencies use EMM solutions to secure sensitive enterprise data and provide customizable workflows to manage the life cycle of the mobile device. The alignment of the mobile device life cycle and DPC life-cycle steps can prove challenging to agencies that wish to eliminate friction for the end user.

1.2. Solution

This NIST Cybersecurity Practice Guide demonstrates how commercially available technologies can meet an organization's need to issue multifactor credentials to mobile devices for authenticating to IT systems in operational environments.

We built an environment that resembles an enterprise network by using commonplace components such as identity repositories, supporting certificate authorities, and web servers. Next, products and capabilities were identified that, when linked together, provide two example implementations demonstrating life-cycle guidelines outlined in NIST SP 800-157 [6]. These example implementations leverage cloud services where possible through a software as a service (SaaS) component. The federal government encourages the use of SaaS or shared service providers (SSPs) [11] that operate under federal policy, such as certificate authorities operating in accordance with policy developed by the Federal PKI Policy Authority. The security controls for these SSPs are periodically assessed, allowing the organization to focus on its primary mission and avoid the costs associated with ongoing maintenance of these systems.

One of our example implementations includes integration of an EMM and a DPC solution. EMMs are useful in applying NIST SP 800-157 life-cycle guidelines by integrating an organization's mobile device issuance process with DPC issuance. EMMs can also assist with terminating the DPC by remotely destroying the EMM's software container.

Finally, this practice guide documents two methods of securely storing the DPCs on a device, demonstrating the flexibility of NIST SP 800-157 guidance. One option uses a software-only solution while the other leverages hardware built into many computing devices used today.

The NCCoE developed a collaborative team uniquely qualified to create two example implementations of DPCs. We partnered with the subject matter experts who wrote NIST SP 800-157 to better understand its requirements and to ensure that the integrations of commercial products were within the document's guidelines.

1.3. Benefits

For an organization that is planning and looking for solutions to issue DPCs to its workforce, the example implementations described in this guide will help the organization navigate through the various options by:

- Providing visibility into how the different device vendors and CMS vendors are implementing solutions for storing the credentials
- Demonstrating the use of managed services for the DPC issuance and life-cycle management
- Demonstrating integration with an EMM solution

2. How to Use This Guide

This NIST Cybersecurity Practice Guide demonstrate standards-based reference designs and provides users with the information they need to replicate the DPC example implementations. These reference designs are modular and can be deployed in whole or in part.

This guide contains three volumes:

- NIST SP 1800-12A: *Executive Summary*
- NIST SP 1800-12B: *Approach, Architecture, and Security Characteristics* – what we built and why (you are here)
- NIST SP 1800-12C: *How-To Guides* – instructions for building the example solutions

Depending on your role in your organization, you might use this guide in different ways:

Business decision makers, including chief security and technology officers, will be interested in the *Executive Summary,* NIST SP 1800-12A, which describes the following topics:

- Challenges that enterprises face in issuing strong multifactor credentials to mobile devices
- The example solutions built at the NCCoE
- Benefits of adopting the example solutions

Technology or security program managers who are concerned with how to identify, understand, assess, and mitigate risk will be interested in this part of the guide, NIST SP 1800-12B, which describes what we did and why.

The following sections will be of particular interest:

- Section 3.5.3, Risk, provides a description of the risk analysis we performed
- Section 3.5.4, Security Control Map, maps the security characteristics of the example solutions to cybersecurity standards and best practices

You might share the *Executive Summary,* NIST SP 1800-12A, with your leadership team members to help them understand the importance of adopting a standards-based DPC solution.

IT professionals who want to implement an approach like this will find the whole practice guide useful. You can use the How-To portion of the guide, NIST SP 1800-12C, to replicate all or parts of the builds created in our lab. The how-to portion of the guide provides specific product installation, configuration, and integration instructions for implementing the example solutions. We do not re-create the product manufacturers' documentation, which is generally widely available. Rather, we show how we incorporated the products together in our environment to create the example solutions.

This guide assumes that IT professionals have experience implementing security products within the enterprise. While we have used a suite of commercial products to address this challenge, this guide does not endorse these particular products. Your organization can adopt either solution or one that adheres to these guidelines in whole, or you can use this guide as a starting point for tailoring and implementing parts of the DPC example solutions. Your organization's security experts should identify the products that will best integrate with your existing tools and IT system infrastructure. We hope that you will seek products that are congruent with applicable standards and best practices. Section 3.6, Technologies, lists the products we used and maps them to the cybersecurity controls provided by the reference solutions.

3. Approach

To develop our example solutions, the Derived PIV Credentials Project team followed an approach common to projects across the NCCoE. First, a project description was published on the website followed by a Federal Register Notice (FRN) [12]. In response to the FRN, several vendors expressed interest in helping the NCCoE build example solutions. Technology companies with relevant products then signed a Cooperative Research and Development Agreement (CRADA) with the NCCoE for the project. After the CRADAs were signed, the NCCoE sponsored a kickoff meeting for the project team, collaborating vendors, and other members of the Derived PIV Credentials Community of Interest (COI).

During the kickoff, we gathered requirements and lessons learned from project stakeholders; this helped establish objectives for our example implementations. In addition to input from collaborators and COI members, we performed a risk assessment during the architecture design phase and on our final DPC example implementations. This assessment included risk factors to both the functions of the system (e.g., DPC issuance or revocation) and to its parts, such as the mobile devices into which a DPC would be provisioned.

The Derived PIV Credentials Project used a phased approach that took direct advantage of previous work by NIST in this area. NIST Internal Report 8055 [10], *Derived Personal Identity Verification (PIV) Credentials (DPC) Proof of Concept Research*, presents a scheme for provisioning a DPC to an organization-managed mobile device. This project applied these technologies as a starting point, then sought to expand on the DPC ecosystem to provide greater diversity across mobile device models, platforms, authenticators, Derived PIV Credential Management Systems (DCMSes), and EMM products.

3.1. Audience

This guide is intended for IT and security managers and for system administrators responsible for deploying secure solutions to support the evolving mobile ecosystem of an organization. With mobile devices rapidly becoming the computing resources of choice within many organizations, there is growing pressure on IT personnel to ensure that the organization has best practices in place for securely accessing the organization's assets when using these devices. As mentioned previously, DPC solutions are still evolving, and no one solution will fit all organizations.

This guide aims to help IT personnel understand the options, capabilities, and limitations of the solutions available in the market today and to deploy the solutions that fit organizational needs.

3.2. Scope

The scope of NIST SP 800-157, *Guidelines for Derived Personal Identity Verification (PIV) Credentials* [6], is to provide PIV-enabled authentication services on the mobile device to authenticate the credential holder to remote systems. The current phase of the Derived PIV Credentials Project and this practice guide focus on only a portion of NIST SP 800-157—the life-cycle activities. Specifically, we evaluated the example solutions against the requirements related to initial issuance, maintenance, and termination of DPCs.

For the proof-of-concept research documented in NIST Internal Report 8055 [10], NIST used a single-vendor CMS product to demonstrate DPC life-cycle management. The device platforms documented in NIST Internal Report 8055 were Windows, Android, and iOS. The CMS vendor's software key store implementation for Android and iOS devices was used for the research effort, and Microsoft's Virtual Smart Card implementation was used for the Windows platform. For the first phase of the NCCoE project, we documented an additional CMS product to demonstrate DPC life-cycle management.

Only Derived PIV Authentication certificates that support remote issuance are addressed in this practice guide. To support a higher level of assurance, we would need to address additional in-person life-cycle requirements that were deemed out of scope for this project. Section 6 offers some future build considerations.

This project integrates an EMM component into one of our documented example implementations. EMMs are essential to securing mobile end points; however, this project defers to the Mobile Device Security: Corporate-Owned Personally-Enabled Project at the NCCoE for specific security control recommendations. Section 3.5, Risk Assessment, includes threats specific to DPCs issued to authenticators contained within mobile devices. For privacy considerations as they pertain to risk, readers of this publication are encouraged to review the NIST SP 800-63-3 discussion on privacy.

PIV Card life-cycle management is not within the scope of the project. However, tests were conducted on test PIV credentials prior to issuing DPCs and to validate that a DCMS performs all required checks of a DPC subscriber's PIV Card and associated PIV Authentication certificate per NIST SP 800-157.

3.3. Relationship to NIST SP 800-63-3

The NIST SP 800-63-3 series of documents published in June 2017 retired the level of assurance (LOA) concept and in its place introduced Identity Assurance Level (IAL), Authenticator Assurance Level (AAL), and Federation Assurance Level components to assist in risk management decisions. At the time of this writing, FIPS 201-2 [2] and NIST SP 800-157 refer to the earlier LOA terminology for electronic authentications. We have mapped the authenticators used in this project to an AAL in Section 5.4. IAL is not applicable in the context of DPC because deriving identity is accomplished by proving possession and successful authentication of an authenticator (on the PIV Card) that is already bound to the original, proofed digital identity [7].

3.4. Assumptions

To implement this practice guide, readers should have a thorough understanding of NIST SP 800-157 and other supporting standards and guidelines. In addition, readers should be aware that the example implementations presented have the following assumptions:

- An implementer who works for a U.S. federal agency will be complying with FIPS 201-2, *Personal Identity Verification (PIV) of Federal Employees and Contractors* [2].
- The mobile devices in an organization's DPC solution are organization-provided [13], and the organization centrally manages them with security policies and controls.

3.4.1. Modularity

Specific assumptions on modularity are based on one of the NCCoE core operating tenets: that organizations already have the PIV Card issuance solution and the associated PKI services in place. We make no further assumptions regarding how the solutions have been deployed; they may combine on-premises operations, cloud deployments, and managed services. Instead, we intend this guide to offer options for adding the DPC life-cycle management solution into a diverse set of existing deployments.

3.4.2. Security

A second assumption is that adopters of our example implementations have already invested in the security of the organization's network and IT systems. We assume that the existing PIV CMS is implemented in a manner consistent with the Cybersecurity Framework and the guidelines presented in NIST SP 800-63-3. Further, we assume that the security features of each product integrated into our example implementations will perform as described by the respective product vendor.

3.4.3. Existing Infrastructure

This guide may help in designing an entirely new infrastructure. However, it is geared toward organizations with an established infrastructure, as that represents the largest portion of readers. Federal agencies and other organizations that are mature enough to implement DPCs are likely to have some combination of the capabilities described in the example implementations, such as solutions to manage mobile devices. Before applying any measures addressed in this practice guide, we recommend reviewing and testing them for applicability to the existing environment. No two organizations are the same, and the impact of applying security controls will differ.

3.4.4. Architecture Components

We have chosen to align the components, where possible, used in this project to the architectural components described in the Federal Identity, Credential, and Access Management (FICAM) program, which helps federal agencies enable access to systems and facilities. The FICAM architecture is the federal government's approach for designing, planning for, and implementing identity, credential, and access management (ICAM). Figure 3-1 presents a view of the different ICAM solutions, applications, and software components that work together to run a functional, secure ICAM program.

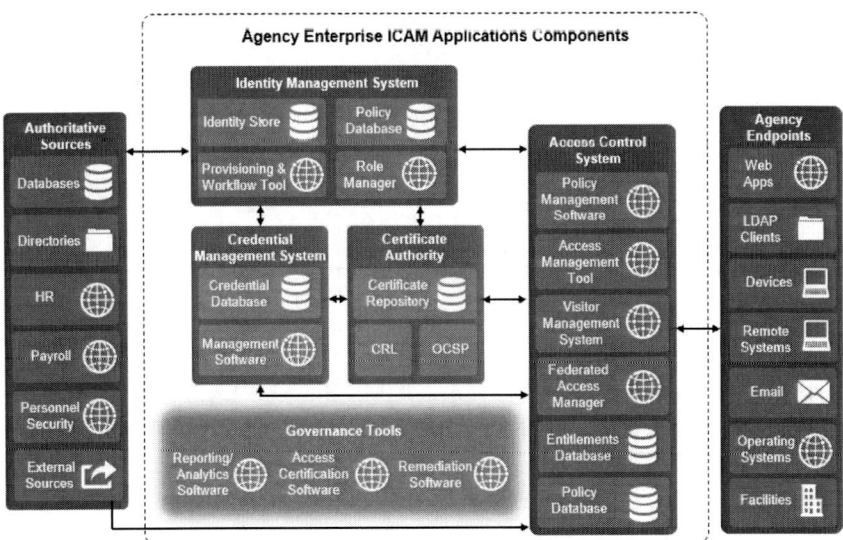

Figure 3-1. Federal ICAM enterprise architecture.

3.4.4.1. Credential Management System

A CMS contains management software and is central to executing the life-cycle operations, typically sponsorship, registration, issuance, maintenance, and termination of authentication credentials. Usually, information related to the life-cycle operations is stored within a database. In our architecture, we depict two types of CMSes: PIV and Derived PIV. The PIV CMS is responsible for enforcing life-cycle activities in accordance with FIPS 201-2, and the DCMS enforces the life-cycle activities in accordance with NIST SP 800-157. Readers will need to be familiar with the PIV standard [2] and associated guidelines before implementing a DPC solution.

3.4.4.2. Public Key Infrastructure

The PKI (also referred to as the certificate authority or certification authority [CA]) issues, maintains, and revokes digital certificates. References to PKI in this document will focus only on digital certificates stored on PIV Cards and mobile devices. The PKI can be operated as part of an on-premises infrastructure and is also offered as a managed service. PIV CMS service providers partner with PKI service providers for issuing the digital certificates that are provisioned to the PIV Card and the mobile device. Typically, certificate status services such as a certificate revocation list (CRL) repository and online certificate status protocol (OCSP) services are also offered by PKIs.

3.4.4.3. Enterprise Mobility Management

An EMM is typically used by organizations to provide security services commonly needed for security management of mobile devices such as remote device wiping, device encryption enforcement, and application restrictions. An EMM within the DPC context enforces the use of secure container solutions and eases the issuance process of the DPC. For example, a DPC enrollment can be combined with enrollment of a device with an EMM (assuming PIV Card issuance and activation have been completed before mobile device enrollment). This reduces the complexity of the enrollment process for the DPC applicant.

A tight integration between the DCMS and the EMM also potentially reduces maintenance life-cycle tasks of the DPC. For instance, if a mobile device is lost by the DPC subscriber, an EMM administrator initiates revocation of the Derived PIV Authentication certificate and destroys the software container that stores the DPC.

3.4.4.4. Mobile Device

For the purposes of this publication, the term *mobile device* refers to a device that stores the DPC. Typically, this is a device such as a smartphone or a tablet running a rich operating system, as defined in NIST SP 800-53 Revision 4, *Security and Privacy Controls for Federal Information Systems and Organizations:*

> A portable computing device that: (i) has a small form factor such that it can easily be carried by a single individual; (ii) is designed to operate without a physical connection (e.g., wirelessly transmit or receive information); (iii) possesses local, non-removable or removable data storage; and (iv) includes a self-contained power source. Mobile devices may also include voice communication capabilities, on-board sensors that allow the devices to capture information, and/or built-in features for synchronizing local data with remote locations. Examples include smart phones, tablets, and E-readers.

In this publication, we use only mobile devices as the "devices" shown in Figure 3-1. In one scenario, we use a hybrid device, a laptop that does not have a built-in smart card reader but that can leverage PIV Card capabilities in a hardware-enhanced container.

3.4.4.5. Authenticator

This publication uses the definition from NIST SP 800-63-3B:

> Something the claimant possesses and controls (typically a cryptographic module or password) that is used to authenticate the claimant's identity.

The authenticator in the context of DPCs is a cryptographic module, referred to in NIST SP 800-157 as a cryptographic token.

3.5. Risk Assessment

NIST SP 800-30 Revision 1, *Guide for Conducting Risk Assessments,* states that risk is "a measure of the extent to which an entity is threatened by a potential circumstance or event, and typically a function of (i) the adverse impacts that would arise if the circumstance or event occurs; and (ii) the likelihood of occurrence." The guide further defines risk assessment as "the process of identifying, estimating, and prioritizing risks to organizational operations (including mission, functions, image, reputation), organizational assets, individuals, other organizations, and the Nation, resulting from the operation of an information system. Part of risk management incorporates threat and vulnerability analyses, and considers mitigations provided by security controls planned or in place."

The NCCoE recommends that any discussion of risk management, particularly at the enterprise level, begins with a comprehensive review of NIST SP 800-37 Revision 2, *Risk Management Framework for Information Systems and Organizations* [4]—material that is available to the public. The Risk Management Framework (RMF) guidance, as a whole, proved to be invaluable in giving us a baseline to assess risks, from which we developed the project, the security characteristics of the builds, and this guide.

This section discusses risk from two perspectives. First, we review the risk mitigation that a DPC system is meant to address in terms of Cybersecurity Framework Functions. Next, we address the residual risk of an implemented DPC system.

Allowing users access to services from a mobile device leads to a more efficient and effective workforce. There are risks, however, and the security objectives [13] of confidentiality, integrity, and availability need to be maintained on the mobile end point. The threats to weak single-factor authentication mechanisms, such as passwords, are well documented by industry [14] and government [9]. Further, the 2017 Department of Homeland Security (DHS) *Study on Mobile Device Security* [15] found the failure to use strong multifactor authentication mechanisms to protect critical cloud services to be a gap in the defense of current mobile devices. This finding is underscored by the move of organizations to cloud services that provide critical services such as email and calendaring. The DHS study recommends enhancing mobile Federal Information Security Modernization Act metrics for authentication methods.

A DPC solution is part of an overall mobile security architecture that protects enterprise data by using strong multifactor authentication to access remote resources. A DPC solution also supplements a basic centralized enterprise mobility security policy, as NIST Special Publication 800-123, *Guidelines for Managing the Security of Mobile Devices in the Enterprise,* recommends. The publication further recommends that organizations design and acquire one or more solutions that collectively mitigate current workforce mobile device security risk. For an in-depth discussion on digital identity risk management, we encourage review of Section 3.5.1, which presents a list of possible identity risks and how they are addressed by DPCs, based on NIST SP 800-63-3 guidelines related to digital identity risk. An organization can apply the guidelines while executing all relevant Cybersecurity Framework and RMF life-cycle phases [7].

Federal cybersecurity risk management has taken on increased emphasis with release of the Presidential Executive Order on Strengthening the Cybersecurity of Federal Networks and Critical Infrastructure [16]. In this memo, the president directs each agency head to use NIST's *Framework for Improving Critical Infrastructure Cybersecurity*, "or any successor document, to manage the agency's cybersecurity risk."

In response, NIST released NIST Internal Report 8170, *The Cybersecurity Framework: Implementation Guidance for Federal Agencies* [17]. This NIST Internal Report guides agencies on how the Cybersecurity Framework can be used to augment current NIST security and privacy risk management publications.

We recommend that organizations, especially federal agencies that implement a DCMS, follow the recommendations presented in NIST Internal Report 8170. For instance, the framework's Example 1— Integrate Enterprise and Cybersecurity Risk Management—recommends using the five cybersecurity Functions (Identify, Protect, Detect, Respond, and Recover) to organize cybersecurity risk management activities at the highest level. Section 3.5.4 presents a list of possible functions that a DPC implementation can address. We recommend that this information be used when communicating risk throughout an organization.

3.5.1. Threats

NIST SP 800-63-3 provides a general identity framework by incorporating authenticators, credentials, and assertions into a digital system [7]. Included in the publication are threat analyses in the areas of authenticator and life-cycle threats. Table 3-1 and Table 3-2 use these threats as a basis for a discussion of threats applicable to a DPC system.

Table 3-1. Enrollment and issuance threats

Activity	Threat/Attack	Example	Applicability to DPC
Enrollment	Falsified identity proofing evidence	An applicant attempts to use a forged PIV Card to obtain a DPC.	PKI-AUTH check by DCMS rejects forged PIV Card (e.g., determines that the certificates were not issued by a trusted CA or user cannot prove control of the private key corresponding to the certificate).

Table 3-1. (Continued)

Activity	Threat/Attack	Example	Applicability to DPC
	Fraudulent use of another's identity	An applicant attempts to use a PIV Card associated with a different individual to obtain a DPC.	Multifactor authentication performed as part of the PKI-AUTH prevents the malicious actor from activating the PIV Card.
	Repudiation of enrollment	A subscriber denies enrollment, claiming that they did not enroll with the credential service provider (CSP).	Denial of DPC enrollment, while possible, would be difficult due to PKI-AUTH authentication and validation requirements during enrollment.
	Use of revoked credential	A subscriber attempts to use a PIV Card authentication certificate that is revoked to obtain a DPC.	The PKI-AUTH check determines the credential is revoked. To lessen the possibility of the PIV Card being very recently revoked and not being detected as such during enrollment, the seven-day revocation check will cause the DPC to be revoked.
Issuance	Disclosure	A key created by the CSP for a subscriber is copied by an attacker as it is transported from the CSP to the subscriber during authenticator issuance.	Not applicable if key is generated within the subscriber's mobile device. If the key is generated by the CSP and transported to the subscriber, then mutually authenticated secure transport as required by NIST SP 800-157 will protect the key.
	Tampering	A new password created by the subscriber to protect the private key is modified by an attacker to a value of the attacker's choosing.	A DPC subscriber's mobile device could contain malware that intercepts the personal identification number (PIN)/password for a software container-based DPC. Use mobile security best practices to prevent and/or detect malware on the end point.
	Unauthorized issuance	A person falsely claiming to be the subscriber is issued credentials for that subscriber.	An attacker could steal a onetime password (OTP) through a man-in-the-middle attack or other means. Use an EMM to authenticate the device requesting the DPC. Furthermore, ensure an appropriate channel is used to

Activity	Threat/Attack	Example	Applicability to DPC
			distribute the OTP, and ensure the OTP is resistant to attempts by an attacker to brute force attack (or use other means) to discover the value of the OTP.
	Social engineering	A malicious person manipulates an individual at the CSP responsible for issuance to obtain a credential bound to another valid subscriber.	An attacker could manipulate an administrator of the DCMS to make a PIV subscriber eligible for a DPC. Use an EMM to authenticate the device and verify it is operated by the person requesting the DPC.

Table 3-2. Authenticator threats to DPC

Authenticator Threats/Attacks	Examples	Applicability to DPC
Theft	A hardware cryptographic device is stolen.	An external USB drive or microSD card can be readily stolen. Multifactor authentication prevents unauthorized use of the private key.
	A cell phone is stolen.	A mobile device that stores the DPC in software or in an embedded cryptographic token can be readily stolen. Use mobile locking mechanisms, remote wipe, and other mobile device security best practices to mitigate risk of a stolen device. Furthermore, multifactor authentication prevents unauthorized use of the private key.
Duplication	A software PKI authenticator (private key) is copied.	A DPC stored in a software-based container on a mobile device could be copied from the device. Use device sandboxing mechanisms, cryptographic techniques, and malware detection mechanisms as mitigation.
Eavesdropping	Memorized secrets are obtained by watching keyboard entry.	Through shoulder surfing, an attacker could observe a PIN/password that protects the cryptographic token. Educate users to be mindful of surroundings when entering PINs/passwords. Use authentication end points that employ trusted input and trusted display capabilities. Note: This attack compromises only one factor of the multifactor authentication mechanisms provided by DPC.
	Memorized secrets or authenticator outputs are intercepted by key-stroke-logging software.	An attacker could use malware to intercept a PIN/password that protects the crypto-graphic token. Use mobile security best practices to prevent and/or detect malware on the end point. Also, native cryptographic

Table 3-2. (Continued)

Authenticator Threats/Attacks	Examples	Applicability to DPC
		token storage on some devices can leverage trusted paths for PIN/password entry.
Offline cracking	A software PKI authenticator is subjected to a dictionary attack to identify the correct password or PIN to use to decrypt the private key.	A DPC stored in a software-based container on a mobile device could be copied from the device and would be subject to offline cracking. Use PIN/password throttling, device encryption, and malware detection mechanisms as mitigation.
Side-channel attack	A key is extracted by differential power analysis on a hardware cryptographic authenticator.	A mobile device is susceptible to side-channel attacks only if the PIN/password has been successfully entered. Use key and/or PIN usage time-out/limits and adopt other countermeasures described in NIST SP 800-63-3B and PHY-5 [9].
	A cryptographic authenticator secret is extracted by analysis of the response time of the authenticator over many attempts.	
End-point compromise	A cryptographic authenticator connected to the end point is used to authenticate remote attackers (i.e., malicious code on the end point is used as a proxy for remote access to a connected authenticator without the subscriber's consent).	A DPC that leverages an external token, such as a USB token, may be vulnerable to this threat. Multifactor authentication prevents unauthorized use of the DPC private key.
	Authentication is performed on behalf of an attacker rather than the subscriber.	An attacker could use malware to intercept a PIN/password that protects the cryptographic token. Use sandboxing and mobile security best practices to prevent and detect malware on the end point. Also, native cryptographic token storage on some devices can leverage trusted paths for PIN/password entry.
	Malicious code is used as a proxy for authentication or exports authenticator keys from the end point.	A DPC stored in a software-based container on a mobile device could be copied from the device and would be subject to offline cracking. Use sandboxing, device encryption, and malware detection mechanisms as mitigation.

3.5.1.1. Other Threats

Mobile devices like those featured in our example implementations are subject to the broader set of mobile ecosystem threats. From NIST Internal Report 8144 [18]:

> Mobile devices pose a unique set of threats to enterprises. Typical enterprise protections, such as isolated enterprise sandboxes and the ability to remote wipe a device, may fail to fully mitigate the security challenges associated with these complex mobile information systems. With this in mind, a set of security controls and countermeasures that address mobile threats in a holistic manner must be identified, necessitating a broader view of the entire mobile security ecosystem. This view must go beyond devices to include, as an example, the cellular networks and cloud infrastructure used to support mobile applications and native mobile services.

We strongly encourage organizations implementing the reference architectures in whole or part to consult the NIST Mobile Threat Catalogue (MTC) [9] when assessing relevant threats to their own organization. Each entry in the MTC contains several pieces of information: an identifier, a category, a high-level description, details on its origin, exploit examples, examples of common vulnerabilities and exposures (CVEs), possible countermeasures, and academic references.

In broad strokes, the MTC covers 32 different threat categories that are grouped into 12 distinct classes as shown in Table 3-3. Of these categories, two, highlighted in green in the table, are covered by the guidance presented in this practice guide and, if implemented correctly, will help mitigate those threats.

The other categories, while still important elements of the mobile ecosystem and critical to the health of an overall mobility architecture, are out of scope for this document. The entire mobile ecosystem should be considered when analyzing threats to the architecture; this ecosystem is depicted below in Figure 3-2, taken from NIST Internal Report 8144. Each player in the ecosystem—the mobile device user, the enterprise, the network operator, the application developer, and the original equipment manufacturer—can find suggestions to deter other threats by reviewing the MTC and NIST Internal Report 8144. Many of these share common solutions, such as using EMM software to monitor device health and restricting installation of applications from only authorized sources.

Table 3-3. Mobile threat classes and categories

Threat Class	Threat Category	Threat Class	Threat Category
Application	Malicious or Privacy-Invasive Application	Local Area Network and Personal Area Network	Network Threats: Bluetooth
	Vulnerable Applications		Network Threats: Near-Field Communication (NFC)
Authentication	Authentication: User or Device to Network		Network Threats: Wi-Fi
	Authentication: User or Device to Remote Service	Payment	Application-Based
	Authentication: User to Device		In-Application Purchases
Cellular	Carrier Infrastructure		NFC-Based
	Carrier Interoperability	Physical Access	Physical Access
	Cellular Air Interface	Privacy	Behavior Tracking
	Consumer-Grade Femtocell	Supply Chain	Supply Chain
	Short Messaging Service/Multimedia Messaging Service/Rich Communications Services	Stack	Baseband Subsystem
	Unstructured Supplementary Service Data		Boot Firmware
	Voice over Long-Term Evolution		Device Drivers
Ecosystem	Mobile Application Store		Isolated Execution Environments
	Mobile Operating System (OS) and Vendor Infrastructure		Mobile Operating System
EMM	Enterprise Mobility		SD Card
Global Positioning System (GPS)	GPS		Universal Subscriber Identity Module/Subscriber Identity Module/ Universal Integrated Circuit Card (UICC) Security

Derived Personal Identity Verification (PIV) Credentials

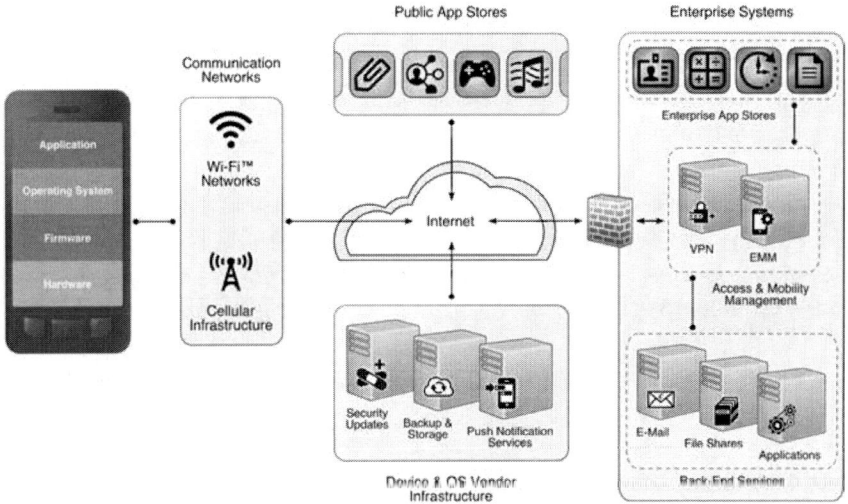

Figure 3-2. The mobile ecosystem.

Because threats to organizationally controlled infrastructure are addressed by normal computer security controls (e.g., separation of duties, record keeping, independent audits), they are outside the scope of this practice guide. See NIST SP 800-53 Revision 4, *Security and Privacy Controls for Federal Information Systems and Organizations* [5], for appropriate security controls.

3.5.2. Vulnerabilities
Vulnerabilities can exist within mobile applications, mobile and desktop operating systems, and network applications that are employed in the storage and use of a mobile credential. Vulnerabilities can be exploited at all levels in the information stack. For up-to-date information regarding vulnerabilities, this guide recommends that security professionals leverage the National Vulnerability Database (NVD) [19]. The NVD is the U.S. government repository of standards-based vulnerability management data.

3.5.2.1. Mobile Device Vulnerabilities
Vulnerabilities discovered within mobile applications and rich operating systems are important to any deployment of DPC. The DPC issuer must ensure strong protections on use of the credential via a PIN or pass phrase [6] Section 3 while also making sure that other applications on the device cannot access the credential. Sensitive cryptographic material can be stored in software at AAL-2, leaving the mobile device open to exploits that attack vulnerable code.

To thwart these types of attacks, it is common for mobile applications to be sandboxed in some manner to prevent unexpected and unwanted interaction among the system, its applications, and data access between disparate applications (including user data) [18]. However, a search of the NVD yields examples of software vulnerabilities [20] that might allow exploits to *break* sandboxing protections. A full discussion on these topics, including mitigations, can be found in NIST Interagency Report 8144, *Assessing Threats to Mobile Devices & Infrastructure: the Mobile Threat Catalogue* [18] and NIST SP 800-163, *Vetting the Security of Mobile Applications* [21].

Vulnerabilities are also introduced by downloading nonapproved applications. We recommend that only vetted and approved applications be downloaded. NIST's AppVet is an example of an application vetting platform.

3.5.2.2. Network Vulnerabilities

Considering that DPC enrollment may happen remotely [6], issuing organizations will want to mitigate network vulnerabilities before deploying a DPC solution for the organization. For example, a DPC applicant may be required to enter an OTP into the DPC mobile provisioning application to complete enrollment as described in NIST SP 800-157 (Section C.1, Appendix C). The organization will want to maintain confidentiality, integrity, and authenticity of the OTP as it traverses potentially untrustworthy networks.

This guide suggests two resources to assist network vulnerability analyses as input to a risk assessment. The CVE database [22] lists more than 100,000 vulnerabilities that can affect web servers, Structured Query Language (SQL) servers, domain name system (DNS) servers, firewalls, routers, and other network components. These vulnerabilities include denial of service, code execution, overflow, cross-site scripting, directory traversal, process bypass, unauthorized gaining of information, SQL injection, file inclusion, memory corruption, cross-site request forgery, and hypertext transfer protocol (http) response splitting.

Many of these vulnerabilities are operating system- or application-based. Others are protocol-based (e.g., vulnerabilities inherent in IPv6, Transport Layer Security [TLS], DNS, Border Gateway Protocol, Simple Mail Transfer Protocol, and other network protocols). The U.S. NVD is an additional resource that builds upon the information included in CVE entries to provide enhanced information for each CVE Identifier. As in the case of mobile device vulnerabilities, NIST frequently updates the NVD so it remains a viable source of vulnerabilities that affect network servers.

3.5.3. Risk

As with the topic of threats, a discussion on DPC risk closely parallels that of risk management when implementing a PIV program within an organization. As such, this document defers to NIST SP 800-63-3 [7] Section 5 on the topic of digital identity risk management.

An implementer of DPC should refer to the NIST SP 800-63-3 discussion of digital identity risk management and the corresponding risk assessment guidelines that supplement the RMF. Specifically, this section provides guidelines on selection of the DPC vendor AAL based on risk.

3.5.4. Security Control Map

An organization may benefit from examples in NIST Interagency Report 8170 [17]. For instance, the framework's Example 1—Integrate Enterprise and Cybersecurity Risk Management—recommends using the five cybersecurity Functions (Identify, Protect, Detect, Respond, and Recover) to organize cybersecurity risk management activities at the highest level. Table 3-4 presents a list of possible functions that a DPC implementation can address.

Table 3-4. Security control mappings

Cybersecurity Framework Function	Cybersecurity Framework Category	Cybersecurity Framework Subcategory	NIST SP 800-53 Rev. 4	NIST SP 800-181 Work Roles
PROTECT (PR)	Access Control (PR.AC)	PR.AC-1: Identities and credentials are issued, managed, verified, revoked, and audited for authorized devices, users, and processes.	IA-2, IA-4, IA-5, AC-2	Software Developer SP-DEV-001), Product Support Manager (OV-PMA-003)
		PR.AC-3: Remote access is managed.	AC-17, AC-19	Information Systems Security Developer (SP-SYS-001), System Administrator (OM-ADM-001)
		PR.AC-6: Identities are proofed and bound to credentials and asserted in interactions.	AC-2, AC-19, IA-2, IA-4,	Security Control Assessor (SP-RSK-002), Product Support Manager (OV-PMA-003)

Table 3-4. (Continued)

Cybersecurity Framework Function	Cybersecurity Framework Category	Cybersecurity Framework Subcategory	NIST SP 800-53 Rev. 4	NIST SP 800-181 Work Roles
			IA-5, IA-8	
		PR.AC-7: Users, devices, and other assets are authenticated (e.g., single factor, multifactor) commensurate with the risk of the transaction.	AC-7, AC-11, IA-2, IA-5	Systems Requirements Planner (SP-SRP-001), Information Systems Security Manager (OV-MGT-001)
	Data Security (PR.DS)	PR.DS-2: Data in transit is protected.	SC-8, SC-12	Data Analyst (OM-DTA-002), Cyber Defense Analyst (PR-CDA-001)
		PR.DS-5: Protections against data leaks are implemented.	SC-13	Research and Development Specialist (SP-TRD-001), Cyber Defense Analyst (PR-CDA-001)
	Information Protection (PR.IP)	PR.IP-3: Configuration change control processes are in place.	CM-3	Software Developer (SP-DEV-001), Systems Security Analyst (OM-ANA-001)

In addition, for each Cybersecurity Framework Subcategory, a mapping was made to NIST SP 800-181, *National Initiative for Cybersecurity Education (NICE) Cybersecurity Workforce Framework* [8], to show what types of work roles are needed to implement and maintain a DPC solution. We recommend that this information be used when communicating risk throughout an organization.

Example 3 documented in Draft NIST Interagency Report 8170—Integrate and Align Cybersecurity and Acquisition Processes—may help in acquiring and integrating a DCMS into an organization's environment. As the framework notes, an organization could ask a vendor to include its Cybersecurity Framework Profile in response to a request for information for a DPC solution. Receiving this data allows an objective comparison of solutions.

3.6. Technologies
The following sections describe the vendors and products we used for our example implementations.

3.6.1. Entrust Datacard
Entrust Datacard, provider of trusted identity and secure transaction technologies, offers solutions for PKI and for PIV Card life-cycle management activities within its portfolio. Organizations can choose to operate these solutions in-house or use Entrust Datacard's managed service offerings.

Entrust's IdentityGuard product is an identity-based authentication platform that includes a web-based self-service module (SSM). It supports a wide range of authenticators, including smart cards.

Following NIST SP 800-157, Entrust expanded IdentityGuard and SSM products to support DPC issuance and life-cycle management. The solution includes a mobile smart credential application and is available for use on Apple iOS, Google Android, and Blackberry operating systems.

The Entrust Datacard Managed PKI solution is a trusted service managed through legal and technology agreements and regular auditing of the services, procedures, and practices [23]. Through a set of standard protocols, the PKI service issues and manages credentials for identities of individual persons. In this project, the Entrust Managed PKI issued X.509 credentials for PIV and Derived PIV applicants.

3.6.2. Intel Authenticate
Intel® Authenticate is a hardware-based multifactor authentication solution that allows IT to define an authentication policy that is secured and enforced in the Intel client hardware systems. Intel Authenticate provides hardware to protect multiple user factors (protected PIN, fingerprint, phone, location, etc.) and to secure IT-defined authentication policies. These policies are evaluated and enforced on the client hardware, leading to release of cryptographic tokens (e.g., PKI-based signatures as used in DPCs) to meet the authentication needs of the applications based on DPCs.

The technology uses the Derived PIV Authentication certificate where the private key is stored in a hybrid firmware/hardware solution. The PKI authentication key is released for the cryptographic operations only when the multifactor authentication condition, as defined by enterprise IT, has been met. The multiple factors that protect the Derived PIV Authentication private key are protected by a PIN. The PIN is protected by a technology called Protected Transaction Display, which is based on a PIN pad that is directly rendered by the graphics engine and verified in hardware. In this way, it adds security features beyond native operating systems mechanisms.

Intel Authenticate technology is available on all Ultrabook devices and other Intel-capable devices with sixth-, seventh-, and eighth-generation and higher Intel Core vPro processors running Microsoft Windows 7, 8, and 10.

3.6.3. Intercede
Intercede contributed an identity and credential management product for PIV credentials that additionally supports DPCs and MyID as a software solution that can be hosted in the cloud or deployed in-house. The MyID server platform comprises an application server, a database, and a web server. It provides connectors to infrastructure components such as network shares and PKI, and application programming interfaces (APIs) to enable integration with the organization's identity and access management system. For mobile devices, the MyID Identity Agent runs as an application and interfaces with the MyID server to support iOS and Android mobile devices and credential stores, including the device's native key store, software key store, and microSD storage.

3.6.4. MobileIron
Vendors that provide products and solutions to manage mobile devices may enter into partnerships with identity and credential management product vendors to deliver integrated solutions. MobileIron, one such vendor, has partnered with Entrust Datacard and is offering an integrated solution for the life-cycle management of DPC for mobile device users.

MobileIron offers an EMM platform that enables organizations to secure and manage mobile devices, applications, and content. Three tools of the EMM product suite—Core, Sentry, and Mobile@Work—are relevant to the integration with Entrust Datacard's IdentityGuard for supporting DPCs. MobileIron Core, the software engine, enables organizations to set policies for managing mobile devices, applications, and content. It integrates with an organization's back-end IT platforms and can be deployed on premises or in the cloud.

MobileIron Sentry functions as an in-line gateway to manage and secure the traffic between mobile devices and back-end systems, such as Microsoft Exchange Server with ActiveSync. The third component, the Mobile@Work application, interfaces with MobileIron Core and configures the device, creates a secure container, and enforces the configuration and security policies set by the organization. As a suite, the MobileIron EMM platform protects enterprise data and applications.

3.6.5. Verizon Shared Service Provider

The Verizon SSP solution is a trusted PKI service for federal agencies managed through legal and technology agreements and regular auditing of the services, procedures, and practices. Through a set of standard protocols, the PKI service issues and manages credentials for identities of individual persons.

The following edited description is taken from the General Services Administration (GSA) IT Schedule 70 contract:

> The SSP solution is built as a scalable architecture that may be complemented (at the Agency's option) with Card Management Services, Lightweight Directory Access Protocol (LDAP)-based Directory services, and Simple Certificate Validation Protocol Validation Services. The core Verizon SSP offering provides all the digital certificate profiles required to be implemented on FIPS-201 approved smart cards.
>
> Verizon SSP PKI services offer fully managed options to archive and recover end user encryption keys, post certificates and CRLs to a publicly accessible directory, and validate certificate status in real time through OCSP. Verizon SSP service platforms are built on open standards, [and] they are well integrated and highly interoperable.

3.6.6. Mobile End Points

Table 3-5 lists the devices used to complete our example implementations. OS versions are current as of the writing of this document. Readers should consult vendor documentation for the latest compatibility requirements.

Table 3-5. Mobile end points

Manufacturer	Model	OS/Version
Apple	iPhone	iOS 11.0.3
Apple	iPad Mini	iOS 11.0.3
Samsung	Galaxy S6	Android 6.0.1
Lenovo	ThinkPad	Windows 10

3.6.7. Technology Mapping

Table 3-6 lists all of the technologies used in this project, and provides a mapping among the generic application term, the specific product used, and the security control(s) that the product provides. Refer to Table 3-4 for an explanation of the NIST Cybersecurity Framework Subcategory codes. Note: Some of our components are marked in the version column as not applicable. This is due to the use of SaaS [24] cloud services.

Table 3-6. Products and technologies

Component	Product	Version	Function	Cybersecurity Framework Subcategories
PKI Certificate Authority	Entrust Datacard Managed PKI	Not applicable	Entity that issues an authentication certificate, which is an X.509 public key certificate that has been issued in accordance with the requirements of NIST SP 800-157 and the X.509 Certificate Policy for the U.S. Federal PKI Common Policy Framework [25]	PR.AC-1
	Verizon Shared Service Provider	Not applicable		
Derived PIV Credential Management System	Entrust Datacard IdentityGuard	Not applicable	Entity that implements Derived PIV life-cycle activities in accordance with NIST SP 800-157	PR.AC-1, PR.IP-3
	Intercede MyID	10.8		
PIV Credential Management System	Entrust Datacard IdentityGuard	Not applicable	Entity that implements PIV life-cycle activities in accordance with FIPS 201-2	PR.AC-1, PR.IP-3
	Intercede MyID	10.8		
Enterprise Mobility Management System	MobileIron Core	9.3	Entity that provides security services commonly needed for security management of mobile devices [13]	PR.AC-1, PR.AC-3
Authenticator	Entrust PIV-D	1.3.0.4	Software component that stores the private key associated with the Derived PIV Authentication certificate	PR.DS-2, PR.DS-5
	Intercede Identity Agent	3.14		
	Intel Authenticate	Not applicable	Hybrid component that stores the private key associated with the Derived PIV Authentication certificate	

4. Architecture

In this section, we describe how the components defined in Section 3.4.4, as implemented by our partner technologies (see Section 3.6, Technologies), were integrated to produce the final example implementations (Section 4.2 and Section 4.3). Note that these architectures were based on time and resource constraints and are focused on supporting DPC life-cycle activities. In future phases of the project, architectures may be expanded to include a managed PIV Card component, broader application of DPCs to mobile applications, and other enhancements. Refer to Section 6 for further details.

Though these capabilities are implemented as integrated solutions in this guide, organizational requirements may dictate that only a subset of these capabilities be implemented. These reference architectures were designed to be modular to support such use cases.

4.1. Architecture Description

Many federal agencies have opted to use a managed shared solution for issuing PIV Cards for their employees rather than deploy and operate their own PKI. GSA's Managed Service Office established the USAccess program to offer federal agencies a managed shared service solution for PIV Card issuance to help agencies meet the HSPD-12 mandate [1]. USAccess provides participating agencies with a comprehensive set of services, including issuance and life-cycle management of PIV credentials, administration, and reporting [1].

Assuming that many agencies use a managed service for their PIV Card issuance and a shared service provider for the PKI services, we considered a few of the different deployment architectures while planning our example implementations. Further, managing mobile devices with EMM products is an integral part of mobile device security for most organizations. Therefore, we considered architectures for DPC provisioning solutions both independent of and integrated with an EMM solution.

As a result, this practice guide documents two reference architectures that are described in the following sections. To assist readers in putting our architectures in the context of the Federal ICAM Enterprise Architecture, as discussed in Section 3.4.4, below we have highlighted (in green) the components that are used within each architecture.

Note that Figure 4-1 is slightly modified from the original FICAM architecture to allow an EMM component to be included within the access control system. An EMM can execute the access processes from policy stored within an access management database.

4.2. Managed Architecture with EMM Integration

Figure 4-2 depicts the final example implementation for this reference architecture, in which cloud services are used to manage the PIV and DPC life-cycle activities. It also introduces an EMM into the workflow, recognizing the need for organizations to apply a consistent set of security policies on the device. In this scenario, the same vendor operates the PIV and DPC management services to simplify the life-cycle linkage requirements between the DPC and PIV so that integration efforts across two solutions are not necessary. This simplification also allows recovery of the PIV user's key management key onto the mobile device with relatively little difficulty, again because of the single-vendor solution. This type of scenario, however, may not be suitable if an organization prefers a more modular architecture.

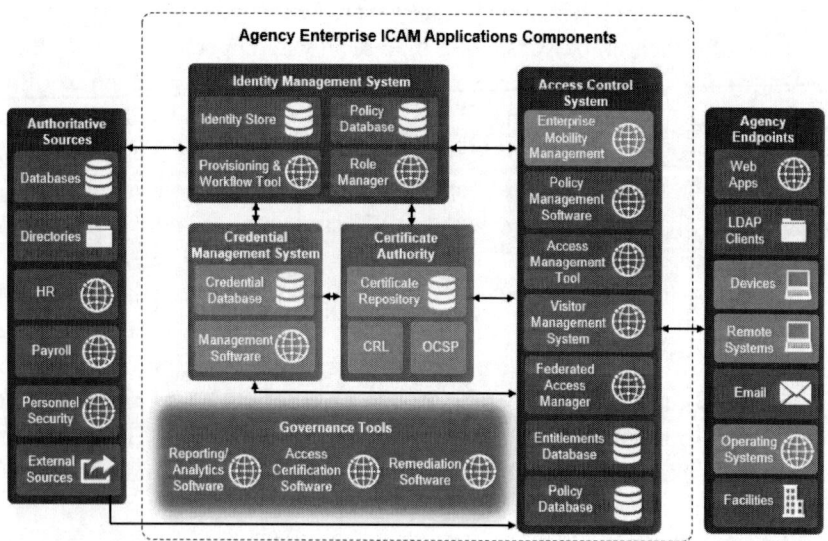

Figure 4-1. Federal ICAM Enterprise Architecture.

The back-end EMM components, MobileIron Core and MobileIron Sentry, were deployed on premises in the demilitarized zone (DMZ) of a simulated enterprise network. MobileIron Core allows administration of users and devices by applying policies and configurations to them based on their assigned labels.

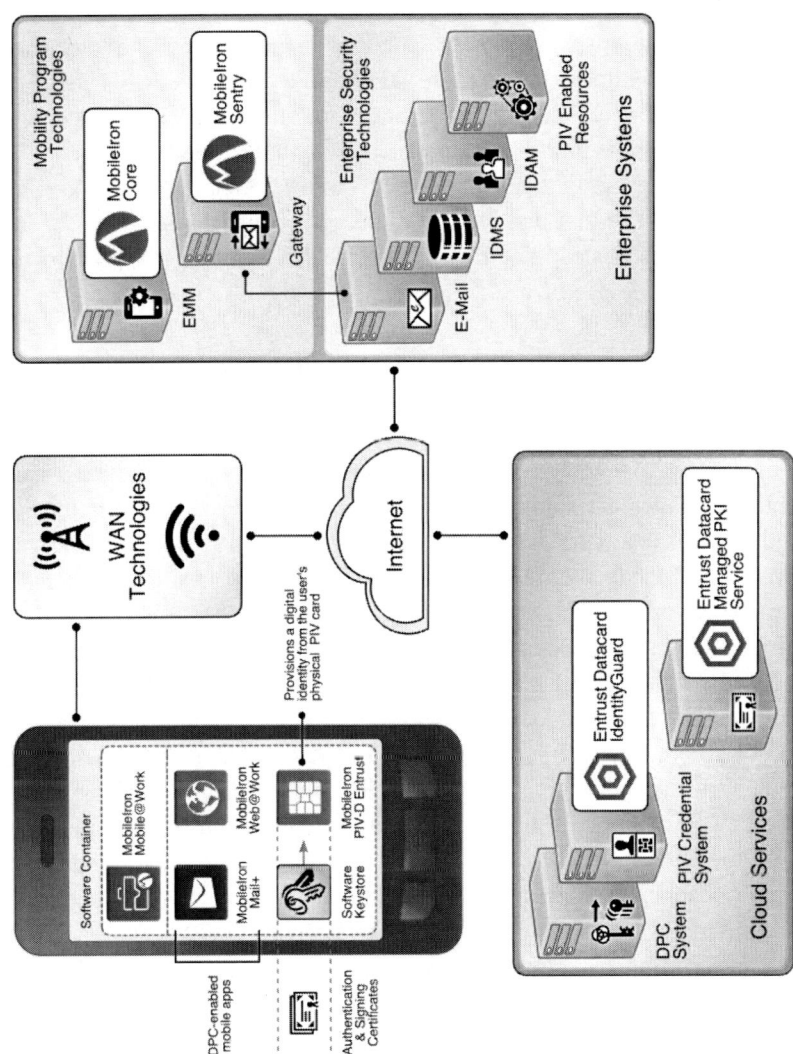

Figure 4-2. PIV and DPC cloud service life-cycle management with EMM integration.

MobileIron Sentry provides a virtual private network (VPN) end point, which creates an authenticated and protected channel between managed devices and on-premises resources, such as internal email. Sentry was included in this architecture to explore DPC usage scenarios as discussed in Section 6. However, as Sentry is not required for any life-cycle management activities of DPCs, it is not further documented by this guide.

The enterprise network also includes Active Directory (AD) and an Exchange server. The instance of AD was used to store the identities of the test users in this scenario. The EMM used AD as its trusted repository of authorized mobile device owners.

4.3. Hybrid Architecture for PIV and DPC Life-Cycle Management

This architecture is described as *hybrid,* in that it utilizes resources that are located both on premises and in the cloud. Organizations have chosen this architectural path to leverage previous investments in enterprise systems, such as identity management solutions, while simultaneously gaining efficiencies and agility from cloud services. In this scenario, the PIV Card and Derived PIV Credential Management Systems are deployed within a simulated internal enterprise network. A self-service kiosk, which serves as the enrollment station for DPC initial issuance, is also deployed on the internal network. The cloud-based managed PKI service is integrated with the on-premises CMS through a toolkit available for the CMS software.

In this example implementation, the life-cycle management capabilities of the DPC are an extension of the PIV issuance capabilities of a vendor product. PIV Card and DPC life-cycle management are tightly integrated, and the DPC applicant interacts with the same self-service portal that is used for PIV Card issuance. Fulfillment of PIV Card linkage requirements is simplified because of the close integration between PIV Card and DPC issuance. There is also a level of transparency and familiarity for users as they access the self-service capabilities of the solution.

This architecture supports traditional mobile devices and hybrid devices that run full desktop operating systems. Hybrid devices, sometimes referred to as convertible laptops, exhibit characteristics of both traditional laptops and mobile devices, such as having both integrated keyboards and touchscreens. Thus, two embedded cryptographic tokens are documented: software tokens for Android/iOS-based mobile devices and Intel processor-based hybrid devices that meet the hardware requirements documented in Section 3.6.2. Additionally, there are Intel-specific support software versioning requirements that are documented in Part C of this guide that an implementer should consider.

This architecture also includes the Verizon SSP managed PKI service for issuing Derived PIV Authentication certificates, which can be reached by traversing the internet. While the selected CMS software can integrate with on-premises or cloud-based certificate authorities, in this example implementation the PKI service is cloud-based. The DPC applicant downloads and installs the MyID Identity Agent application from Intercede. The architecture uses the MyID Identity Agent application, which manages provisioning the Derived PIV Authentication certificate to the device and other life-cycle activities, and can be downloaded and installed by using Google Play and the Apple App Store.

This architecture supports options for mobile and Intel-based devices, which use software- and hardware-backed authenticators, respectively. The DPC applicant experience for initial issuance differs slightly, depending on the authenticator type. When requesting a DPC for a mobile device, the applicant is prompted to scan a quick response (QR) code by using the enrollment application once the back-end system has validated the PIV Authentication certificate. In Intel-based hybrid devices, however, the applicant is sent an OTP through an out-of-band notification scheme, which in this example implementation uses email. Knowledge of the OTP verifies that the user attempting to collect the DPC is the same user who requested it. More details of this process can be found in Section 5.2.2.1.

An implementer should consider using an EMM to automatically deploy the Identity Agent application to mobile devices and to take advantage of secure application containers provided by the EMM. This capability was not implemented due to project constraints but may be included in future revisions of this guide. The Identity Agent communicates directly with the MyID CMS for provisioning and other functions over the network. The back-end MyID CMS system is composed of components that can be deployed in a layered fashion if desired to support a large user population. Table 4-1 lists the components and corresponding descriptions.

Table 4-1. MyID CMS component descriptions

MyID Web Server	Hosts the MyID web services used to deliver functions to the MyID Self-Service Kiosk and MyID Identity Agent application
MyID Application Server	Hosts the MyID business object layer and connector to the Verizon SSP
MyID Database	Hosts the MyID database (SQL server) used to store information credential policy, key management information, and audit records

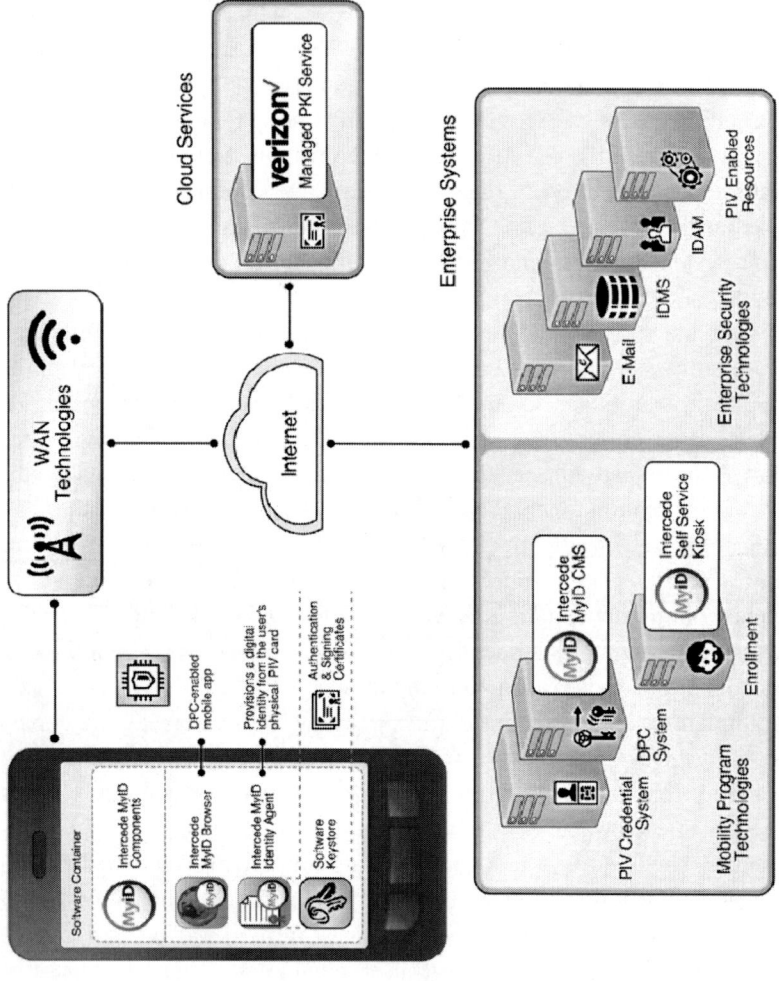

Figure 4-3. Mobile device hybrid architecture for both PIV card and DPC life-cycle management.

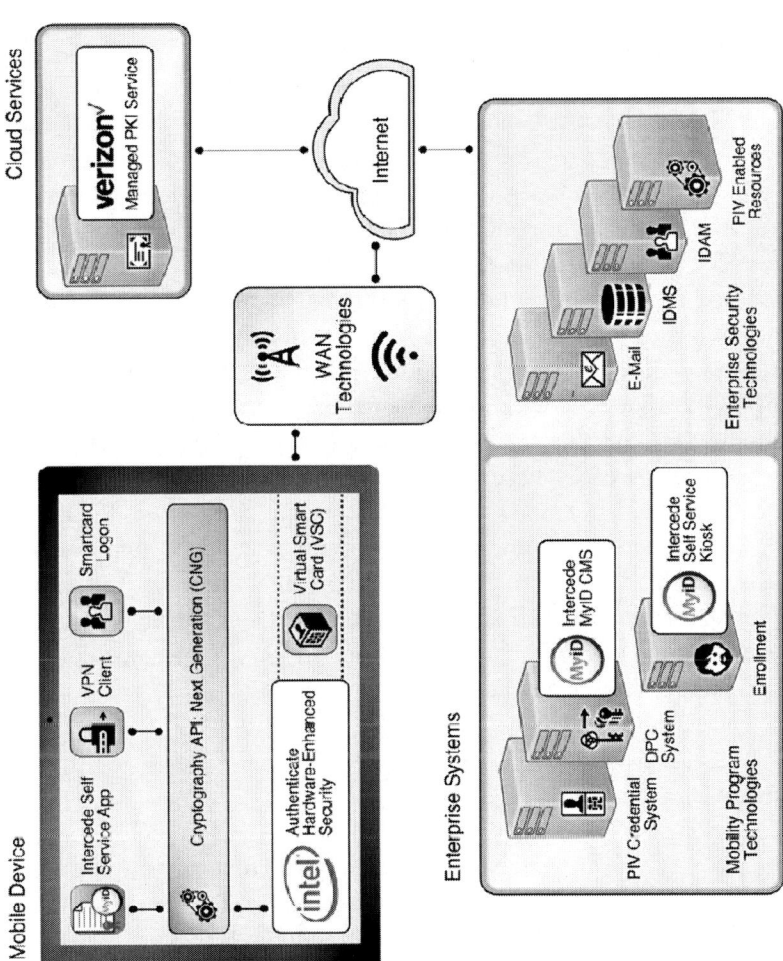

Figure 4-4. Intel-based hybrid architecture for both PIV card and DPC life-cycle management.

Implementers of similar architectures should consider the deployment options that are available after assessing existing infrastructure and security requirements. For instance, the web server component used to provision DPC can be deployed on a separate web server to communicate with the self-service kiosk. For remote enrollment this allows the web server component to be placed on a DMZ, isolating the traffic from local networks. Additionally, this configuration supports a reverse proxy that can be placed between the mobile device and the MyID web service. This breaks the connection between the mobile device and the web service, allowing the traffic to be inspected before it is forwarded to the web service.

The previous figures depict high-level views of the example implementations of the hybrid architecture used for this solution for DPCs. Detailed, system-level figures can be found in Part C of this guide. Figure 4-3 focuses on the mobile device implementation. Here, the Identity Agent application is used to manage the DPC. The Derived PIV Authentication key is stored in a software key store within the secure container. The supporting cloud and enterprise systems as described above are also shown. Figure 4-4 depicts the architecture when an Intel-based device that supports Intel Authenticate is used to store the DPC. Here, the Intercede self-service application is used to manage issuing the DPC. The DPC is then available for smart card log-on and VPN authentication. In this implementation, we exercised smart card log-on to observe usage of the DPC.

5. Security Characteristic Analysis

The purpose of the security characteristic analysis is to understand the extent to which the project meets its objective of demonstrating the life cycle of DPC requirements specified in NIST SP 800-157. In addition, it seeks to understand the security benefits and drawbacks of the example solutions. Readers may also find Section 3.5 helpful when evaluating DPC security characteristics for their own organization.

5.1. Assumptions and Limitations
The security characteristic analysis has the following limitations:

- It is neither a comprehensive test of all security components nor a red-team exercise.

- It cannot identify all weaknesses.
- It does not include the lab infrastructure. It is assumed that devices are hardened. Testing these devices would reveal only weaknesses in implementation that would not be relevant to those adopting these reference architectures.

5.2. Build Testing

This project uses Table 5, Requirements Definition and Implementation Mappings, from NIST Internal Report 8055 [10] as a basis for testing the example implementations. Using the table as a foundation (see Appendix C), we created a test plan that specifies test cases with traceability to DPC requirements. We collected artifacts from each test case execution, such as screen captures and network packet traces, and documented the results. In cases where a requirement could not be tested from our lab environment, we collaborated with our build partners to document how a requirement could be fulfilled in a production environment.

The sections below are a summary of the test case execution structured by NIST SP 800-157 life-cycle stages: initial issuance, maintenance, and termination. Screenshots of certain operations aid the narrative. Detailed workflow steps for these example implementations are found in Volume C of this practice guide.

5.2.1. Managed Architecture Build Testing

5.2.1.1. Initial Issuance

With our Entrust Datacard example solution, the mobile device connects to the IdentityGuard system, and the IdentityGuard connects to the CA, thereby handling delivery of the public certificate to the mobile device, which follows the same process for issuing a PIV Card except that a QR is involved. In this case, the DPC key pairs are generated on the mobile device, and the user's public key and certificate signing request are securely passed to the CA for certificate issuance by IdentityGuard.

To test this example implementation, Entrust Datacard gave us access to a development instance of its IdentityGuard service and populated it with identities of users who were issued test PIV Cards. These users were also granted preapproval to request a DPC. We observed that the prescribed DPC initial issuance workflow, summarized below, adhered to the requirements in NIST SP 800-157 [6].

Note that the figures below are screenshots from a shared IdentityGuard test infrastructure and feature an AnyBank Self-Service logo. This image is configurable and is not intended to exclude federal agencies from using this service.

As a prerequisite to issuance, we added our test DPC applicant's user account to an Active Directory group associated with users authorized to use DPCs. Users of this group are managed by a MobileIron AppConnect policy configured to achieve compliance with NIST SP 800-157. The policy enforces multiple issuance requirements, such as the need for a DPC applicant to create a six-to-eight-digit password to protect access to the private key associated with the DPC's PIV Authentication certificate. Additionally, the test applicant has a mobile device enrolled into management by MobileIron Core. Two MobileIron applications are employed: PIV-D Entrust, which is used in the DPC issuance workflow; and Mobile@Work, which maintains the target software token where the DPC will be stored.

Issuance begins with the test DPC applicant (Matteo) authenticating to the Entrust IdentityGuard self-service portal via PKI-AUTH multifactor authentication by using a computer and the applicant's valid PIV Card (Figure 5-1 and Figure 5-2). The applicant then makes appropriate selections within the portal to request issuance of a new DPC.

Entrust IdentityGuard presents a QR code and a numeric OTP (see Figure 5-3). These time-limited shared secrets link Matteo's (the DPC applicant's) session from a computer to the Entrust IdentityGuard self-service portal to the subsequent session between his target mobile device and Entrust IdentityGuard.

The applicant launches the MobileIron PIV-D Entrust application on the mobile device and uses it to scan the QR code and enter the OTP. See Figure 5-4 and Figure 5-5.

The application then creates a TLS 1.2-secured session with Entrust IdentityGuard and authenticates with the OTP. Once authenticated, the application generates asymmetric key pairs for Derived PIV Authentication and digital signing certificates and transmits the certificate requests to Entrust IdentityGuard. The IdentityGuard service verifies that the requested certificates match information on file for the PIV subscriber for whom the OTP was generated (i.e., Matteo). Once verified, it forwards the certificate requests to the Entrust CA, receives the Derived PIV Authentication certificates, then relays them to the MobileIron PIV-D Entrust application, where they are stored in the software token.

Derived Personal Identity Verification (PIV) Credentials 43

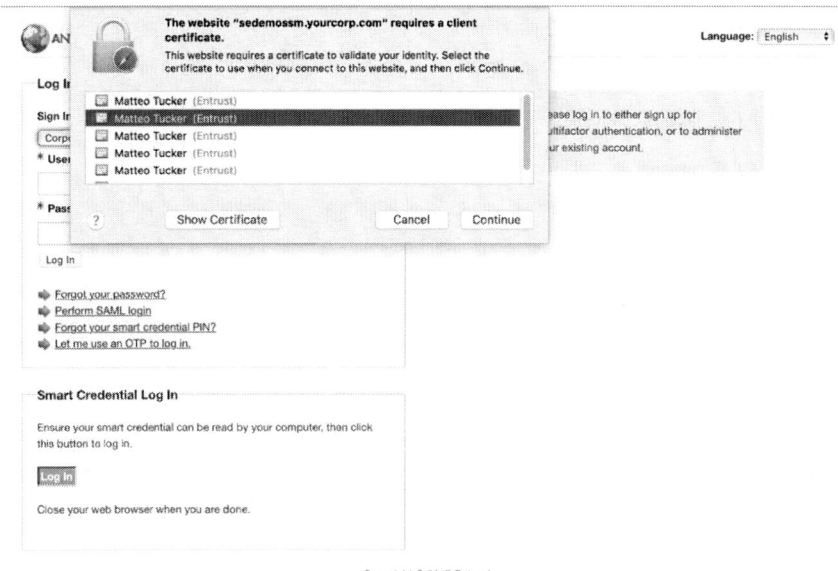

Figure 5-1. PIV authentication certificate selection for PKI-AUTH.

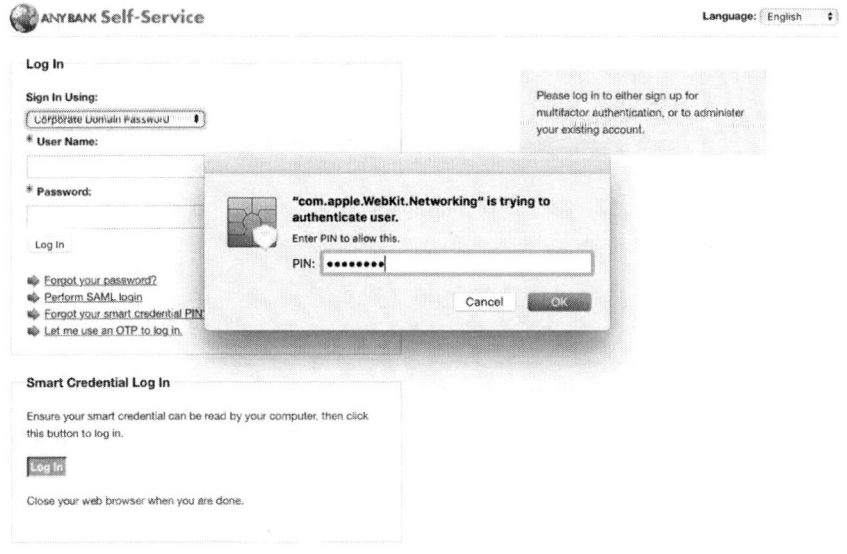

Figure 5-2. Password-based subscriber authentication via PIN.

Figure 5-3. Entrust IdentityGuard DPC activation codes.

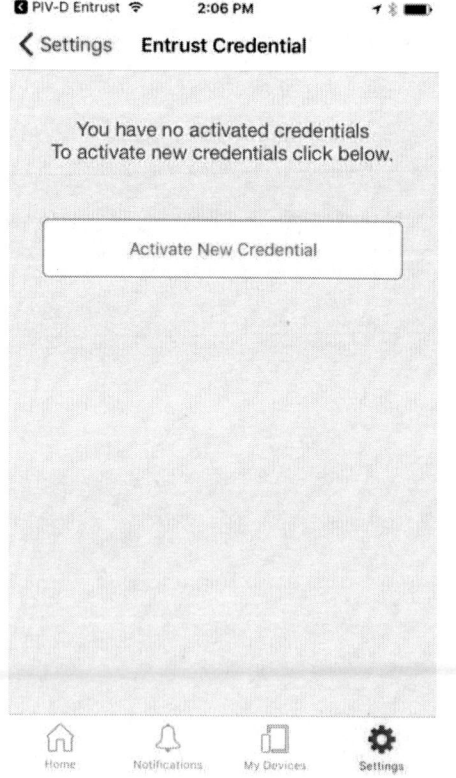

Figure 5-4. MobileIron PIV-D Entrust application.

Derived Personal Identity Verification (PIV) Credentials

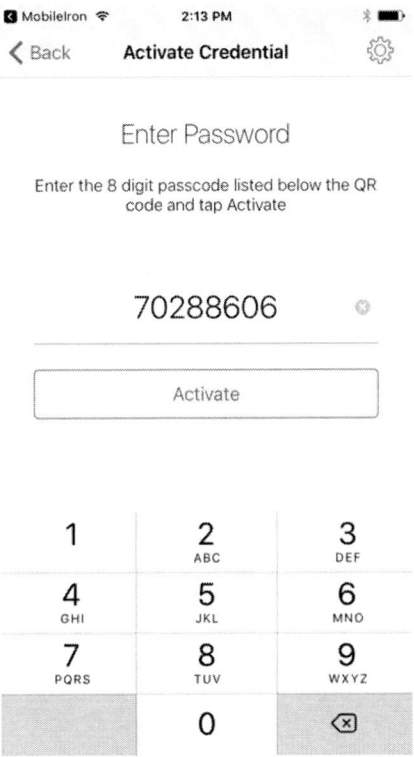

Figure 5-5. Entrust DPC activation.

The DPC subscriber must authenticate to the MobileIron PIV-D Entrust container by using the created password before Derived PIV Authentication certificates or their associated private keys can be used by any application integrated with MobileIron. See Figure 5-6 and Figure 5-7.

5.2.1.2. Maintenance

Maintenance activities for a DPC issued within this architecture are managed in two ways. Operations that require generating a new PIV Authentication certificate (certificate modification or rekey) require the DPC subscriber to repeat the initial issuance process as described in Section 5.2.1.1.

Linkage requirements between the status of the subscriber's PIV Card and DPC are covered by both the CA and CMS being under control of Entrust Datacard. These systems exchange identity management system data, and any necessary changes to the status of the subscriber's DPC will occur automatically.

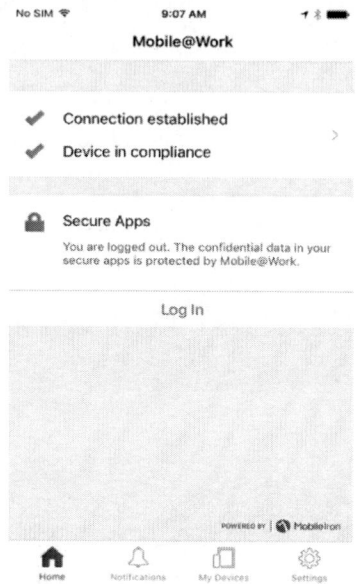

Figure 5-6. PIV-D application.

Figure 5-7. PIV-D passcode entry.

5.2.1.3. Termination

Should the mobile device with a software token be lost or compromised, a DPC sponsor-initiated workflow will specifically destroy the DPC by triggering the Retire Device operation available through the MobileIron administrative console. This process removes the MobileIron and all Web@Work applications and cryptographically wipes the MobileIron PIV-D Entrust software token containing the DPC. Triggering a remote wipe of all data on the device will also achieve this result. Further, the Derived PIV Authentication certificate can be directly revoked from the Entrust IdentityGuard interface (see Figure 5-8).

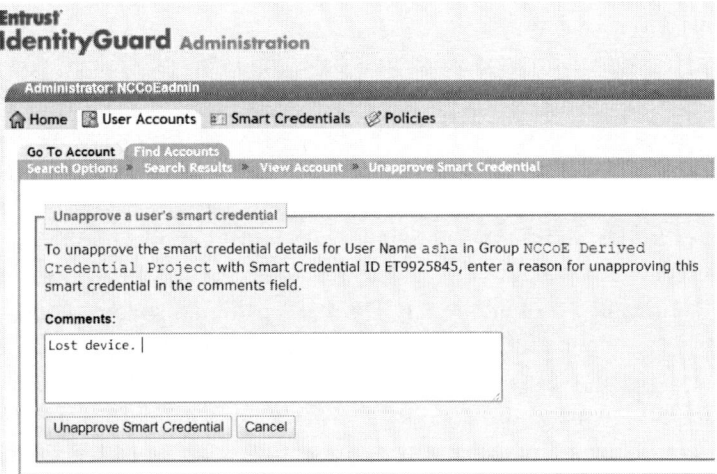

Figure 5-8. DPC IdentityGuard termination.

5.2.1.4. Derived PIV Authentication Certificate Management

PKI management instructions between the Entrust IdentityGuard service and the Entrust Datacard Managed CA use a combination of the Public Key Infrastructure X.509—Certificate Management Protocol (PKIX-CMP) and the XML Administration Protocol (XAP). PKIX-CMP [26] provides online interactions between PKI components, including an exchange between a CA and a client system—in this case, the Entrust IdentityGuard service. PKIX-CMP is defined as a standard by the IETF, which standardizes many network-based protocols, in RFC 4210. The XAP protocol was developed by Entrust Datacard and is used for administration tasks within the Entrust Datacard Managed CA.

The Entrust IdentityGuard service uses an XAP credential to securely communicate with the XAP subsystem on the Entrust Datacard Managed CA. The Entrust IdentityGuard service uses XAP to obtain an activation code, which is then used to create a PKIX-CMP General Message. The DPC certificate request is then forwarded to the Entrust Datacard Managed CA in the Public Key Cryptography Standards (PKCS) #10 format over PKIX-CMP. The Entrust Datacard Managed CA returns the signed DPC certificate to the Entrust IdentityGuard service.

5.2.2. Hybrid Architecture Build Testing

5.2.2.1. Initial Issuance
Issuing the DPC in this test scenario is based upon the subscriber's ownership of a PIV credential and DPC eligibility. In this example solution, the MyID CMS fulfills the role of a PIV Card issuer, a prerequisite to enrollment for a DPC, having been configured with profiles that were compatible with the test PIV Cards used in the example implementation. Next, we uploaded test PIV identities to the MyID CMS through a specialized application that included required PIV data to be stored on the card. An Issue Card workflow completed the PIV issuance within the MyID Desktop administrative console. PIV holders were eligible for a Derived PIV when the identities were mapped to a local MyID group. See Figure 5-9 for a screenshot of the test PIV Card user.

The DPC issuance process begins with a DPC applicant using the PKI-AUTH authentication mechanism from Section 6.2.3.1 of FIPS 201-2 [1] at the MyID Self-Service Kiosk. Once the applicant's PIV Card is inserted into the kiosk, the applicant is prompted for the PIV Card PIN as depicted in Figure 5-10. After successful PIV Card authentication, the kiosk transmits PIV Card information to the MyID CMS through secure transport, where a job is created to handle the second phase of issuance to the end point.

The DPC issuance process requires the use of the Identity Agent mobile application or the self-service application to complete the workflow. In the case of an iOS or Android-based mobile device, the applicant launches the Identity Agent application and scans a QR code presented by the self-service kiosk. The QR code contains the information needed for the Identity Agent mobile application to communicate securely with the MyID CMS back end.

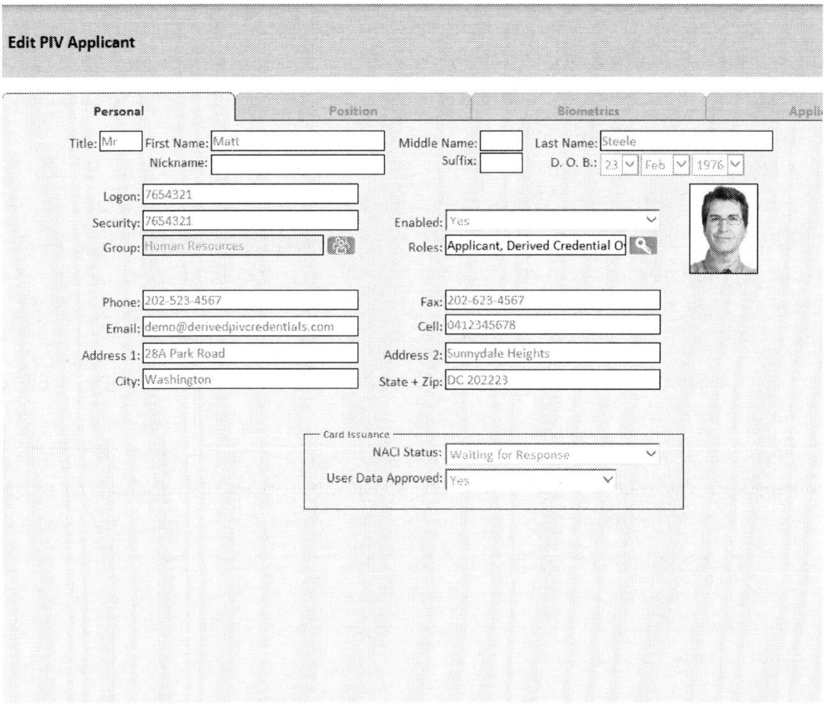

Derived Personal Identity Verification (PIV) Credentials 49

Figure 5-9. Test PIV card user.

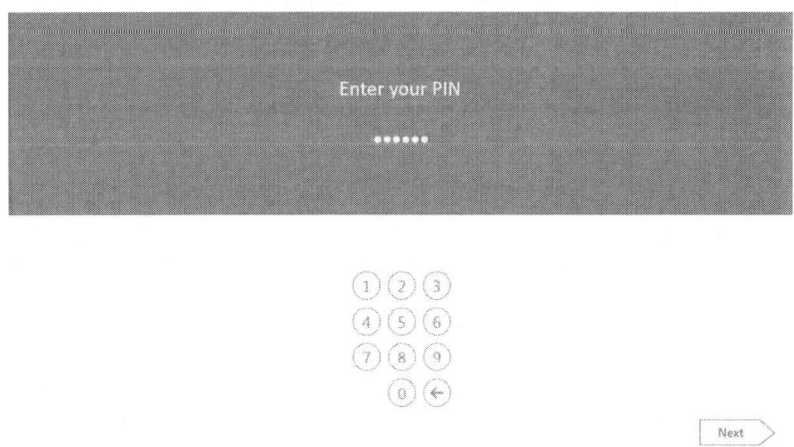

Figure 5-10. Kiosk workflow.

After the MyID CMS has received and validated the OTP obtained from the scanned QR code, the Identity Agent creates containers and generates a key pair on the device by using a third-party FIPS 140-2-certified OpenSSL library for cryptographic services.

The public key is transmitted to the Intercede MyID back end in the form of a PKCS #10 request. We configured our MyID back-end instance to run within a local Internet Information Services instance that uses a TLS end point. An implementer should consult NIST SP 800-52, Revision 1, *Guidelines for the Selection, Configuration, and Use of Transport Layer Security (TLS) Implementations* for configuration guidance in this area [27].

The authentication certificate request is then relayed to the Verizon Managed PKI. We used a test instance of the Verizon Managed PKI in this project; however, the production version for U.S. federal agencies has been granted an authority to operate (ATO) that requires a security controls assessment. We encourage reviewing the ATO and associated security certification as part of an organization's risk management process.

The DPC stored within the software container was protected with a PIN that can be configured to more complex schemes within the MyID Desktop console. A PIN is required before the certificate is delivered to the end point.

The MyID Identity Agent mobile application displays a virtual image of the associated PIV Card, as shown in Figure 5-11.

For Windows-based devices, the initial issuance process starts with the self-service kiosk, the same as for mobile devices. Figure 5-12 shows an example.

Instead of a QR code, however, an OTP is emailed to the DPC applicant (see Figure 5-13).

The DPC applicant then starts the self-service application on the device to collect the DPC (see Figure 5-14).

Once the DPC is issued to the Intel Authenticate token, it can be activated only by using a PIN set by the DPC applicant through the Intel Authenticate client (see Part C for details).

The client allows the user to choose one or more additional *factors* to protect PKI-based keys; however, the PIN-based protection scheme was chosen in this implementation to meet the guidelines in NIST SP 800-157 and NIST SP 800-63-3.

Derived Personal Identity Verification (PIV) Credentials 51

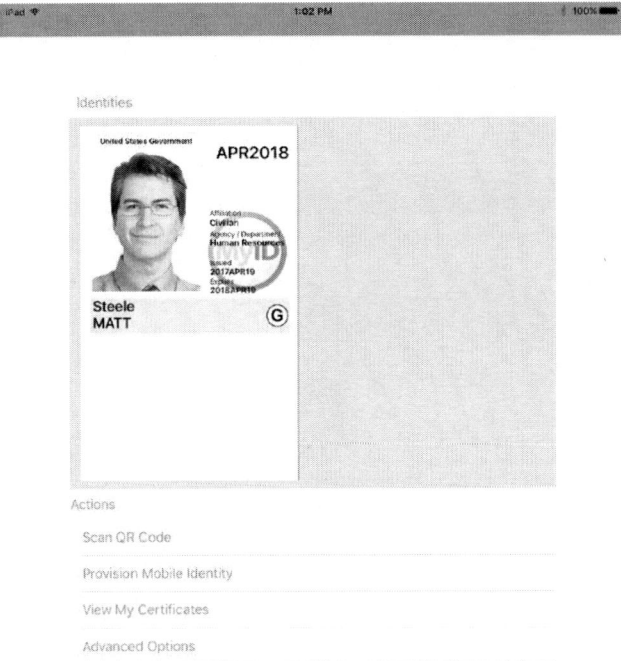

Figure 5-11. DPC in MyID Identity Agent.

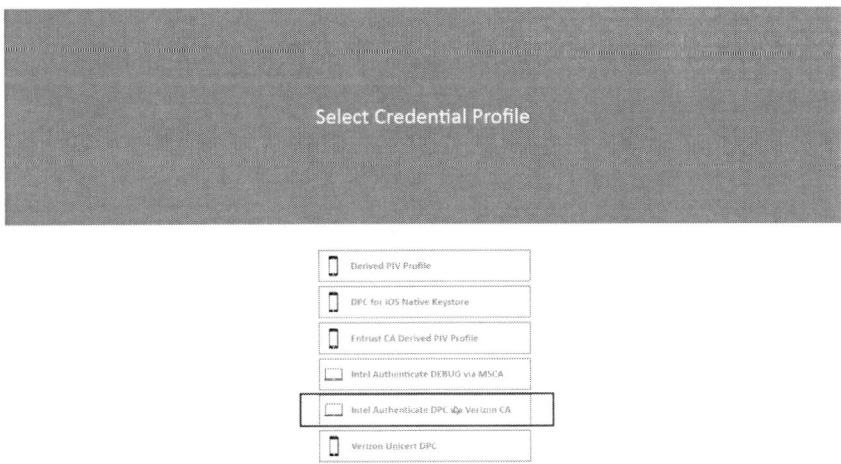

Figure 5-12. DPC applicant chooses Intel Credential Profile.

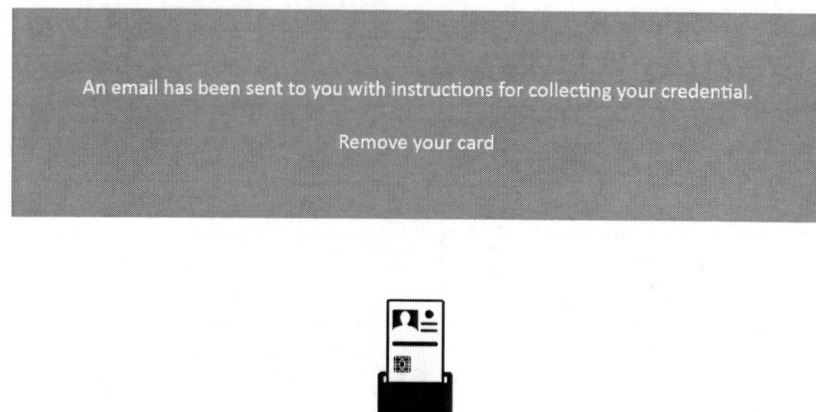

Figure 5-13. Email notification message via Self-Service Kiosk.

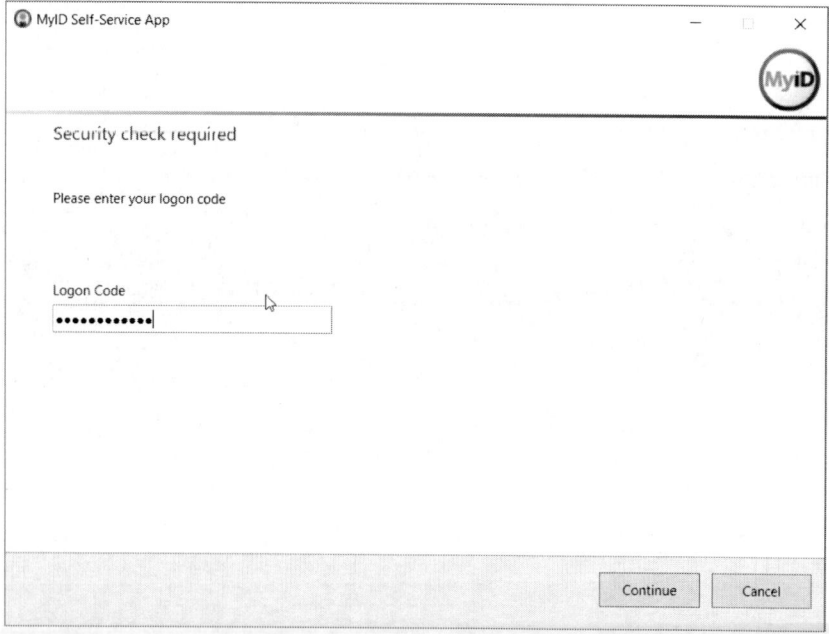

Figure 5-14. DPC applicant inputs the onetime code.

Furthermore, there is an additional layer of security provided by the Intel-protected PIN input user interface. The PIN pad exhibits the following security enhancements:

- Software-based screen scraping or malware attacks that attempt to perform a screen capture of the keypad cannot view the actual layout of the numbers. Instead, the entire keypad is blacked out.
- Each time the keypad window is presented, the numeric keypad is randomized. This means the locations used to enter the PIN change every time. An attacker that captures the PIN entry pattern for successful authenticator activation cannot use it for subsequent PIN entries.
- Authenticator activation input for the PIN entry is translated and used within the protective hardware. The actual PIN value is not exposed outside the hardware.
- A "PIN throttling" mechanism tracks the number of incorrect PIN entry attempts, and at specific intervals will refuse additional PIN attempts for a specific period. This feature minimizes brute force attacks on the PIN.
- Keyboard entry of the PIN is not allowed. This feature minimizes keyboard logger attacks.

Post-issuance, the Derived PIV Authentication certificate, along with an indication that the user controls the associated private key, is visible through the Windows certificate Microsoft Management Console in the Personal folder as shown in Figure 5-15.

5.2.2.2. Maintenance

Maintenance activities for a DPC issued within this architecture are managed in two ways. Operations that require generating a new PIV Authentication certificate (modification, rekey) require the DPC subscriber to repeat the initial issuance process as described in Initial Issuance.

Linkage requirements between the status of the subscriber's PIV Card and DPC are covered by both the PIV and DCMS database being shared within the same system; therefore, DPC processes have direct access to PIV Card information.

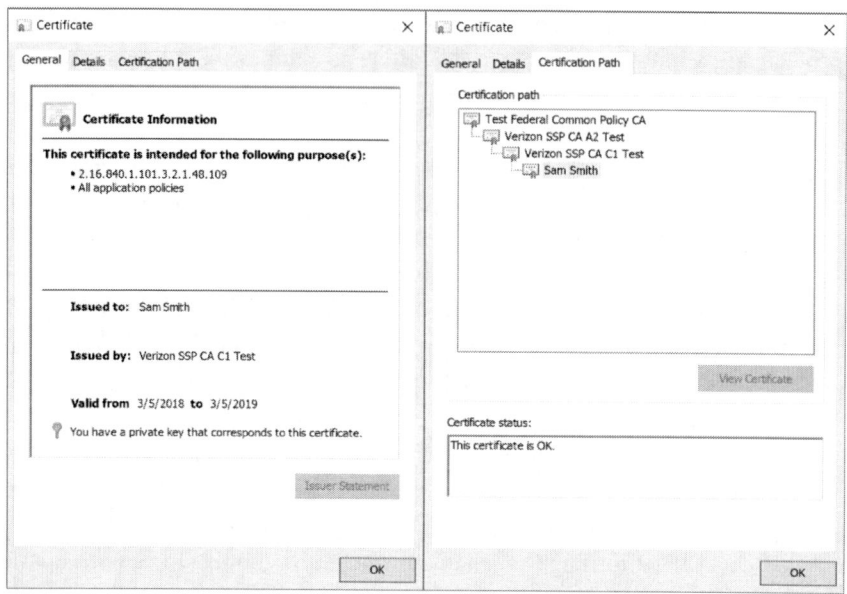

Figure 5-15. Verizon SSP derived PIV authentication certificate.

5.2.2.3. Termination

Direct termination of the DPC is managed through the MyID Desktop console by executing the Cancel Credential workflow. An administrator first finds the DPC subscriber within the database. After the subscriber is found, all credentials issued to them are displayed, including the PIV credential linked to the DPC. An administrator then selects the DPC targeted for termination. This action revokes all certificates associated with the DPC for the target mobile device.

5.2.2.4. Derived PIV Authentication Certificate Management

In this reference architecture, the Verizon SSP issued X.509 credentials for PIV and Derived PIV identities. The Verizon SSP is integrated with the Intercede CMS through a software development kit called the UniCERT Programmatic Interface Java Toolkit. This toolkit communicates to the Verizon SSP through an API that provides PKI functions (enrollment, management, and termination of certificates). Confidentiality, integrity, and authenticity are protected by using TLS 1.2 to protect all operations. In a production setting, availability is ensured through load balancing, redundant systems, and disaster recovery sites. Contact a Verizon SSP representative to received detailed infrastructure diagrams.

5.3. Scenarios and Findings

One aspect of our security evaluation involved assessing how well the reference architectures address the security characteristics that they were intended to support. The Cybersecurity Framework Subcategories were used to provide structure to the security assessment by consulting the specific sections of each standard that are cited in reference to a Subcategory. The cited sections provide validation points that the example solutions would be expected to exhibit. Using the Cybersecurity Framework Subcategories as a basis for organizing our analysis allowed us to systematically consider how well the reference designs support the intended security characteristics.

Our reference architectures primarily support the Function known as Protect (PR) of the Cybersecurity Framework, which features Identity Management and Access Control (AC) as an outcome Subcategory. We discuss the associated Subcategories in the following subsections.

5.3.1. PR.AC-1: Identities and Credentials Are Issued, Managed, Verified, Revoked, and Audited for Authorized Devices, Users, and Processes

To address the Function known as Protect of the Cybersecurity Framework, users of the Derived PIV CMS in the *managed architecture* are administered through group and role membership. In this reference architecture, a privileged user managed the CMS configuration and security options in the Entrust Datacard IdentityGuard administrative website. Furthermore, the on-premises deployment of MobileIron Core used a local privileged credential to manage configuration of the mobile device policies.

In the managed architecture, we worked with Entrust Datacard engineers to populate sample PIV information within IdentityGuard. This sample PIV user data was linked to local user data in an Active Directory repository that was also leveraged by the MobileIron Core user management system.

Similarly, in the hybrid architecture, access privileges for administrative functions are managed through group and role membership. For instance, the administrator role, which has the highest level of privilege, is separately defined from the manager role that is responsible only for requests from individual DPC holders.

The hybrid architecture also supports management of DPC users by obscuring authenticator feedback through a protected PIN pad when the DPC Authentication keys are stored by Intel Authenticate. The protected PIN pad reduces the threat of shoulder surfing from unauthorized individuals by randomizing the numeric keypad.

When an organization is ready for its own production deployment, we encourage a review of security controls mapped to this Subcategory and for organizations to use Best Practices for Privileged User PIV Authentication [28] as a resource.

5.3.2. PR.AC-3: Remote Access Is Managed

To address the Function known as Protect, the organizationally owned mobile devices of DPC subscribers are managed through an EMM to establish usage restrictions, configuration requirements, connection requirements, and implementation guidance for organization-controlled mobile devices [5]. While we used a basic set of security policies in our project to enforce DPC requirements, such as using an application passcode to unlock the DPC before use, holistic mobile device security implementation is out of scope for the example implementations within this practice guide. Readers should refer to the Mobile Device Security for Enterprises Project at the NCCoE for guidance that will enable tailoring the work in this practice guide for their organization's needs.

5.3.3. PR.AC-6: Identities Are Proofed and Bound to Credentials and Asserted in Interactions

To address the Function known as Protect, a DPC solution can help authenticate nonorganizational users to logical systems. Implementers of systems that require PIV Authentication as part of access control can (if appropriate) accept DPCs from outside their organization. This is due to the DPC linkage to the PIV Card that leverages the processes and technical standards documented in NIST SP 800-63-3 and FIPS 201-2.

5.3.4. PR.AC-7: Users, Devices, and Other Assets Are Authenticated (e.g., Single-Factor, Multifactor) Commensurate with the Risk of the Transaction (e.g., Individuals' Security and Privacy Risks and Other Organizational Risks)

To address the Function known as Protect, the managed architecture with EMM integration example implementation allows an organization to create a policy to lock and/or wipe the device after an organization-set number of unsuccessful authenticator unlock attempts. This results in the DPC becoming unusable until an administrator acts to either unlock the device or force reenrollment for the DPC.

5.3.5. *PR.DS-2: Data in Transit Is Protected*

To address the Function known as Protect, the example implementations protect data in transit by ensuring the integrity and confidentiality through client/server mutually authenticated internet protocols. For example, network traffic originating from the mobile device transmitted to the EMM server and cloud services is protected through logical means by using TLS. Further, the cryptographic modules used in the DPC provisioning applications on the mobile device were validated to FIPS 140-2 Level 1. Table 5-1 lists the FIPS-validated modules used in the reference architectures.

Table 5-1. FIPS 140-2 validation of cryptographic modules

Cryptographic Token FIPS 140-2 Validation	Cryptographic Token Type	Module Name	Module Type	Source
Level 1	MobileIron Container Software Token	OpenSSL FIPS Object Module	Software	https://csrc.nist.gov/projects/crypto-graphic-module-validation-program/Certificate/1747
Level 1	Intercede Container Software Token	OpenSSL FIPS Object Module	Software	https://csrc.nist.gov/projects/crypto-graphic-module-validation-program/Certificate/1747
Level 1	Intel Authenticate	Cryptographic Module for Intel vPro Platforms' Security Engine Chipset	Firmware—Hybrid	https://csrc.nist.gov/projects/crypto-graphic-module-validation-program/Certificate/2720

5.3.6. *PR.DS-5: Protections against Data Leaks Are Implemented*

To address the Function known as Protect, we used the client/server mutually authenticated internet protocols as mentioned in Section 5.3.5 as a boundary protection device, enforcing the flow control of DPC-related life-cycle information. The example implementations also protect against data leaks by restricting privileged accounts to specific personnel and by using local accounts. We also used subnetworks and DMZs to logically separate sensitive systems from other internal enterprise workstations.

5.3.7. *PR.IP-3: Configuration Change Control Processes Are in Place*

To address the Function known as Protect, DPC processes and procedures in NIST SP 800-157 are managed through technical controls provided by the Derived PIV Credential Management Systems (Entrust Datacard Identity-

Guard, Intercede MyID CMS). For example, if the PIV Card status is terminated, there is a process in place to revoke the Derived PIV Authentication certificate.

5.4. Authenticator AAL Mapping

Based on NIST's Digital Identity Guidelines, the strength of an authentication transaction is measured by the AAL. A higher AAL authenticator requires more resources and capabilities by attackers to subvert the authentication process. This DPC Project meets the requirements for the AAL-2 software multifactor authenticator. Table 5-2 lists the authenticator requirements at AAL-2, which provide high confidence that the claimant controls the authenticator(s) bound to the subscriber's account and maps it to the corresponding requirement in NIST SP 800-157.

Table 5-2. AAL-2 authenticator requirements mapping

Requirement Identifier	NIST SP 800-63-3 Authenticator Requirement	NIST SP 800-157 Guideline
1	Multifactor software cryptographic authenticators encapsulate one or more secret keys that are unique to the authenticator and are accessible only through the input of an additional factor—either a memorized secret or a biometric.	Use of the Derived PIV Authentication private key, or access to the plain text or wrapped private key, shall be blocked prior to password-based subscriber authentication. ... The required password length shall be at least six characters.
2	The key SHOULD be stored in suitably secure storage available to the authenticator application (e.g., key chain storage, Trusted Platform Module, Trusted Execution Environment).	Many mobile devices on the market provide a hybrid approach where the key is stored in hardware, but a software cryptographic module uses the key during an authentication operation. ... Therefore, the hybrid approach is recommended when supported by mobile devices and applications.
3	The key SHALL be strongly protected against unauthorized disclosure by access controls that limit access to the key to only those software components on the device requiring access.	No mapping exists.
4	Multifactor cryptographic software authenticators SHOULD discourage and SHALL NOT facilitate cloning of the secret key onto multiple devices.	For Derived PIV Authentication certificates issued under id-fpki-commonpivAuth-derived (LOA-3), the Derived PIV Authentication key pair shall be generated within a cryptographic module that has been validated to [FIPS 140] Level 1 or higher.

Requirement Identifier	NIST SP 800-63-3 Authenticator Requirement	NIST SP 800-157 Guideline
5	Any memorized secret used by the authenticator for activation SHALL be a randomly chosen numeric value at least six decimal digits in length or other memorized secret meeting the requirements of Section 5.1.1.2 (Memorized Secret Verifiers).	Use of the Derived PIV Authentication private key or access to the plain text or wrapped private key shall be blocked prior to password-based subscriber authentication. ... The required password length shall be at least six characters.
6	Any memorized secret used by the authenticator for activation SHALL be rate limited as specified in Section 5.2.2.	Throttling mechanisms may be used to limit the number of attempts that may be performed over a given period.
7	A biometric activation factor SHALL meet the requirements of Section 5.2.3, including limits on the number of consecutive authentication failures.	Biometric activation is outside the bounds of NIST SP 800-157.
8	The unencrypted key and activation secret or biometric sample, and any biometric data derived from the biometric sample such as a probe produced through signal processing, SHALL be zeroized immediately after an authentication transaction has taken place.	No mapping exists. Biometric sample not collected for activation of the authenticator

In Table 5-3, we have documented how each authenticator used in the reference architectures satisfies AAL-2 requirements identified in Table 5-2.

Table 5-3. AAL technology mappings for authenticators used

Requirement Identifier	Authenticator		
	MobileIron Container Software Token	Intercede Container Software Token	Intel Authenticate
1	PIN required to activate token	PIN required to activate token	PIN required to activate token
2	Encrypted software container	Encrypted software container	Hardware/firmware protection
3	Authentication key available only to other MobileIron secure container applications with PIN	Authentication key available only to other Intercede secure container applications with PIN	Authentication key available for domain log-on and VPN with PIN

Table 5-3. (Continued)

Requirement Identifier	Authenticator		
	MobileIron Container Software Token	Intercede Container Software Token	Intel Authenticate
4	No export mechanism available, and device encryption discourages cloning	No export mechanism available, and device encryption discourages cloning	Authentication key binds to unique hardware key
5	Configurable PIN length and complexity rules	Configurable PIN length and complexity rules	Configurable PIN length and complexity rules
6	Configurable PIN lock after failed attempts	Configurable PIN lock after failed attempts	Protected PIN input has built-in throttling mechanism.
7	Biometric activation is outside the bounds of NIST SP 800-157.	Biometric activation is outside the bounds of NIST SP 800-157.	Biometric activation is outside the bounds of NIST SP 800-157.

6. Future Build Considerations

Mobile technologies such as DPC are constantly evolving. This project seeks to keep reasonable pace with the changing mobile landscape while sustaining an attainable scope bound by current policies. Moving forward, we will consider additional challenges for future DPC projects, including:

- *Application Enablement*–To leverage DPCs, an organization needs to enable applications on its mobile devices and from the relying-party perspective. Mobile device application development is complicated by the various operating systems, cryptographic token options, and third-party software development kits provided by software containers. Further, modifying the source code of third-party closed mobile applications can be difficult or impossible. Relying parties face similar challenges with legacy systems that can be difficult to make ready for DPCs. Future work might focus on adopting native embedded cryptographic tokens provided by hardware manufacturers and on using federations for relying parties such as cloud service providers.
- *Architecture Expansion*–Integrate with an identity management system (IDMS), which retains identity data that is retrieved from authoritative sources, to provide DPC subscriber PIV eligibility status

information. NIST SP 800-157 recommends that the issuer of the DPC prevent further use of the DPC when the subscriber is no longer eligible for a PIV Card. Integration with an IDMS would store the eligibility of the DPC subscriber to help determine when DPC should be revoked, and it allows for DPC status to remain independent of the PIV Card status. This is helpful in the case of lost or stolen cards to allow a DPC subscriber to keep working without a PIV Card.
- *Key Management (Encryption) Key Recovery*–Mobile users should be able to recover key management keys from escrow. Unlike a signature key, the same key management key that is stored on the PIV Card is necessary to decrypt encrypted email stored on the device, for example.

The NCCoE DPC Project team welcomes submissions of use cases, noting that such input could become the basis for additional challenges for future projects. Please submit your use cases to piv-nccoe@nist.gov.

Appendix A: List of Acronyms

AAL	Authenticator Assurance Level
AD	Active Directory
APDU	Application Protocol Data Unit
API	Application Programming Interface
ATO	Authority to Operate
CA	Certificate Authority
CMS	Credential Management System
COI	Community of Interest
CRADA	Cooperative Research and Development Agreement
CRL	Certificate Revocation List
CSP	Credential Service Provider
CVE	Common Vulnerabilities and Exposures
DCMS	Derived PIV Credential Management System
DHS	Department of Homeland Security
DMZ	Demilitarized Zone
DNS	Domain Name System
DPC	Derived PIV Credential
EMM	Enterprise Mobility Management

(Continued)

FICAM	Federal Identity, Credential, and Access Management
FIPS	Federal Information Processing Standard
FRN	Federal Register Notice
GSA	General Services Administration
HR	Human Resources
HSPD-12	Homeland Security Presidential Directive-12
HTTP	Hypertext Transfer Protocol
IAL	Identity Assurance Level
ICAM	Identity, Credential, and Access Management
IDAM	Identity and Access Management
IDMS	Identity Management System
IETF	Internet Engineering Task Force
IT	Information Technology
LDAP	Lightweight Directory Access Protocol
LOA	Level of Assurance
microSD	Micro Secure Digital
MTC	Mobile Threat Catalogue
NCCoE	National Cybersecurity Center of Excellence
NFC	Near-Field Communication
NICE	National Initiative for Cybersecurity Education
NIST	National Institute of Standards and Technology
NVD	National Vulnerability Database
OCSP	Online Certificate Status Protocol
OS	Operating System
OTP	Onetime Password
PIN	Personal Identification Number
PIV	Personal Identity Verification
PKCS	Public Key Certificate Standard
PKI	Public Key Infrastructure
PKIX-CMP	Public Key Infrastructure X.509—Certificate Management Protocol
QR	Quick Response
RFC	Request for Comments
RMF	Risk Management Framework
SaaS	Software as a Service

SD	Secure Digital
SP	Special Publication
SQL	Structured Query Language
SSM	Self-Service Module
SSP	Shared Service Provider
TLS	Transport Layer Security
UICC	Universal Integrated Circuit Card
URL	Uniform Resource Locator
U.S.	United States
USB	Universal Serial Bus
VPN	Virtual Private Network
WAN	Wide Area Network
XAP	XML Administration Protocol

Appendix B: Glossary

All significant technical terms used within this document are defined in other key documents, including National Institute of Standards and Technology (NIST) Special Publication (SP) 800-157, *Guidelines for Derived Personal Identity Verification (PIV) Credentials* [6]; and NIST SP 800-63-3, *Digital Identity Guidelines* [7]. As a convenience to the reader, terms critical to an understanding of DPCs are in this glossary.

Applicant	An individual who has applied for but has not yet been issued a Derived PIV Credential
Asymmetric keys	Two related keys, a public key and a private key, that are used to perform complementary operations, such as encryption and decryption or signature generation and signature verification
Authenticated protected channel	An encrypted channel that uses approved cryptography where the connection initiator (client) has authenticated the recipient (server)
Authentication	The process of establishing confidence of authenticity. In this case, it is the validity of a person's identity and the PIV Card.
Card	An integrated circuit card
Cardholder	An individual possessing an issued PIV Card

(Continued)

Card management system	The system that manages the life cycle of a PIV Card application
Card reader	An electronic device that connects an integrated circuit card and the card applications therein to a client application
Certificate revocation list	A list of revoked public key certificates created and digitally signed by a certification authority
Certification Authority	A trusted entity that issues and revokes public key certificates
Credential	Evidence attesting to one's right to credit or authority. In this standard, it is the PIV Card and data elements associated with an individual that authoritatively bind an identity (and, optionally, additional attributes) to that individual.
Cryptographic key (key)	A parameter used in conjunction with a cryptographic algorithm that determines the specific operation of that algorithm
Demilitarized zone	Perimeter network segment that is logically between internal and external networks. Its purpose is to enforce the internal network's information assurance policy for external information exchange and to provide external, untrusted sources with restricted access to releasable information while shielding the internal networks from outside attacks.
Derived PIV Application	A standardized application residing on a removable hardware cryptographic token that hosts a Derived PIV Credential and associated mandatory and optional elements
Derived PIV Credential	An X.509 Derived PIV Authentication certificate with associated public and private key that is issued in accordance with the requirements specified in this document where the PIV Authentication certificate on the applicant's PIV Card serves as the original credential. The Derived PIV Credential (DPC) is an additional common identity credential under Homeland Security Presidential Directive-12 and

	Federal Information Processing Standards (FIPS) 201 that is issued by a federal department or agency and is used with mobile devices.
E-authentication assurance level	A measure of trust or confidence in an authentication mechanism defined in publications Office of Management and Budget (OMB)-04-04 and NIST SP 800-63 in terms of four levels: • Level 1: LITTLE OR NO confidence • Level 2: SOME confidence • Level 3: HIGH confidence • Level 4: VERY HIGH confidence
Federal Information Processing Standards	A standard for adoption and use by federal departments and agencies that has been developed within the Information Technology Laboratory and published by NIST. A standard in FIPS covers a specific topic in information technology to achieve a common level of quality or some level of interoperability.
Identity	The set of physical and behavioral characteristics by which an individual is uniquely recognizable
Identity management system	One or more systems or applications that manage the identity verification, validation, and issuance process
Identity proofing	The process of providing sufficient information (e.g., identity history, credentials, documents) to establish an identity
Identity verification	The process of confirming or denying that a claimed identity is correct by comparing the credentials (something you know, something you have, something you are) of a person requesting access with those credentials previously proven and stored in the PIV Card or system and associated with the identity being claimed
Issuer	The organization that is issuing the PIV Card (or DPC) to an applicant. Typically, this is an organization for which the applicant is working.

(Continued)

Level of assurance	OMB Memorandum M-04-04 describes four levels of identity assurance and references NIST technical standards and guidelines, which are developed for agencies to use in identifying the appropriate authentication technologies that meet their requirements.
Mobile device	A portable computing device that (1) has a small form factor so it can easily be carried by a single individual; (2) is designed to operate without a physical connection (e.g., wirelessly transmit or receive information); (3) possesses local, nonremovable or removable data storage; and (4) includes a self-contained power source. Mobile devices may also include voice communication capabilities, onboard sensors that allow the devices to capture information, and/or built-in features for synchronizing local data with remote locations. Examples are smartphones, tablets, and e-readers.
Multifactor authentication	Authentication using two or more factors to achieve authentication. Factors are (i) something you know (e.g., password/personal identification number); (ii) something you have (e.g., cryptographic identification device, token); and (iii) something you are (e.g., biometric).
Personal identification number	A secret number that a cardholder memorizes and uses to authenticate his or her identity as part of multifactor authentication
Personal identity verification (card)	A physical artifact (e.g., identity card, "smart" card) issued to an individual, which contains a PIV Card application that stores identity credentials (e.g., photograph, cryptographic keys, digitized fingerprint representation) so that the claimed identity of the cardholder can be verified against the stored credentials by another person (human-readable and -verifiable) or an automated process (computer-readable and -verifiable)

PKI-PIV Authentication key (PKI-AUTH)	A PIV Authentication mechanism that is implemented by an asymmetric key challenge/response protocol by using the PIV Authentication key of the PIV Card and a contact reader or a contactless card reader that supports the virtual contact interface
Private key	The secret part of an asymmetric key pair that is typically used to digitally sign or decrypt data
Public key	The public part of an asymmetric key pair that is typically used to verify signatures or encrypt data.
Public key infrastructure	A support service to the PIV system that provides the cryptographic keys needed to perform digital signature-based identity verification and to protect communications and storage of enterprise data
Sponsor	Submits a Derived PIV Credential request on behalf of the applicant
Subscriber	The individual who is the subject named or identified in a Derived PIV Authentication certificate and who holds the token that contains the private key that corresponds to the public key in the certificate

Appendix C. National Institute of Standards and Technology (NIST) Internal Report 8055 [10] Requirements Enumeration and Implementation Mappings

Regulatory Requirement	Req. Number	Req. Section Number	Requirement Name
RC1—Device and Cryptographic Token	RC1.1	2.3.1.1	Private key in cryptographic module
	RC1.2	2.3.1.2	Alternative tokens
	RC1.3	2.3.1.7	Only digital signatures demonstrated (Section 4.8.2)
	RC1.4	2.3.3.5.1	Zeroize or destroy the token due to lost, stolen, damaged, or compromised device
	RC1.5	2.3.3.5.2	Zeroize or destroy the token due to transfer of token or device to another individual
	RC1.6	2.3.3.5.3	Zeroize or destroy the token due to no longer being eligible to have a personal identity verification (PIV) Card

(Continued)

Regulatory Requirement	Req. Number	Req. Section Number	Requirement Name
	RC1.7	2.3.3.5.4	Zeroize or destroy the token due to no longer being eligible to have a Derived PIV Credential
	RC1.8	2.3.5.3.1.1	Removable hardware cryptographic tokens: interface of PIV Card
	RC1.9	2.3.5.3.1.2	Removable hardware cryptographic tokens: secure element
	RC1.10	2.3.5.3.1.3	Removable hardware cryptographic tokens: NIST Special Publication (SP) 800-157 Appendix B Application Protocol Data Unit command interface
	RC1.11	2.3.5.3.1.4	Removable hardware cryptographic tokens: NIST SP 800-157 Appendix B digital signature, key management, authentication private key, and its corresponding certificate
	RC1.12	2.3.5.3.1.5.1	Removable hardware cryptographic tokens: Secure Digital (SD) card with cryptographic module: onboard secure element or security system
	RC1.13	2.3.5.3.1.5.2	Removable hardware cryptographic tokens: SD card with cryptographic module: NIST SP 800-157 Appendix B interface with the card commands
	RC1.14	2.3.5.3.1.6.1	Removable hardware cryptographic tokens: Universal Integrated Circuit Card (UICC): separate security domain for Derived PIV Application
	RC1.15	2.3.5.3.1.6.2	Removable hardware cryptographic tokens: UICC: NIST SP 800-157 Appendix B application protocol data unit (APDU) command interface
	RC1.16	2.3.5.3.1.6.3	Removable hardware cryptographic tokens: UICC: *Global Platform Card Secure Element Configuration v1.0*
	RC1.17	2.3.5.3.1.7.1	Removable hardware cryptographic tokens: Universal Serial Bus (USB) token with cryptographic module: integrated secure element with *Smart Card Integrated Circuit Card Devices Specification for USB Integrated Circuit Card Devices*
	RC1.18	2.3.5.3.1.7.2	Removable hardware cryptographic tokens: USB token with cryptographic module: NIST SP 800-157 Appendix B application protocol data units command interface with bulk-out and bulk-in command pipe

Derived Personal Identity Verification (PIV) Credentials 69

Regulatory Requirement	Req. Number	Req. Section Number	Requirement Name
	RC1.19	2.3.5.3.1.7.2	Removable hardware cryptographic tokens: USB token with cryptographic module: NIST SP 800-96 for APDU support for contact card readers
	RC1.20	2.3.5.3.2.1	Embedded cryptographic tokens: hardware or software cryptographic module
	RC1.21	2.3.5.3.2.2	Embedded cryptographic tokens: software cryptographic module at level of assurance (LOA)-3
	RC1.22	2.3.5.3.2.3	Embedded cryptographic tokens: key stored in hardware with a software cryptographic module using the key at LOA-3
	RC1.23	2.3.5.3.2.4	Embedded cryptographic tokens: id-fpki-common-pivAuth-derived-hardware or id-fpki-common-pivAuth-derived for certificates
	RC1.24	2.3.5.3.2.5	Embedded cryptographic tokens: other keys stored in the same cryptographic module
	RC1.25	2.3.5.4.6	Embedded cryptographic tokens: authentication mechanism implemented by hardware or software mechanism outside crypto-graphic boundary at LOA-3
	RC1.26	2.3.5.4.7	Implementation and enforcement of authentication mechanism by cryptographic module at LOA-4
	RC1.27	2.3.5.4.10	Support password reset per Appendix B of NIST SP 800-157 for removable token and new issuance of certificate for LOA-3
RC2—PIV Card	RC2.1	2.3.1.4	Identity proofing
	RC2.2	2.3.1.5	Proof of possession of a valid PIV Card
	RC2.3	2.3.2.1	Verification of applicant's PIV Authentication for issuance
	RC2.4	2.3.2.2	Revocation status of PIV Authentication certificate checked after seven days of issuance
	RC2.5	2.3.2.10	Issuance of multiple DPCs
RC3—Public Key Infrastructure (PKI)	RC3.1	2.3.1.3	PKI-based DPC at LOA-3 and LOA-4
	RC3.2	2.3.1.6	X.509 public key certificate
	RC3.3	2.3.3.6	Issuance of Derived PIV Authentication certificate because of subscriber name change
	RC3.4	2.3.5.1.2	Worksheet 10: Derived PIV Authentication certificate profile found in *X.509 Certificate and Certificate Revocation List Profile for the Shared Service Providers Program*
	RC3.5	2.3.5.1.3	No dependency with expiration date of the Derived PIV Authentication certificate with PIV Card

(Continued)

Regulatory Requirement	Req. Number	Req. Section Number	Requirement Name
	RC3.6	2.3.5.2.1	NIST SP 800-78 cryptographic algorithm and key size requirements for the Derived PIV Authentication certificate and private key
RC4—Level of Assurance	RC4.1	2.3.2.3	LOA-3 or LOA-4
	RC4.2	2.3.2.4	LOA-3 DPC issued in person or remotely
	RC4.3	2.3.2.5	Authenticated and protected channel for remote issuance
	RC4.4	2.3.2.6	Identification of each encounter in issuance process involving two or more electronic transactions
	RC4.5	2.3.2.7	Identification of applicant by using biometric sample for LOA-4
	RC4.6	2.3.2.8	Identification of each encounter in issuance process involving two or more electronic transactions of applicant by using biometric sample for LOA-4
	RC4.7	2.3.2.9	Retain biometric sample of applicant for LOA-4
	RC4.8	2.3.3.1	Communication over mutually authenticated secure sessions between issuer and cryptographic module for LOA-4
	RC4.9	2.3.3.2	Encrypted and integrity checks for data transmitted between issuer and cryptographic module for LOA-4
	RC4.10	2.3.3.3	Rekey of and expired or compromised DPC
	RC4.11	2.3.3.4	Rekey of and expired or compromised 2.3.3.4 DPC to new hardware token at LOA-4
	RC4.12	2.3.5.1.1	id-fpki-common-pivAuth-derived-hardware (LOA-4) or id-fpki-common-pivAuth-derived (LOA-3) policy of the X.509 Certificate Policy
	RC4.13	2.3.5.2.2	Key pair generated in hardware cryptographic module validated to FIPS 140 level 2 or higher with level 3 physical security protection for LOA-4
	RC4.14	2.3.5.2.3	Key pair generated in cryptographic module validated to FIPS 140 level 1 or higher for LOA-3

Derived Personal Identity Verification (PIV) Credentials

Regulatory Requirement	Req. Number	Req. Section Number	Requirement Name
RC5—Credential Management System	RC5.1	2.3.4.1	Issuance of a DPC based on information of applicant's PIV Card
	RC5.2	2.3.4.2	Periodically check the status of the PIV Card
	RC5.3	2.3.4.3.1	Termination status of PIV Card checked every 18 hours via notification system
	RC5.4	2.3.4.3.2	Termination of the PIV and DPC record on an integrated management system
	RC5.5	2.3.4.4	Track beyond the revocation of the PIV Authentication certificate
	RC5.6	2.3.4.5.1	Direct access to the PIV Card information for integrated PIV and DPC system
	RC5.7	2.3.4.5.2.1	Access to the back-end attribute exchange
	RC5.8	2.3.4.5.2.2	Notification of DPC system issuer with issuer of PIV Card
	RC5.9	2.3.4.5.2.3	Access to the Uniform Reliability and Revocation Service for termination status
	RC5.10	2.3.5.4.1	Password-based subscriber authentication for Derived PIV Authentication private key
	RC5.11	2.3.5.4.2	Password is not guessable or individually identifiable
	RC5.12	2.3.5.4.3	Minimum password length of six characters
	RC5.13	2.3.5.4.4	Block use of Derived PIV Authentication key after a number of consecutive failed activation attempts.
	RC5.14	2.3.5.4.5	Limit number of attempts over period of 2.3.5.4.5 time with throttling mechanisms.
	RC5.15	2.3.5.4.8.1	Password reset in person: authentication via PKI-AUTH mechanism with subscriber's PIV Card
	RC5.16	2.3.5.4.8.2	Password reset in person: biometric match on subscriber PIV Card or stored in the chain of trust
	RC5.17	2.3.5.4.9.1	Password reset remotely: authentication via PKI-AUTH mechanism with subscriber's PIV Card
	RC5.18	2.3.5.4.9.2	Password reset remotely: strong linkage between the PKI-AUTH session and reset session
	RC5.19	2.3.5.4.9.3	Password reset remotely: same subscriber for the DPC and the PIV Card
	RC5.20	2.3.5.4.9.4	Password reset remotely: reset completed over a protected session

Appendix D: References

[1] Department of Homeland Security. *Homeland Security Presidential Directive 12: Policy for a Common Identification Standard for Federal Employees and Contractors*. [Online]. Available: https://www.dhs.gov/homeland-security-presidential-directive-12.

[2] U.S. Department of Commerce, *Personal Identity Verification (PIV) of Federal Employees and Contractors*, Federal Information Processing Standards (FIPS) Publication 201-2, Aug. 2013. Available: https://doi.org/10.6028/NIST.FIPS.201-2.

[3] National Institute of Standards and Technology (NIST). *Framework for Improving Critical Infrastructure Cybersecurity, Version 1.1*. [Online]. Available: https://www.nist.gov/cyberframework.

[4] Joint Task Force Transformation Initiative, *Risk Management Framework for Information Systems and Organizations*, NIST Special Publication (SP) 800-37 Revision 2, Gaithersburg, Md., Dec. 2018. Available: https://doi.org/10.6028/NIST.SP.800-37r1.

[5] Joint Task Force Transformation Initiative, *Security and Privacy Controls for Federal Information Systems and Organizations*, NIST SP 800-53 Revision 4, Gaithersburg, Md., Apr. 2013. Available: https://doi.org/10.6028/NIST.SP.800-53r4.

[6] Ferraiolo, H., et al., *Guidelines for Derived Personal Identity Verification (PIV) Credentials*, NIST SP 800-157, Gaithersburg, Md., Dec. 2014. Available: https://doi.org/10.6028/NIST.SP.800-157.

[7] Grassi, P., et al., *Digital Identity Guidelines*, NIST SP 800-63-3, Gaithersburg, Md., June 2017. Available: https://doi.org/10.6028/NIST.SP.800-63-3.

[8] Newhouse, W., et al., *National Initiative for Cybersecurity Education (NICE) Cybersecurity Workforce Framework*, NIST SP 800-181, Gaithersburg, Md., Aug. 2017. Available: https://doi.org/10.6028/NIST.SP.800-181.

[9] NIST. *Mobile Threat Catalogue*. [Online]. Available: https://pages.nist.gov/mobile-threat-catalogue/.

[10] Bartock, M., et al., *Derived Personal Identity Verification (PIV) Credentials (DPC) Proof of Concept Research,* NIST Internal Report 8055, Gaithersburg, Md., Jan. 2016. Available: https://doi.org/10.6028/NIST.IR.8055.

[11] IDManagement.gov. *Government Identity and Credentials*. [Online]. Available: https://www.idmanagement.gov/trust-services/#gov-identity-credentials.

[12] "Derived Personal Identity Verification Credentials Building Block," 80 *Federal Register* 157, Aug. 14, 2015. Available: https://www.federalregister.gov/documents/2015/08/14/2015-20039/national-cybersecurity-center-of-excellence-derived-personal-identity-verification-credentials.

[13] Souppaya, M., and K. Scarfone, *Guidelines for Managing the Security of Mobile Devices in the Enterprise,* NIST SP 800-124 Revision 1, Gaithersburg, Md., June 2013. Available: https://doi.org/10.6028/NIST.SP.800-124r1.

[14] OWASP. *Top 10 2014-I2 Insufficient Authentication/Authorization.* [Online]. Available: https://www.owasp.org/index.php/Top_10_2014-I2_Insufficient_Authentication/Authorization.

[15] Department of Homeland Security, *Study on Mobile Device Security*, Apr. 2017. Available: https://www.dhs.gov/sites/default/files/publications/DHS%20Study%20on%20Mobile%20Device%20Security%20-%20April%202017-FINAL.pdf.

[16] Executive Order no. 13800, *Strengthening the Cybersecurity of Federal Networks and Critical Infrastructure*, May 11, 2017. Available: https://www.whitehouse.gov/the-press-office/2017/05/11/presidential-executive-order-strengthening-cybersecurity-federal.

[17] Barrett, M., et al., *The Cybersecurity Framework: Implementation Guidance for Federal Agencies*, Draft, NIST Interagency Report 8170, Gaithersburg, Md., May 2017. Available: https://csrc.nist.gov/publications/detail/nistir/8170/draft.

[18] Brown, C., et al., *Assessing Threats to Mobile Devices & Infrastructure: The Mobile Threat Catalogue,* Draft, NIST Interagency Report 8144, Gaithersburg, Md., Sept. 2016. Available: https://csrc.nist.gov/publications/detail/nistir/8144/draft.

[19] NIST. National Vulnerability Database. [Online]. Available: https://nvd.nist.gov/.

[20] NIST. CVE-2016-6716 Detail, National Vulnerability Database. [Online]. Available: https://nvd.nist.gov/vuln/detail/CVE-2016-6716.

[21] Quirolgico, S., et al., *Vetting the Security of Mobile Applications*, NIST SP 800-163, Gaithersburg, Md., Jan. 2015. Available: https://doi.org/10.6028/NIST.SP.800-163.

[22] The MITRE Corporation. Common Vulnerabilities and Exposures (CVE). [Online]. Available: https://cve.mitre.org/.

[23] U.S. General Services Administration, Decision for Standard Assessment & Authorization, Authorization to Operate Letter, Nov. 3, 2016. Available: https://www.idmanagement.gov/wp-content/uploads/sites/1171/uploads/entrust-ato.pdf.

[24] Simmon, E., DRAFT—*Evaluation of Cloud Computing Services Based on NIST 800-145,* NIST SP 500-322, Gaithersburg, Md., Apr. 2017. Available: https://www.nist.gov/sites/default/files/documents/2017/05/31/evaluation_of_cloud_computing_services_based_on_nist_800-145_20170427clean.pdf.

[25] Federal Public Key Infrastructure Policy Authority, *X.509 Certificate Policy for the U.S. Federal PKI Common Policy Framework*, Version 1.24, May 7, 2015. Available: https://www.idmanagement.gov/wp-content/uploads/sites/1171/uploads/Common-Policy-Framework.pdf.

[26] Adams, C., et al., *Internet X.509 Public Key Infrastructure Certificate Management Protocol (CMP)*, Internet Engineering Task Force Request for Comments 4210, Sept. 2005. Available: https://tools.ietf.org/html/rfc4210.

[27] Polk, T., et al., *Guidelines for the Selection, Configuration, and Use of Transport Layer Security (TLS) Implementations*, NIST SP 800-52 Revision 1, Gaithersburg, Md., Apr. 2014. Available: https://doi.org/10.6028/NIST.SP.800-52r1.

[28] Computer Security Division and Applied Cybersecurity Division, *Best Practices for Privileged User PIV Authentication,* NIST Cybersecurity White Paper, Gaithersburg, Md., Apr. 21, 2016. Available: https://doi.org/10.6028/NIST.CSWP.04212016.

Volume C: How-To Guides

Abstract

Federal Information Processing Standards (FIPS) Publication 201-2, "Personal Identity Verification (PIV) of Federal Employees and Contractors," establishes a standard for a PIV system based on secure and reliable forms of identity credentials issued by the federal government to its employees and contractors. These credentials are intended to authenticate individuals to federally controlled facilities, information systems, and applications as part of access management. In 2005, when FIPS 201 was published, authentication of individuals was geared toward traditional computing devices (i.e., desktop and laptop computers) where the PIV Card provides common multifactor authentication mechanisms through integrated or external smart card readers, where available. With the emergence of computing devices, such as tablets, hybrid computers, and, in particular, mobile devices, the use of PIV Cards has proved to be challenging. Mobile devices lack the integrated smart card readers found in laptop and desktop computers and require separate card readers attached to devices to provide authentication services. To extend the value of PIV systems into mobile devices that do not have PIV Card readers, NIST developed technical guidelines on the implementation and life cycle of identity credentials that are issued by federal departments and agencies to individuals who possess and prove control over a valid PIV Card. These NIST guidelines, published in 2014, describe Derived PIV Credentials (DPCs) that leverage identity proofing and vetting results of current and valid PIV credentials.

To demonstrate the DPC guidelines, the NCCoE at NIST built two security architectures using commercial technology to enable the issuance of a Derived PIV Credential to mobile devices that use Identity Credentialing and Access Management shared services. One option uses a software-only solution while the other leverages hardware built into many computing devices used today.

This project resulted in a freely available NIST Cybersecurity Practice Guide that demonstrates how an organization can continue to provide multifactor authentication for users with a mobile device that leverages the strengths of the PIV standard. Although this project is primarily aimed at the federal sector's needs, it is also relevant to mobile device users with smart-card-based credentials in the private sector.

Derived Personal Identity Verification (PIV) Credentials

Keywords: cybersecurity, Derived PIV Credential (DPC), enterprise mobility management (EMM), identity, mobile device, mobile threat, multifactor authentication, personal identity verification (PIV), PIV Card, smart card

1. Introduction

The following volumes of this guide show information technology (IT) professionals and security engineers how we implemented these example solutions. We cover all of the products employed in these reference designs. We do not re-create the product manufacturers' documentation, which is presumed to be widely available. Rather, these volumes show how we incorporated the products together in our environment.

Note: These are not comprehensive tutorials. There are many possible service and security configurations for these products that are out of scope for these reference designs.

1.1. Practice Guide Structure
This National Institute of Standards and Technology (NIST) Cybersecurity Practice Guide demonstrates two standards-based reference designs and provides users with the information they need to replicate a Derived Personal Identity Verification (PIV) Credential (DPC) life-cycle solution. These reference designs are modular and can be deployed in whole or in part.

This guide contains three volumes:

- NIST SP 1800-12A: *Executive Summary*
- NIST SP 1800-12B: *Approach, Architecture, and Security Characteristics* – what we built and why
- NIST SP 1800-12C: *How-To Guides* – instructions for building the example solutions (you are here)

Depending on your role in your organization, you might use this guide in different ways.

Business decision makers, including chief security and technology officers, will be interested in the *Executive Summary,* NIST SP 1800-12A, which describes the following topics:

- Challenges that enterprises face in issuing strong, multifactor credentials to mobile devices
- Example solutions built at the NCCoE
- Benefits of adopting an example solution

Technology or security program managers who are concerned with how to identify, understand, assess, and mitigate risk will be interested in NIST SP 1800-12B, which describes what we did and why. The following sections will be of particular interest:

- Section 3.5.3, Risk, provides a description of the risk analysis we performed.
- Section 3.5.4, Security Control Map, maps the security characteristics of these example solutions to cybersecurity standards and best practices.

You might share the *Executive Summary,* NIST SP 1800-12A, with your leadership team members to help them understand the importance of adopting a standards-based DPC solution.

IT professionals who want to implement an approach like this will find this whole practice guide useful. You can use this How-To portion of the guide, NIST SP 1800-12C, to replicate all or parts of the build created in our lab. This How-To portion of the guide provides specific product installation, configuration, and integration instructions for implementing the example solutions. We do not recreate the product manufacturers' documentation, which is generally widely available. Rather, we show how we incorporated the products together in our environment to create example solutions.

This guide assumes that IT professionals have experience implementing security products within the enterprise. While we have used a suite of commercial products to address this challenge, this guide does not endorse these particular products. Your organization can adopt one of these solutions or one that adheres to these guidelines in whole, or you can use this guide as a starting point for tailoring and implementing parts of a DPC example solution. Your organization's security experts should identify the products that will best integrate with your existing tools and IT system infrastructure. We hope that you will seek products that are congruent with applicable standards and best practices. Volume B, Section 3.6, Technologies, lists the products that we used and maps them to the cybersecurity controls provided by these reference solutions.

1.2. Build Overview

Unlike desktop computers and laptops that have built-in readers to facilitate the use of PIV Cards, mobile devices pose usability and portability issues because they lack a smart card reader.

NIST sought to address this issue by introducing the general concept of DPCs in NIST Special Publication (SP) 800-63-2, which leverages identity proofing and vetting results of current and valid credentials.

Published in 2014, NIST SP 800-157, *Guidelines for Derived Personal Identity Verification (PIV) Credentials,* defined requirements for initial issuance and maintenance of DPCs. NIST's Applied Cybersecurity Division then created a National Cybersecurity Center of Excellence (NCCoE) project to provide an example implementation for federal agencies and private entities that follows the requirements in NIST SP 800-157.

In the NCCoE lab, the team built an environment that resembles an enterprise network by using commonplace components such as identity repositories, supporting certificate authorities (CA), and web servers.

In addition, products and capabilities were identified that, when linked together, provide two example solutions that demonstrate life-cycle functions outlined in NIST SP 800-157. Figure 1-1 depicts the final lab environment.

2. Product Installation Guides

This section of the practice guide contains detailed instructions for installing and configuring key products used for the depicted architectures documented below, as well as demonstration of the DPC life-cycle management activities of initial issuance and termination.

In our lab environment, each example implementation was logically separated by a virtual local area network (VLAN), where each VLAN represented a mock enterprise environment. The network topology consists of an edge router connected to a demilitarized zone (DMZ).

An internal firewall separates the DMZ from internal systems that support the enterprise. All routers and firewalls used in the example implementations were virtual pfSense appliances.

As a basis, the enterprise network had an instance of Active Directory (AD) to serve as a repository for identities to support DPC vendors.

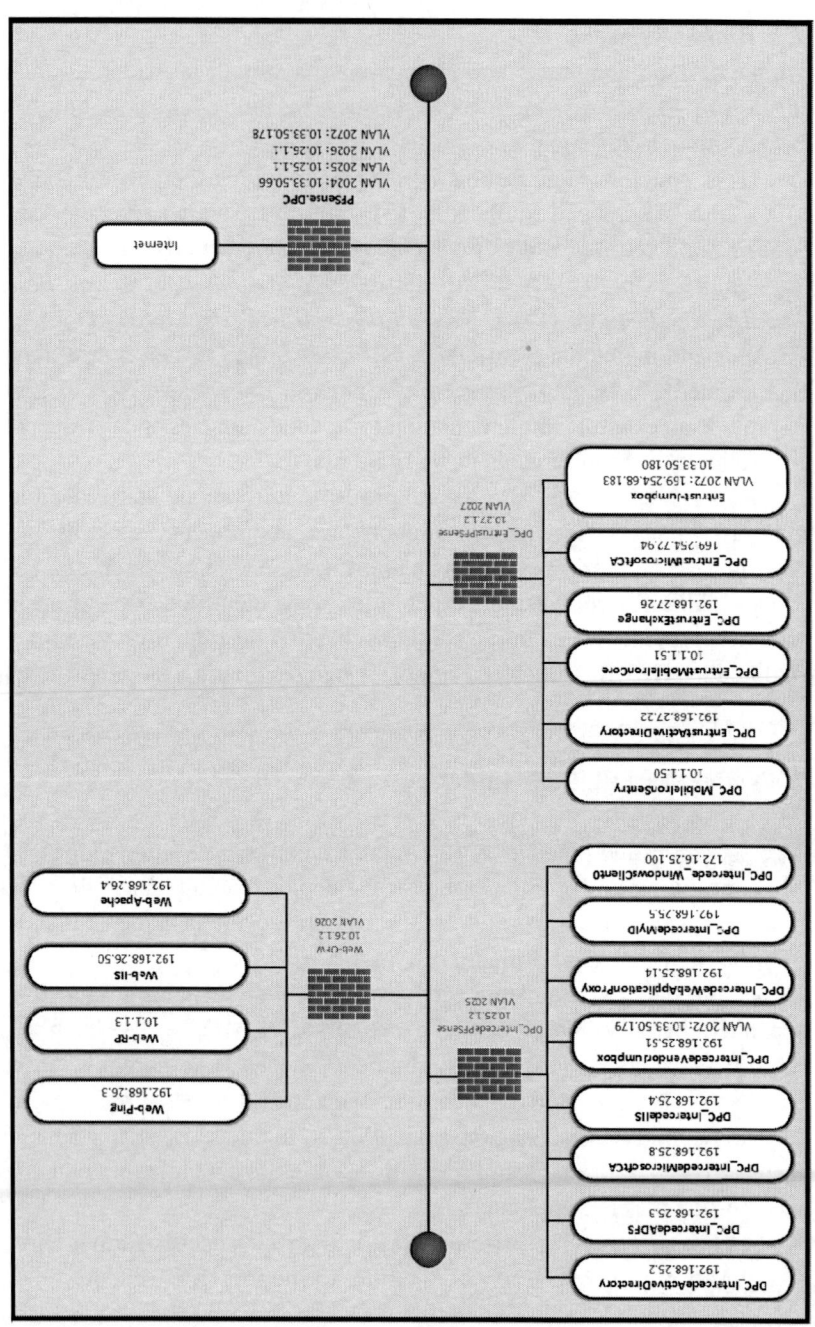

Figure 1-1. Lab network diagram.

2.1. Managed Service Architecture with Enterprise Mobility Management (EMM) Integration

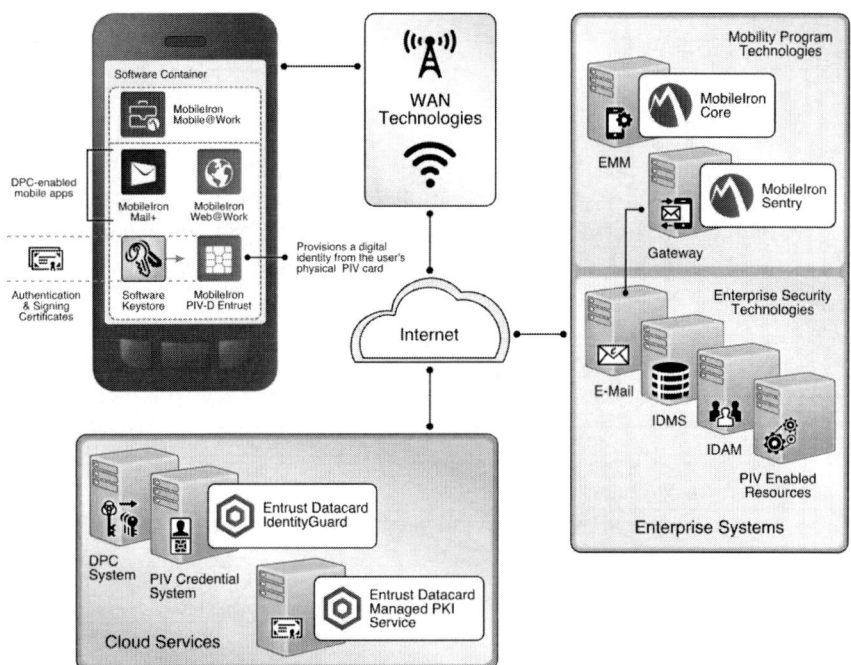

Figure 2-1. Architecture.

2.1.1. Entrust Datacard IdentityGuard (IDG)
Entrust Datacard contributed test instances of its managed public key infrastructure (PKI) service and IdentityGuard products, the latter of which directly integrate with MobileIron to support the use of DPC with MobileIron Mobile@Work applications.

2.1.1.1. Identity Management Profiles
To configure services and issue certificates for DPCs that will work with the organization's user identity profiles, Entrust Datacard will need information on how identities are structured and which users will use PKI services. For this lab instance, Entrust Datacard issued PIV Authentication, Digital Signature, and Encryption certificates for PIV Cards and DPCs for two test identities, as represented in Table 2-1.

Table 2-1. Identity management profiles

Username	Email Address	User Principal Name (UPN)
Patel, Asha	asha@entrust.dpc.nccoe.org	asha@entrust.dpc.nccoe.org
Tucker, Matteo	matteo@entrust.dpc.nccoe.org	matteo@entrust.dpc.nccoe.org

2.1.2. MobileIron Core

MobileIron Core is the central product in the MobileIron suite. The following sections describe the steps for installation, configuration, and integration with Active Directory and the Entrust Datacard IdentityGuard managed service. Key configuration files used in this build are listed in Table 2-2 and are available from the NCCoE DPCs Project website.

Table 2-2. MobileIron core settings

File Name	Description
core.dpc.nccoe.org-Default AppConnect Global Policy-2017-08-14 16-48-36.json	Configures policies such as password strength for the container
core.dpc.nccoe.org-Default Privacy Policy-2017-08-14 16-52-33.json	Configures privacy settings for each enrolled device
core.dpc.nccoe.org-DPC Security Policy-2017-08-14 16-51-07.json	Configures device-level security management settings
shared_mdm_profile.mobileconfig	iOS Mobile Device Management (MDM) profile used when issuing DPC to devices

2.1.2.1. Installation

Follow the steps below to install MobileIron Core:

1. Obtain a copy of the *On-Premise Installation Guide for MobileIron Core, Sentry, and Enterprise Connector* from the MobileIron support portal.
2. Follow the MobileIron Core predeployment and installation steps in Chapter 1 for the version of MobileIron being deployed in the organization's environment. In our lab implementation, we deployed MobileIron Core 9.2.0.0 as a Virtual Core running on VMware 6.0.

Derived Personal Identity Verification (PIV) Credentials

2.1.2.2. General MobileIron Core Setup

The following steps are necessary for mobile device administrators or users to register devices with MobileIron, which is a prerequisite to issuing DPCs.

1. Obtain a copy of *MobileIron Core Device Management Guide for iOS Devices* from the Mobile-Iron support portal.
2. Complete all instructions provided in Chapter 1, Setup Tasks.

2.1.2.3. Configuration of MobileIron Core for DPC

The following steps will reproduce this configuration of MobileIron Core.

2.1.2.3.1. Integration with Active Directory

In our implementation, we chose to integrate MobileIron Core with Active Directory by using lightweight directory access protocol (LDAP). This is optional. General instructions for this process are covered in the Configuring LDAP Servers section in Chapter 2 of *On-Premise Installation Guide for MobileIron Core, Sentry, and Enterprise Connector*. The configuration details used during our completion of selected steps (retaining original numbering) from that guide are given below:

1. From Step 4 in the MobileIron guide, in the *New LDAP Server* dialogue:
   a. Directory Connection:

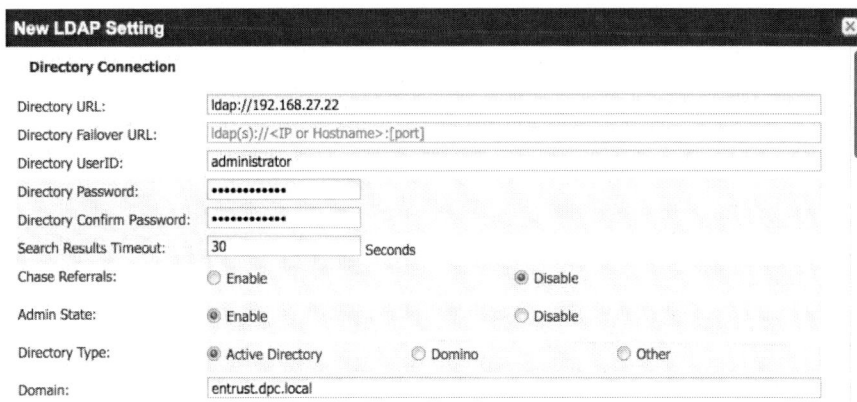

b. Directory Configuration—Organizational Units (OUs):

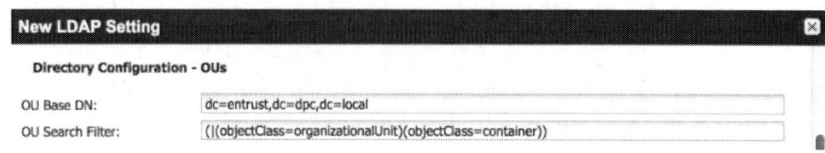

c. Directory Configuration—Users:

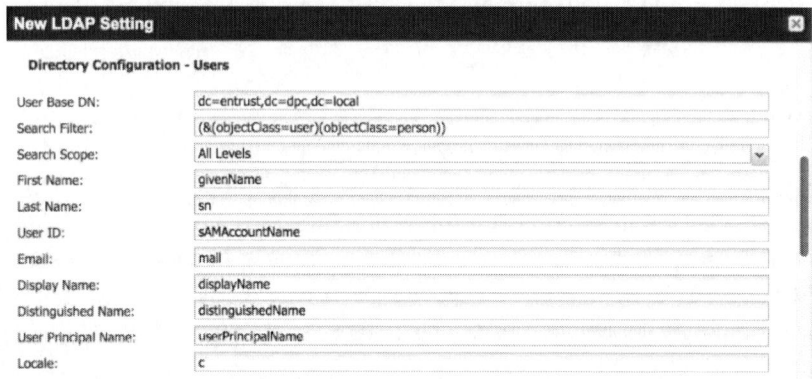

d. Directory Configuration—Groups:

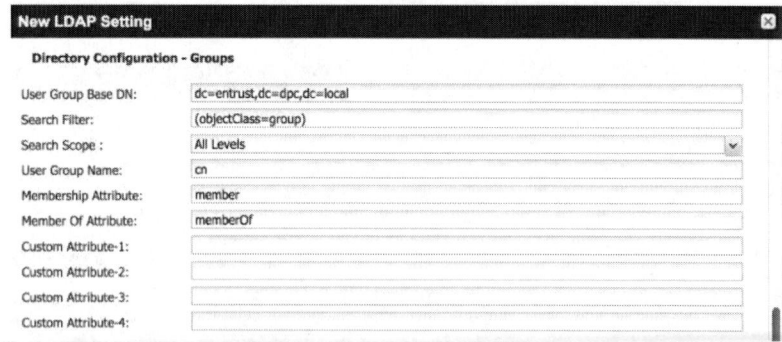

e. LDAP Groups:
- As a prerequisite step, we used Active Directory Users and Computers to create a new security group for DPC-authorized users on the Domain Controller for the

Derived Personal Identity Verification (PIV) Credentials 83

entrust.dpc.local domain. In our example, this group is named DPC Users.

- In the search bar, enter the name of the LDAP group for DPC-authorized users, and click the magnifying glass button; the group name should be added to the Available list.
- In the Available list, select DPC Users, and click the right-arrow button to move it to the Selected list.
- In the Selected list, select the default Users group, and click the left-arrow button to move it to the Available list.

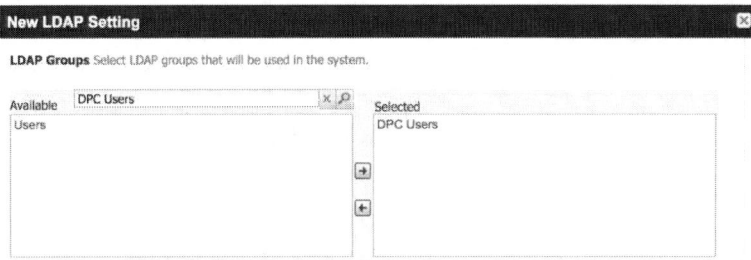

f. Custom Settings: Custom settings were not specified.

g. Advanced Options:

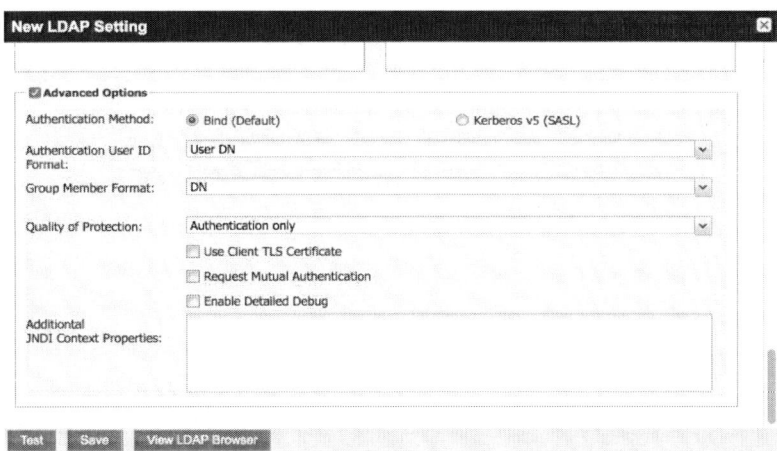

Note: In our lab environment, we did not enable stronger Quality of Protection or enable the Use Client TLS Certificate or Request Mutual Authentication features. However, we recommend that implementers consider using those additional security mechanisms to secure communications with the LDAP server.

2. From Steps 19 to 21 from the MobileIron guide, we tested that MobileIron can successfully query LDAP for DPC Users.
   a. In the **New LDAP Setting** dialogue, click the **Test** button to open the **LDAP Test** dialogue.
   b. In the **LDAP Test** dialogue, enter a **User ID** for a member of the DPC Users group, then click the **Submit** button. A member of the DPC Users group in our environment is **Matteo.**

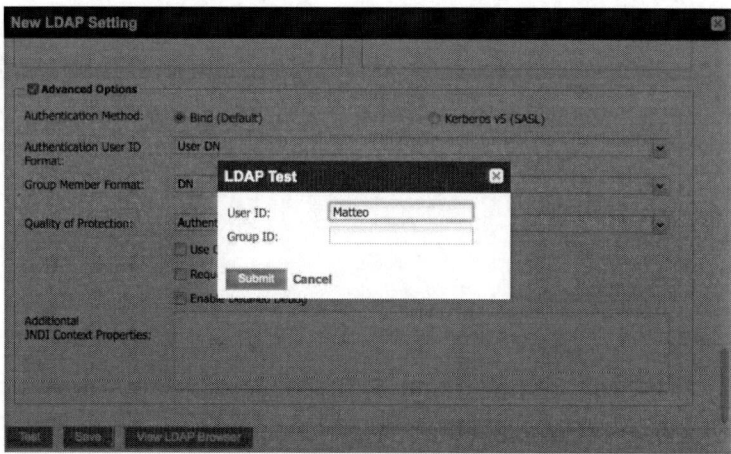

c. The **LDAP Test** dialogue indicates the query was successful:

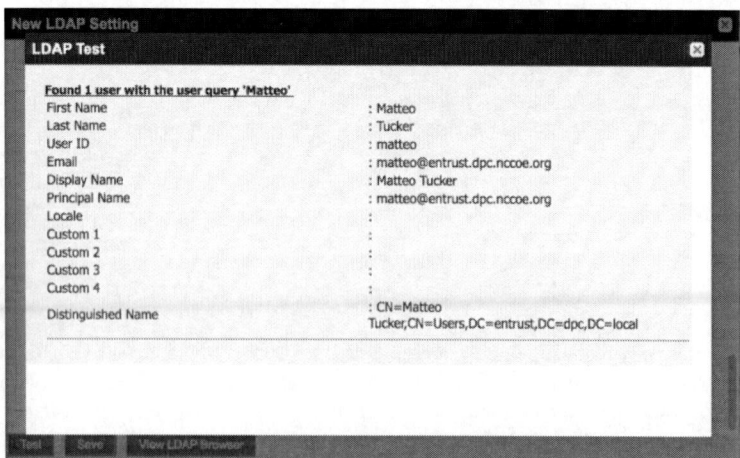

2.1.2.3.2. Create a DPC Users Label

MobileIron uses labels to link policies and device configurations with users and mobile devices. Creating a unique label for DPC users allows mobile device administrators to apply controls relevant for mobile devices provisioned with a derived credential specifically to those devices. We recommend applying DPC-specific policies and configurations to this label, in addition to any others appropriate to an organization's mobile device security policy.

1. In the **MobileIron Core Admin Portal,** navigate to **Devices & Users > Devices.**
2. Select **Advanced Search** (far right).

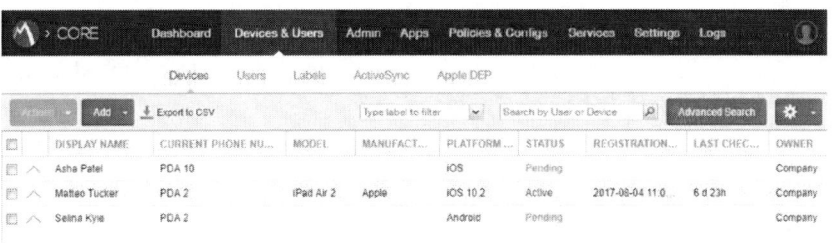

3. In the **Advanced Search** pane:
    a. In the blank rule:
        - In the **Field** drop-down menu, select **User > LDAP > Groups > Name.**
        - In the **Value** drop-down menu, select the Active Directory group created to support DPC-specific MobileIron policies (named **DPC Users** in this example).
    b. Select the **plus sign icon** to add a blank rule.
    c. In the newly created blank rule:
        - In the **Field** drop-down menu, select **Common > Platform.**
        - In the **Value** drop-down menu, select **iOS.**
    d. Optionally, select **Search** to view matching devices.
    e. Select **Save to Label.**

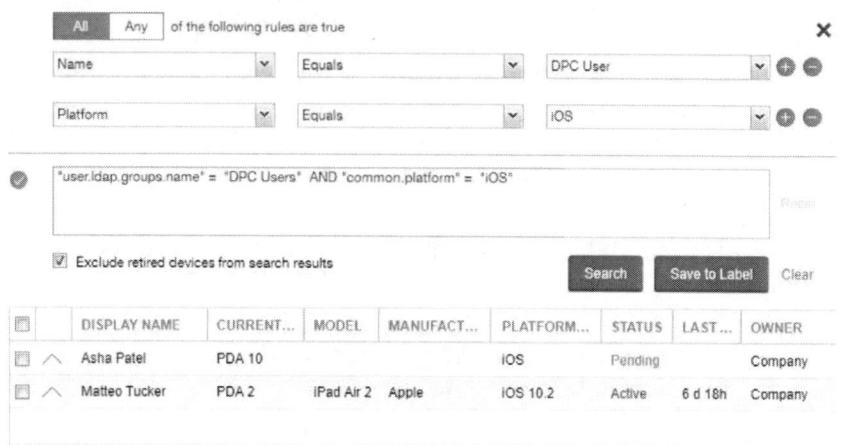

f. In the **Save to Label** dialogue:
   - In the **Name** field, enter a descriptive name for this label (**DPC Users** in this example).
   - In the **Description** field, provide additional information to convey the purpose of this label.
   - Click **Save**.

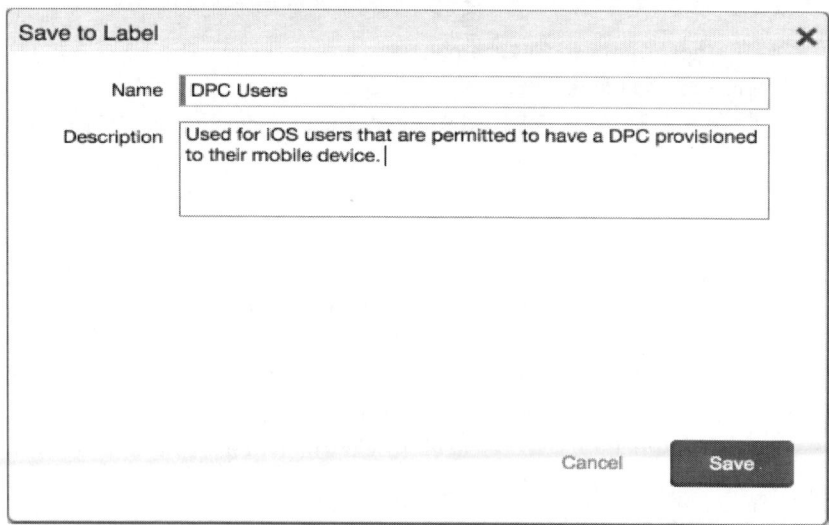

4. Navigate to **Devices & Users > Labels** to confirm that the label was successfully created. It can be applied to DPC-specific MobileIron policies and configurations in future steps.

Derived Personal Identity Verification (PIV) Credentials 87

	NAME	DESCRIPTI...	TYPE	CRITERIA	SPACE	VIEW DE...
	Android	Label for all ...	Filter	"common.platform"="Android" ...	Global	1
	Company-O...	Label for all ...	Filter	"common.owner"="COMPANY...	Global	3
	DPC Users	Used for iO...	Filter	("common.platform" = "iOS" A...	Global	2

2.1.2.3.3. Implement MobileIron Guidance

The following provides the sections from the *MobileIron Derived Credentials with Entrust Guide* that were used in configuring this instance of MobileIron DPC. For sections for which there may be configuration items tailored to a given instance (e.g., local system host names), this configuration is provided only as a reference. We noted any sections in which the steps performed to configure our systems vary from those in the *MobileIron Derived Credentials with Entrust Guide*.

Complete these sections in Chapter 2 of the *MobileIron Derived Credentials with Entrust Guide*:

1. Before beginning:
   a. Configure client certificate authentication to the user portal.
      Note: The root CA certificate or trust chain file can be obtained from Entrust Datacard.
   b. Configure the Entrust IdentityGuard Self-Service Module universal resource locator.
      Note: The URL will be specific to the organization's instance of the IDG service and can be obtained from Entrust Datacard.
   c. Configure PIN-based registration.
   d. Configure user portal roles.
   e. Add the PIV-D Entrust application to the App Catalog and add Web@Work for iOS.
   f. Configure Apps@Work.
      - Set authentication options.
      - Send the Apps@Work web clip to devices.
   g. Configure AppConnect.
      - Configure AppConnect licenses.

- Configure the AppConnect global policy. The **AppConnect Passcode** policy settings for our implementation are presented below.

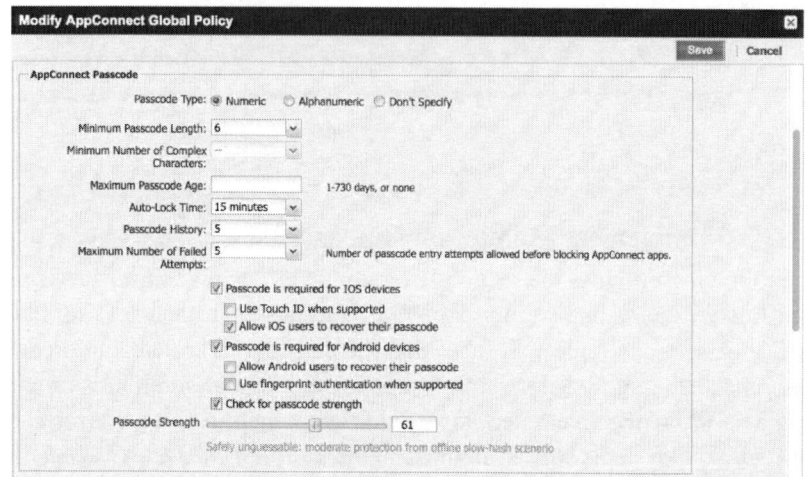

Note: Based on our testing, a **Passcode Strength** of 61/100 or higher prevents easily guessable derived credential passcode combinations (e.g., abc123) from being set by a DPC Applicant.

    h. Configure the PIV-D Entrust application.
    i. Configure client-provided certificate enrollment settings. Note that the configuration items created by completing this section will be used in the following section. Replace Step 2 in this section of the *MobileIron Derived Credentials with Entrust Guide* with the following step:
Select **Add New > Certificate Enrollment > SCEP.**
    j. Configure Web@Work to use DPC:
- Require a device password.
- Configure a Web@Work setting. The **Custom Configurations** key-value pairs set for our instance in Step 4 are presented below.

Note: The value for idCertificate_1 is the descriptive name we applied to the Simple Certificate Enrollment Protocol (SCEP) certificate enrollment configuration for derived credential authentication created in the *MobileIron Derived Credentials with Entrust Guide* section referenced in Step 8.

Derived Personal Identity Verification (PIV) Credentials

KEY	VALUE	i
IdCertificate_1_host	*	✖
IdCertificate_1	DC Authentication	✖

2.1.3. DPC Life-Cycle Workflows

This section describes how to perform the DPC life-cycle activities of initial issuance, maintenance, and termination.

2.1.3.1. DPC Initial Issuance

This section provides the steps necessary to issue a DPC onto a target mobile device.

2.1.3.1.1. Register Target Device with MobileIron

The following steps will register the target mobile device with MobileIron, which will create the secure Mobile@Work container into which a DPC is later provisioned.

1. Insert a valid PIV Card into the card reader attached to or integrated into your laptop or computer workstation.
2. Using a web browser, visit the MobileIron Self-Service Portal URL provided by the administrator.
3. In the MobileIron Self-Service Portal, click **Sign in with certificate.**

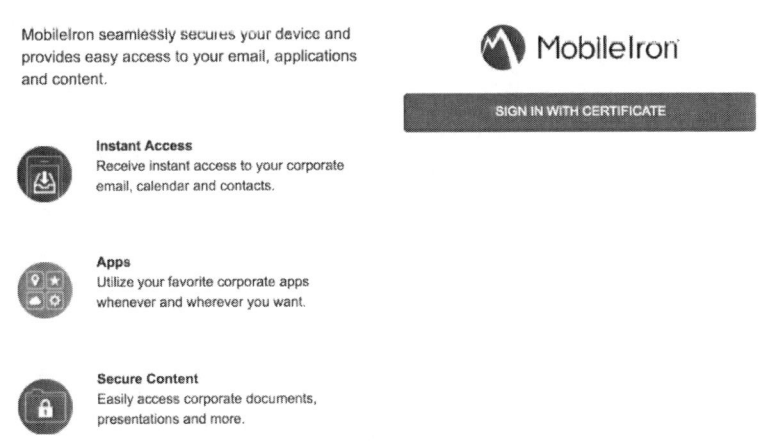

4. In the certificate selection dialogue:
    a. If necessary, identify your PIV Authentication certificate:
        - Highlight a certificate.
        - Select **Show Certificate.**

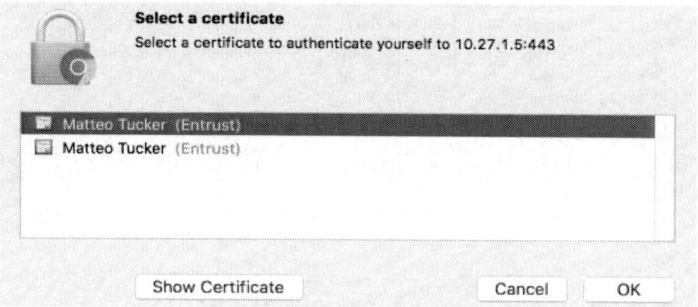

   - Navigate to the **Details** tab.
   - The PIV Authentication certificate contains a **Field** named **Certificate Policies** with a **Value** that contains **Policy Identifier=2.16.840.1.101.3.2.1.3.13.**
   - Repeat Steps i–iii above as necessary.

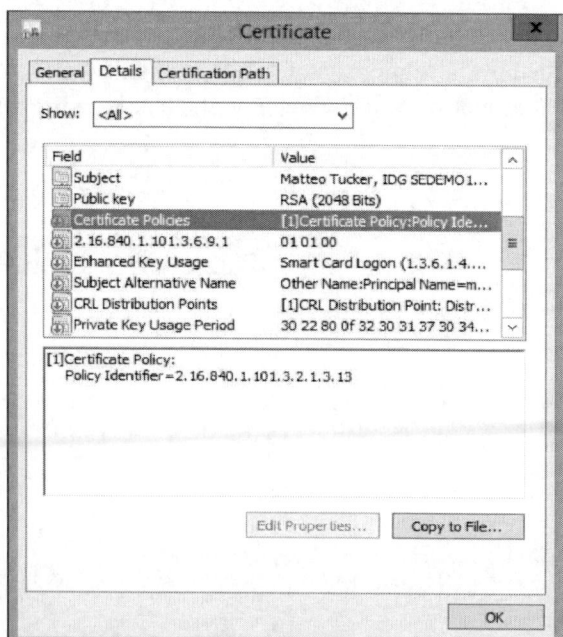

Derived Personal Identity Verification (PIV) Credentials 91

    b. Select your PIV Authentication certificate in the list of available certificates.
    c. Click **OK**.

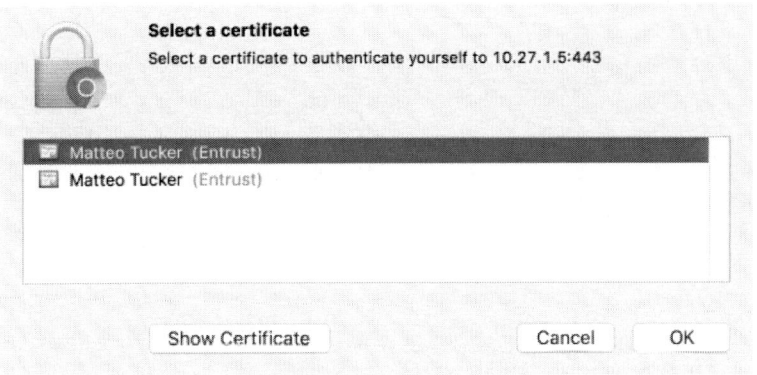

5. In the authentication dialogue:
    a. In the **PIN** field, enter your PIV Card PIN.
    b. Click **OK**.

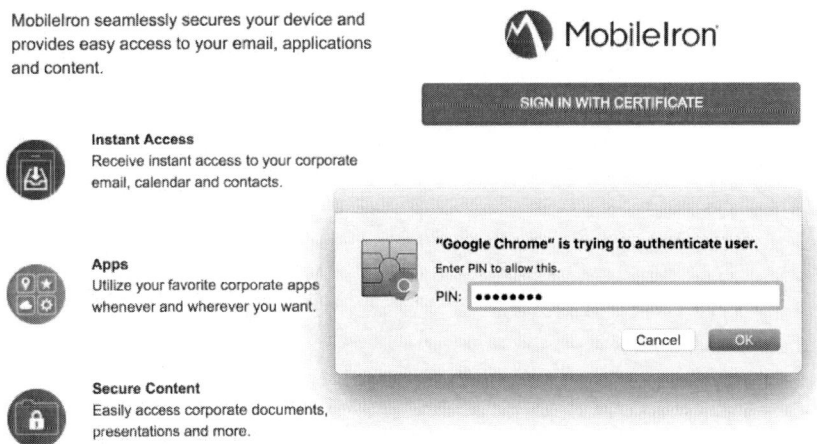

6. In the right-hand sidebar of the device summary screen, click **Request Registration PIN**.

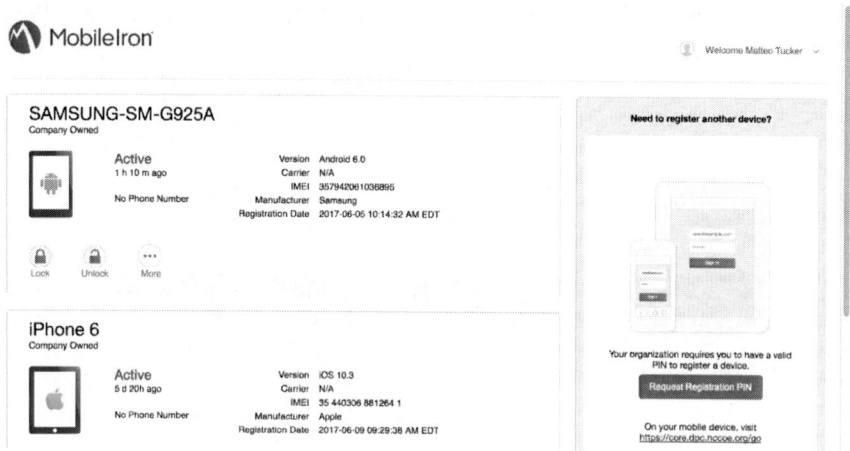

7. In the **Request Registration PIN** page:
   a. Select **iOS** from the **Platform** drop-down menu.
   b. If your device does not have a phone number, check **My device has no phone number.**
   c. If your device has a phone number, enter it in the **Phone Number** field.
   d. Click **Request PIN.**

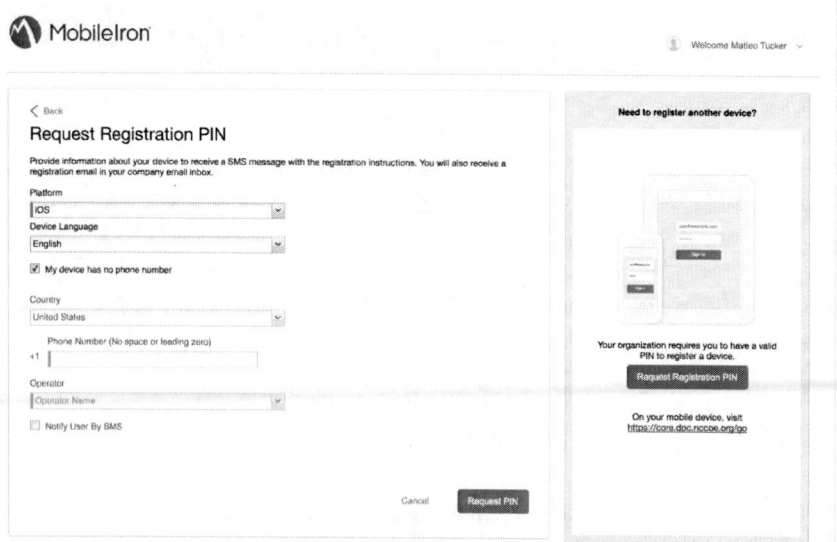

Derived Personal Identity Verification (PIV) Credentials 93

e. The **Confirmation** page, shown in Figure 2-2, displays a unique device **Registration PIN.** Leave this page open while additional registration steps are performed on the target mobile device.

Note: This page may also facilitate the workflow for initial DPC issuance, covered in Section 2.1.3.1.2.

Figure 2-2. MobileIron registration confirmation page.

8. Using the target mobile device, launch the MobileIron **Mobile@Work** application.
9. In the request to grant MobileIron permission to receive push notifications, tap **Allow.**

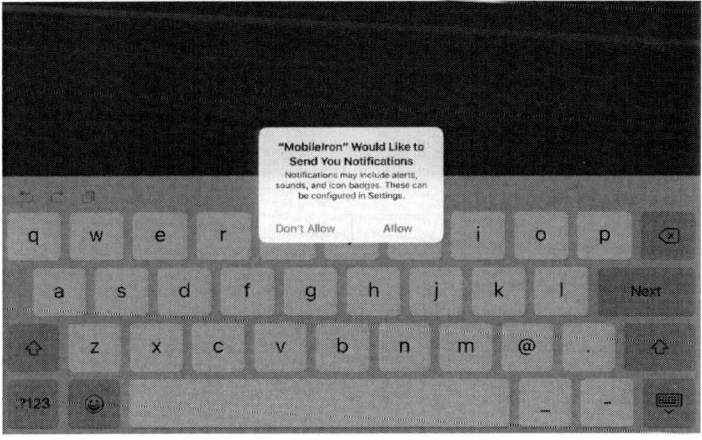

10. In **Mobile@Work:**
    a. In the **User Name** field, enter your LDAP or MobileIron user ID.

b. Tap **Next.**

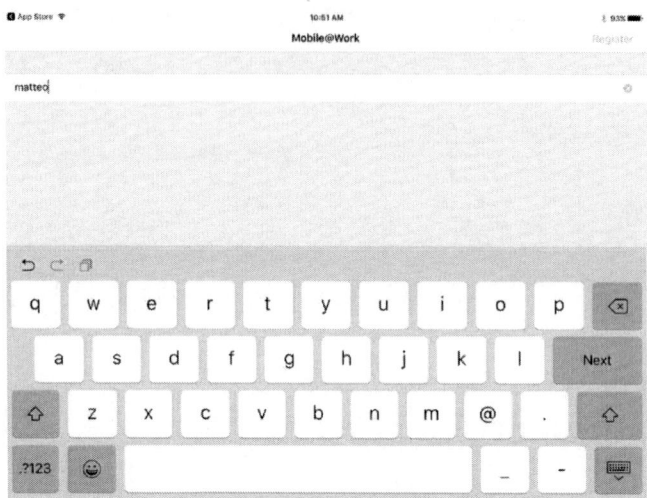

c. In the **Server** field, enter the URL for the organization's instance of MobileIron Core as provided by a MobileIron Core administrator.
d. Tap **Next.**

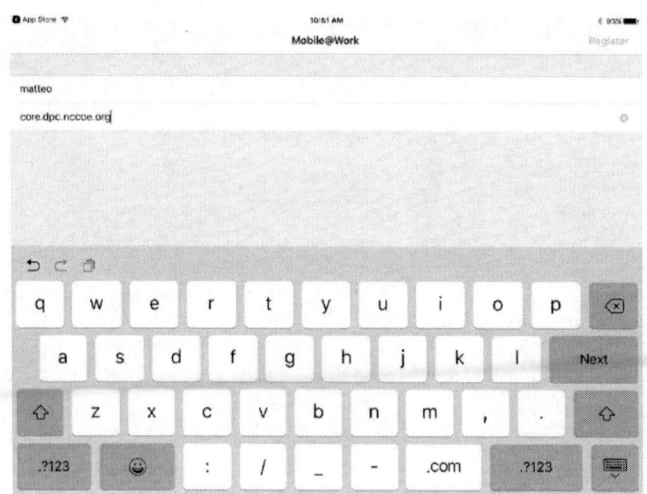

Derived Personal Identity Verification (PIV) Credentials   95

e. In the **PIN** field, enter the **Registration PIN** displayed in the **Confirmation** page (see Figure 2-2) of the MobileIron Self-Service Portal at completion of Step 7e.

f. Tap **Go** on keyboard or **Register** in Mobile@Work.

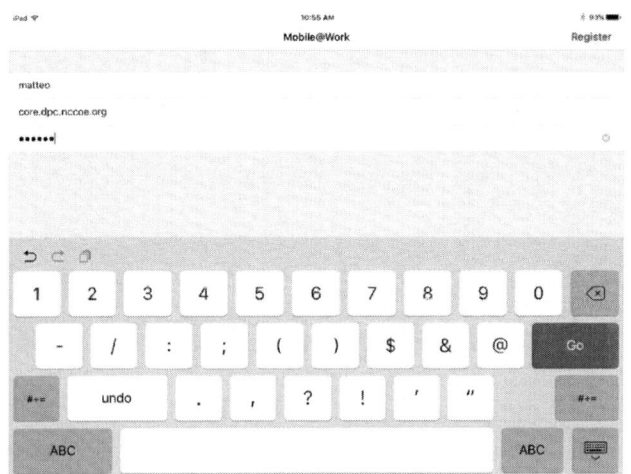

g. In the Privacy screen, tap **Continue**.

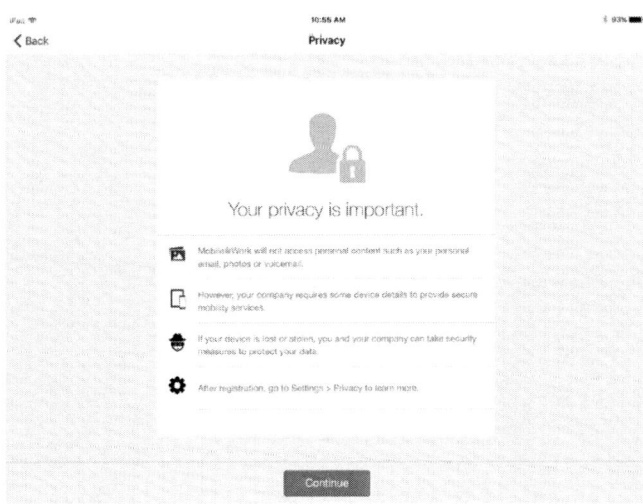

11. In the **Updating Configuration** dialogue, tap **OK;** this will launch the built-in iOS **Settings** application.

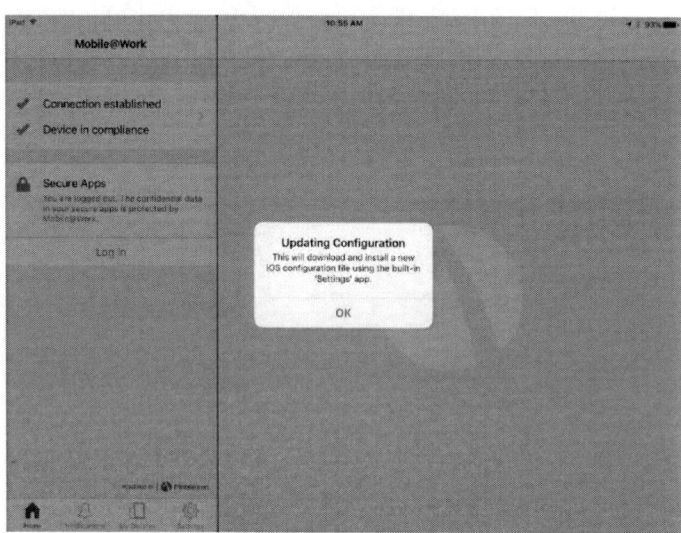

12. In the **Settings** application, in the **Install Profile** dialogue:
    a. In the **Signed by** field, confirm that the originating server identity shows as **Verified**.
       Note: If verification of the originating server fails, contact your MobileIron administrator before resuming registration.
    b. Tap **Install**.

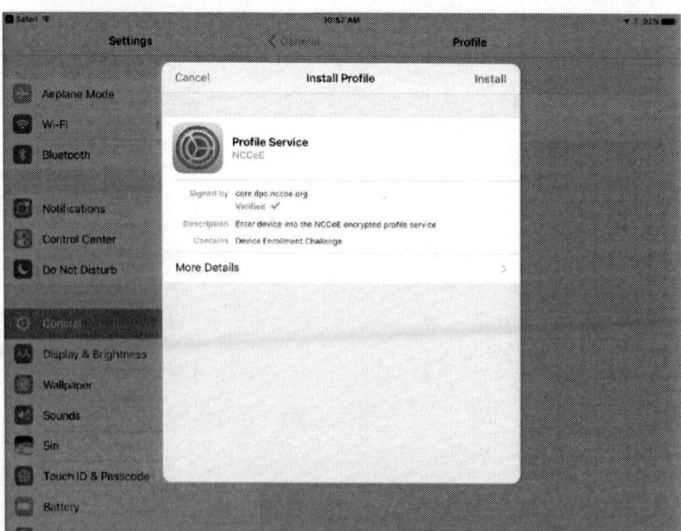

Derived Personal Identity Verification (PIV) Credentials   97

13. In the **Enter Passcode** dialogue:
    a. Enter your device unlock code.
    b. Tap **Done.**

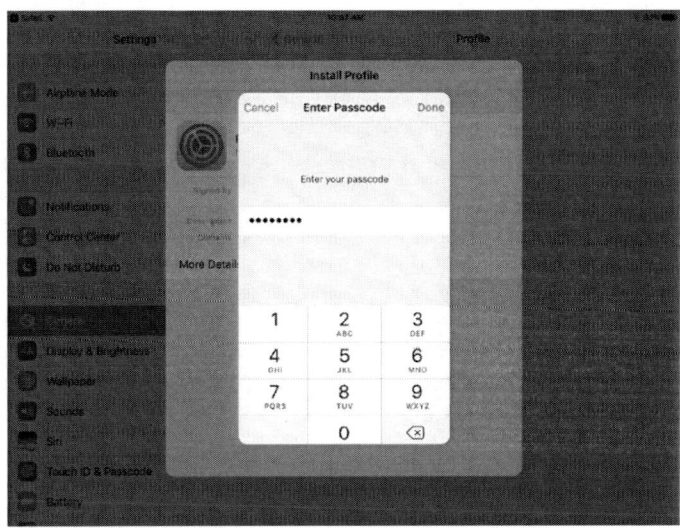

14. In the **Install Profile** dialogue, tap **Install.**

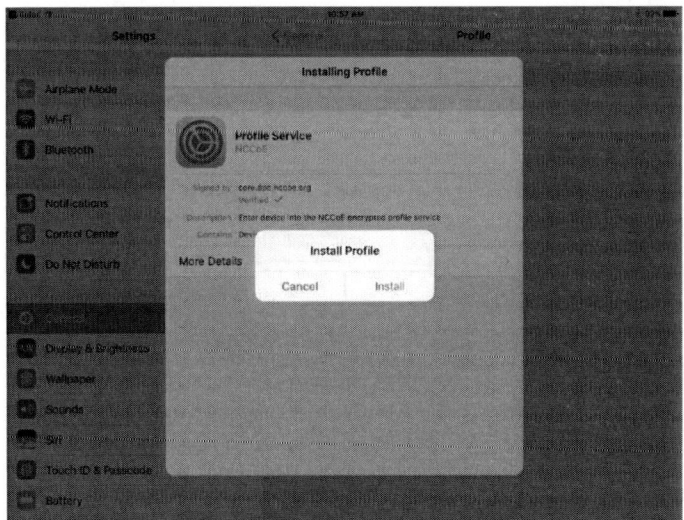

15. In the **Warning** dialogue, tap **Install.**

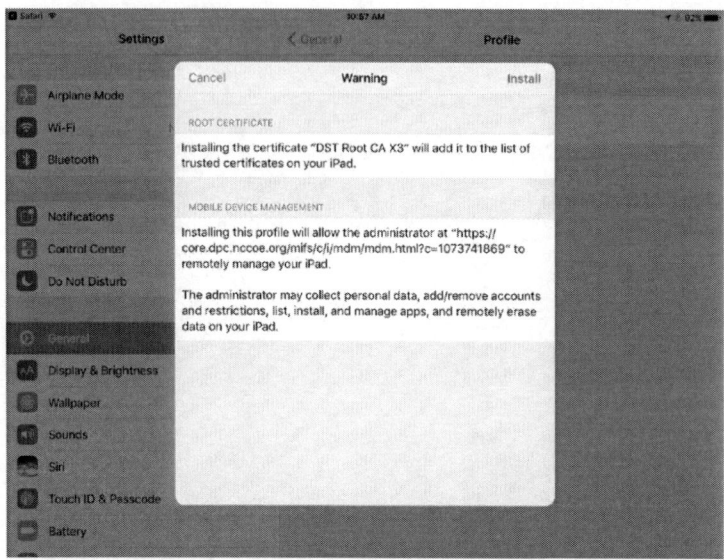

16. In the **Remote Management** dialogue, tap **Trust.**

Note: The root certificate presented in this step may vary based on the CA used to sign the MDM profile. This build uses the Let's Encrypt certificate authority.

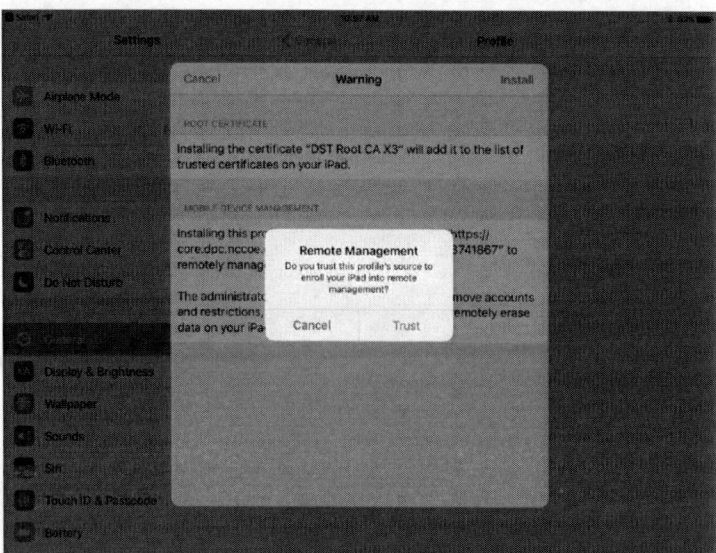

Derived Personal Identity Verification (PIV) Credentials   99

17. In the **Profile Installed** dialogue, tap **Done**.
18. In the **App Management Change** dialogue, tap **Manage**.

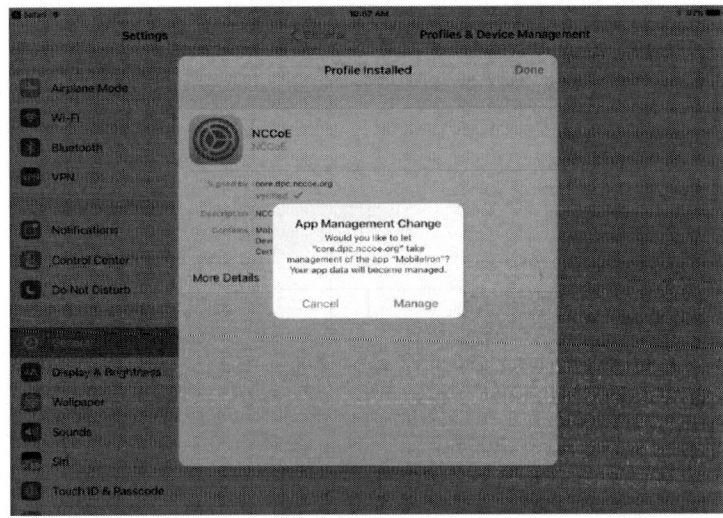

19. If additional Mobile@Work applications (e.g., Email+) are installed as part of the MobileIron management profile (based on your organization's use case), an **App Installation** dialogue will appear for each application. To confirm, tap **Install**.

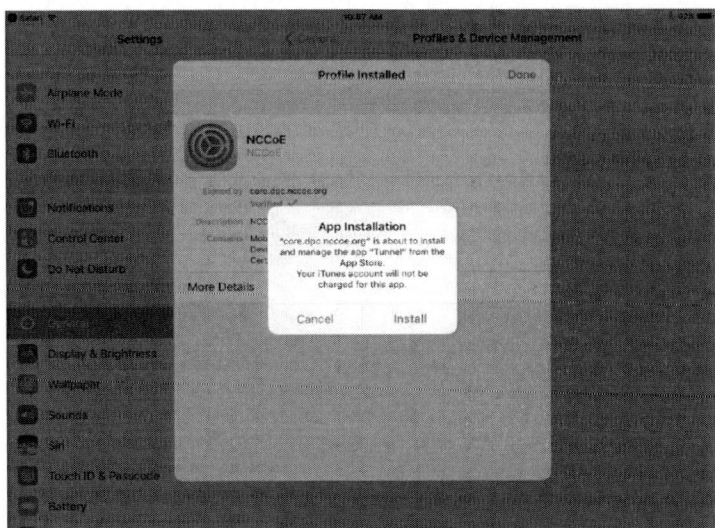

20. In the **Profile Installed** dialogue, tap **Done**.

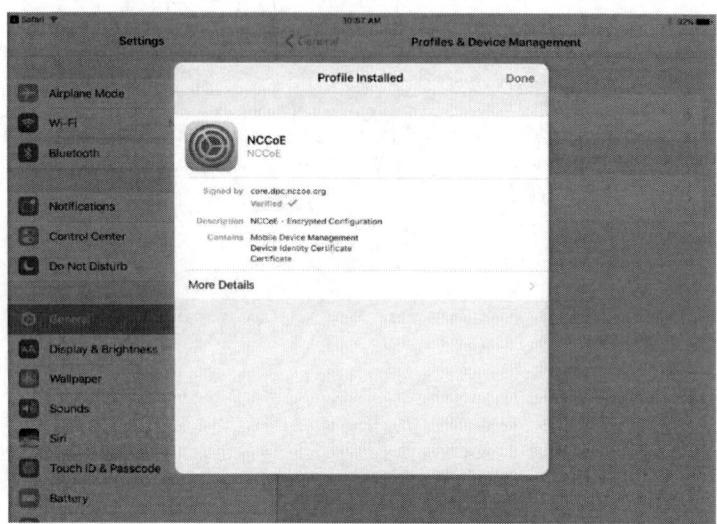

21. The **Mobile@Work > Home** screen should now display check marks for both status indicators of **Connection established** (with MobileIron Core) and **Device in compliance** (with the MobileIron policies that apply to your device).

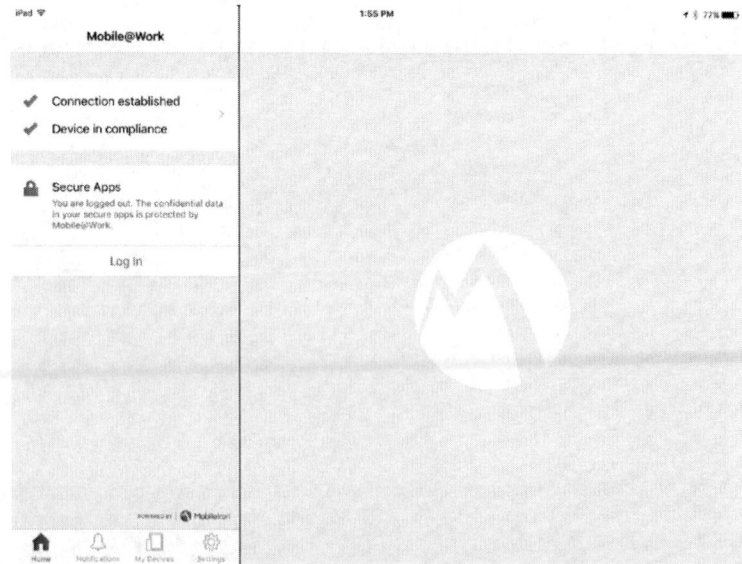

2.1.3.1.2. DPC Initial Issuance

The following steps demonstrate how a DPC is issued to an applicant's mobile device. It assumes the target mobile device is registered with MobileIron (see Register Target Device with MobileIron) and the MobileIron PIV-D Entrust application is installed (see Implement MobileIron Guidance). These steps are completed by the mobile device user who is receiving a DPC.

1. Launch the **MobileIron PIV-D Entrust** application on the target mobile device.
2. If a Mobile@Work Secure Apps passcode has not been set, you will be prompted to create one. In the **Mobile@Work Secure Apps** screen: a. In the **Enter your new passcode** field, enter a password consistent with your organization's DPC password policy. This password will be used to activate your DPC (password-based subscriber authentication) for use by Mobile@Work secure applications.

Note: NIST SP 800-63-3 increased the minimum DPC password length to eight characters.

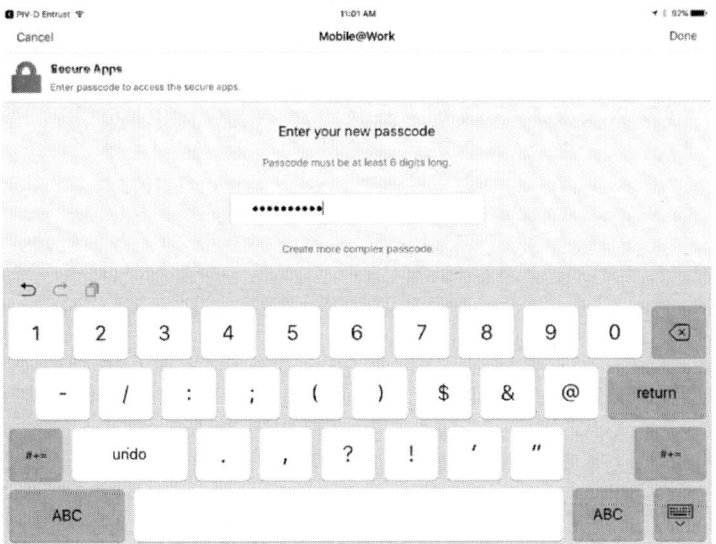

a. In the **Re-enter your new passcode** field, reenter the password you entered in Step 2b.
b. Tap **Done**.

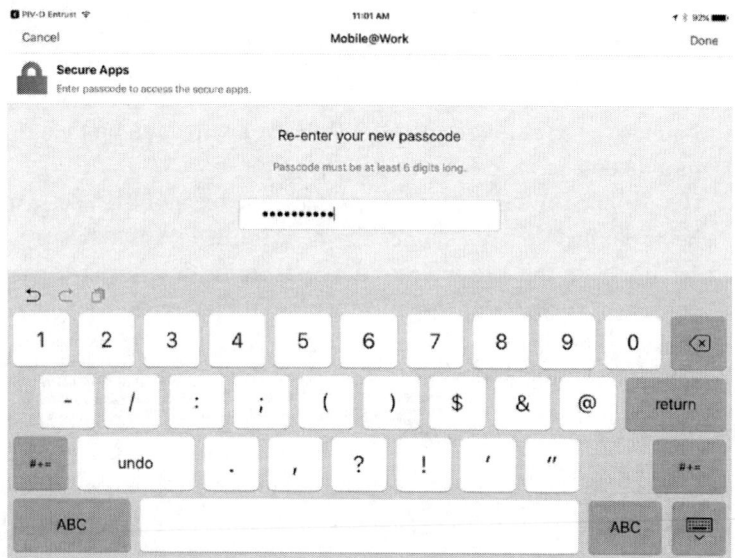

3. Following registration with MobileIron Core and when no DPC is associated with Mobile@Work, **PIV-D Entrust** displays a screen for managing your DPC. You will return to this application in a later step.

4. Insert your valid PIV Card into the reader attached to your laptop or computer workstation.

5. To request a DPC during the same session as registration with MobileIron:
   a. In the MobileIron Self-Service Portal **Confirmation** page (see Figure 2-2), click **Request Derived Credential.**

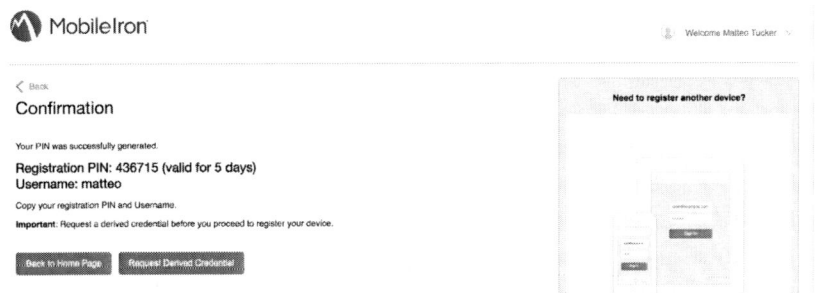

   b. In the certificate selection dialogue:
      - Select your PIV Authentication certificate from the list of available certificates. See Step 4 of Section 2.1.3.1.1 for additional steps to identify this certificate, as necessary.
      - Click **OK.**
      - Continue with Step 6.

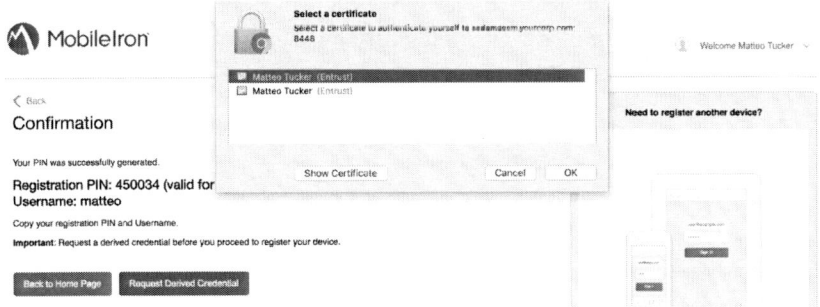

6. To request a DPC in a new session:
   a. Using a web browser, visit the Entrust IDG Self-Service Portal URL provided by an administrator.
   b. In the Entrust IDG Self-Service Portal, under **Smart Credential Log In,** click **Log In.**

Note: The portal used in our test environment is branded as a fictitious company, AnyBank Self-Service.

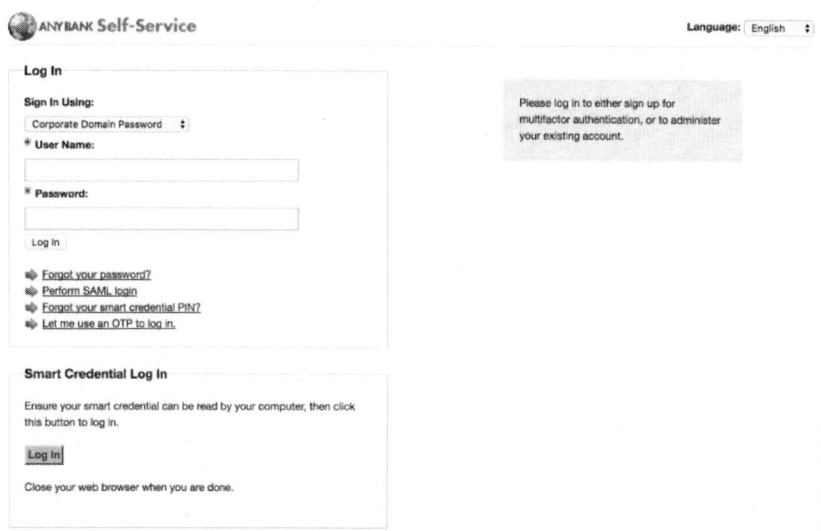

c. In the **Select a certificate** dialogue:
   - Select your PIV Authentication certificate from the list of available certificates. See Step 4 of Section 2.1.3.1.1 for additional steps to identify this certificate, as necessary.
   - Click **OK**.

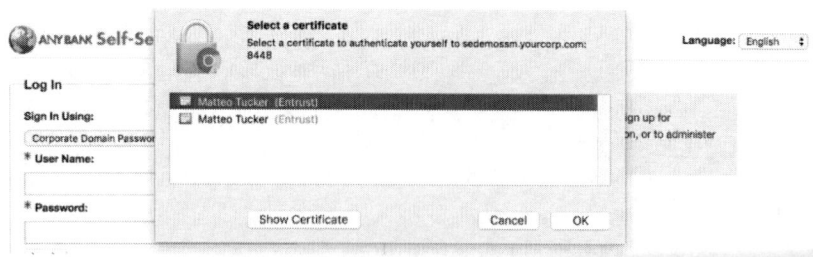

d. In the authentication dialogue:
   - In the **PIN** field, enter the password to activate your PIV Card.
   - Click **OK**.

Derived Personal Identity Verification (PIV) Credentials   105

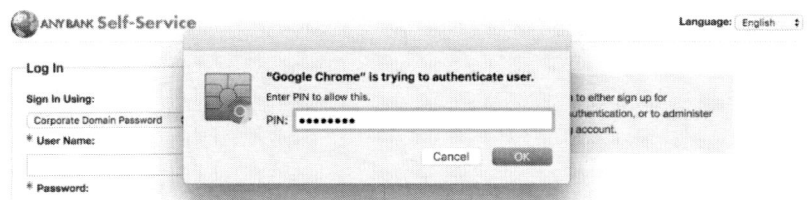

7. On the **Self-Administration Actions** page, follow the **I'd like to enroll for a derived mobile smart credential** link (displayed below as the last item; this may vary based on which self-administration actions your Entrust IDG administrator enabled).

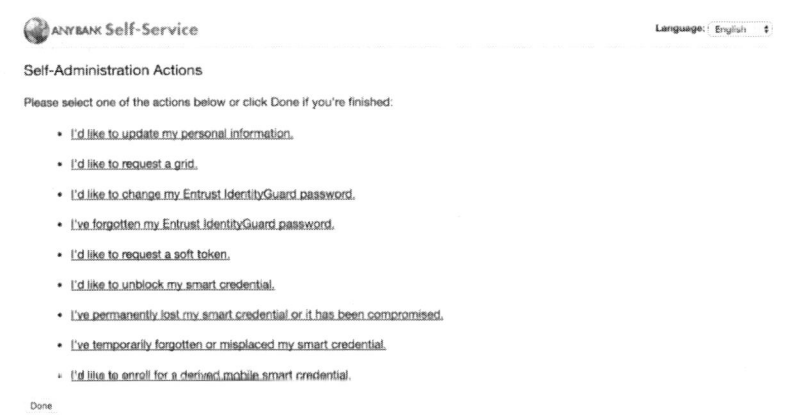

8. On the **Smart Credential enabled Application** page, select **Option 2: I've successfully down-loaded and installed the Smart Credential enabled application.**

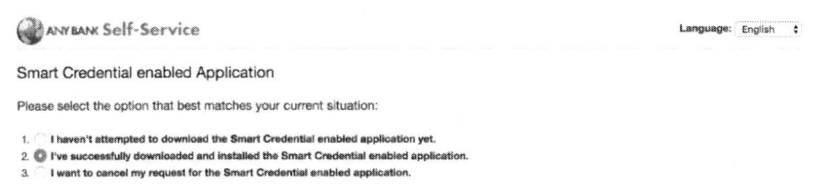

9. On the **Derived Mobile Smart Credential** page:
   a. In the **Identity Name** field, enter your LDAP or MobileIron user ID.

b. Click **OK**.

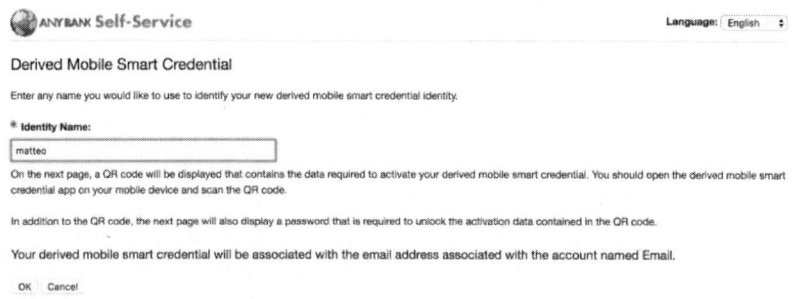

10. The **Derived Mobile Smart Credential Quick Response (QR) Code Activation** page displays infor-mation used in future steps; keep this page displayed. The workflow resumes using the MobileIron PIV-D Entrust application that is open on the target mobile device.

Note: Steps 11–13 must be completed by using the target mobile device within approximately three minutes, otherwise Steps 7–10 must be repeated to generate new activation codes.

Figure 2-3. Derived mobile smart credential QR code activation page.

Derived Personal Identity Verification (PIV) Credentials   107

11. In the **PIV-D Entrust** application that is running on the target mobile device, tap **Activate New Credential.**

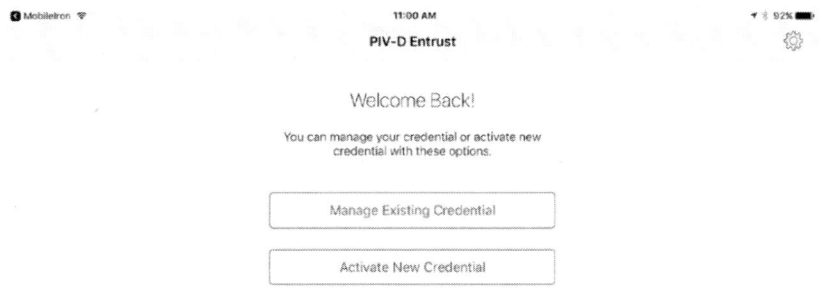

12. Use the device camera to capture the QR code displayed on the **Derived Mobile Smart Credential QR Code Activation** page as represented in Figure 2-3.

13. On the **Activate Credential** screen:
    a. Enter the **password** below the QR code that is displayed on the **Derived Mobile Smart Credential QR Code Activation** page

(displayed by the same device used to perform Steps 4–10) as represented in Figure 2-3.

b. Tap **Activate.**

14. If issuance was successful, the PIV-D Entrust application should automatically launch Mobile-Iron. Go to **Mobile@Work > Settings > Entrust Credential** to view its details.

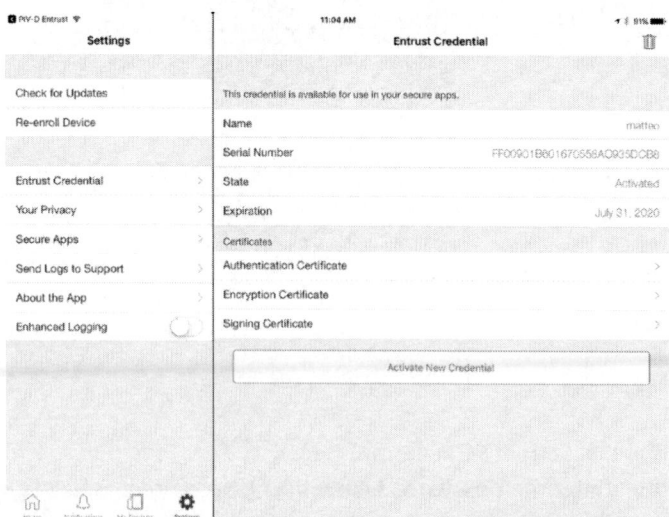

2.1.3.2. DPC Maintenance

Changes to a DPC subscriber's PIV Card that result in a rekey or reissuance (e.g., official name change) require the subscriber to repeat the initial issuance workflow as described in the previous section. The issued DPC will replace any existing DPC in the MobileIron Apps@Work container.

2.1.3.3. DPC Termination

Termination of a DPC can be initiated from the MobileIron Admin Console. Upon completion of this workflow, the DPC stored in the MobileIron Apps@Work container will be cryptographically wiped (destroyed). These steps are performed by a MobileIron Core administrator.

1. In the MobileIron Admin Console, navigate to **Devices & Users > Devices.**

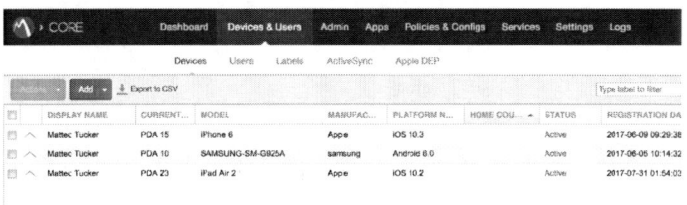

2. Select the checkbox in the row identifying the mobile device to be retired.

3. Select **Actions > Retire.**

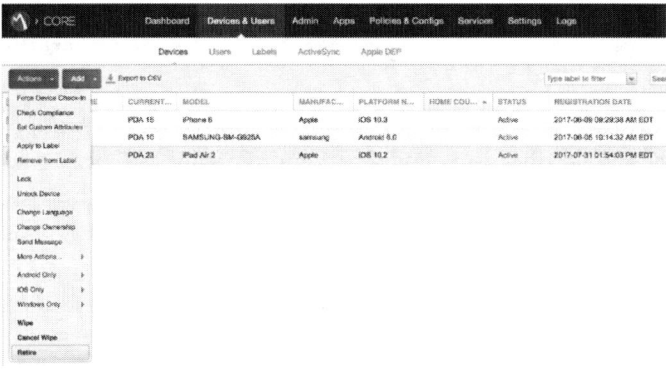

2. In the **Retire** dialogue that appears:
   a. In the **Note** text box, enter the reason(s) the device is being retired from MobileIron.
   b. Select **Retire**.

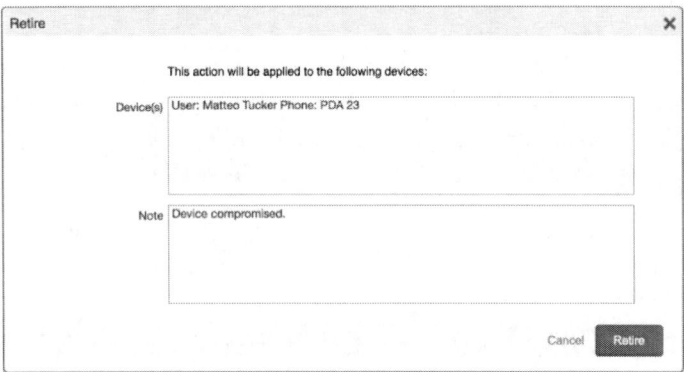

3. The **Devices** tab no longer displays the retired mobile device in the list of the devices.

The MobileIron PIV-D Entrust application now no longer reflects management by MobileIron. As a result, the DPC has been cryptographically wiped (destroyed) and its recovery is computationally infeasible.

2.2. Hybrid Architecture for PIV and DPC Life-Cycle Management

This section describes installation and configuration of key products for the architecture depicted in Figure 2-4 and Figure 2-5, as well as demonstration of the DPC life-cycle management activities of initial issuance and termination.

Derived Personal Identity Verification (PIV) Credentials   111

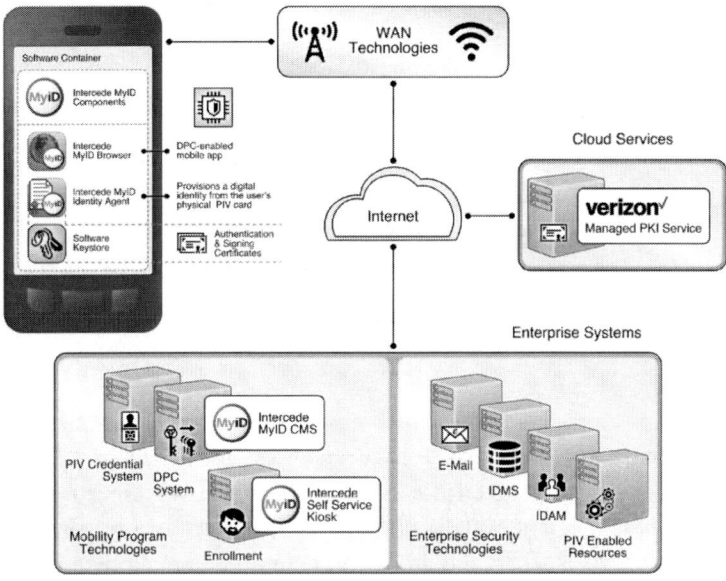

Figure 2-4. Mobile device hybrid architecture for PIV card and DPC life-cycle management (software keystore).

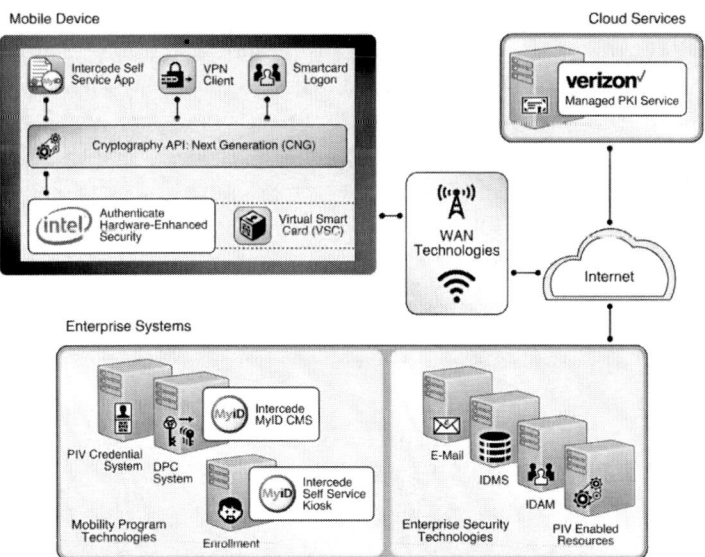

Figure 2-5. Mobile device hybrid architecture for PIV card and DPC life-cycle management (intel authenticate).

Figure 2-4 focuses on the mobile device implementation. Here, the Identity Agent application is used to manage the DPC. The DPC authentication key is stored in a software keystore within the secure container. The supporting cloud and enterprise systems as described above are also shown. Figure 2-5 depicts the architecture when an Intel-based device that supports Intel Authenticate is used to store the DPC.

2.2.1. Intercede MyID CMS

Intercede offers its identity and credential management system (CMS) product, MyID, as a software solution that can be hosted in the cloud or deployed on premises. The MyID server platform is composed of an application server, database, and web server. It provides connectors to infrastructure components such as directories and PKIs, and application programming interfaces to enable integration with the organization's identity and access management system. The MyID CMS is the core component for the architecture; as such, it should be fully configured and operational before other components.

2.2.1.1. Installation

Detailed instructions to install an instance of the MyID CMS are in the Intercede document *MyID Version 10.8 Installation and Configuration Guide*. Here, we document specific installation instructions for our environment.

The MyID system is modularly designed with web, application, and database tiers. In a production environment, it is likely that these tiers are separated onto multiple systems depending on performance and disaster recovery requirements. However, in our architecture, all tiers were installed on a Windows Server 2012 system due to resource constraints. Finally, role separation within the MyID system is not addressed here but should be considered before any deployment.

Install a supported version of Microsoft Structured Query Language (SQL) Server on the target MyID server. Our environment uses SQL Server 2012 with the SQL Server Database Engine and SQL Server Management Tools. See Table 2-3 SQL Server Components for specific component versions. A full settings document *(Exported-2017-07-27.vssettings)* is available from the NCCoE DPC Project website. Refer to Microsoft's online documentation for specific installation procedures.

Derived Personal Identity Verification (PIV) Credentials 113

Table 2-3. SQL server components

Microsoft SQL Server Management Studio	11.0.5058.0
Microsoft Analysis Services Client Tools	11.0.5058.0
Microsoft Data Access Components	6.3.9600.17415
Microsoft Extensible Markup Language	3.0 6.0
Microsoft Internet Explorer	9.11.9600.18739
Microsoft .NET Framework	4.0.30319.42000
Operating System (OS)	6.3.9600

2.2.1.2. Verizon Shared Service Provider (SSP) PKI Integration

Detailed instructions to integrate Verizon SSP with MyID are in Intercede's *UniCERT UPI Certificate Authority Integration Guide*. Here, we document the specific configurations used within our builds.

1. Install the following prerequisites on the MyID server:

Component	Comment
Java Runtime Environment 8.0	Download and install the latest update from the Oracle website. This build uses 8u121.
Java Cryptography Extension Unlimited Strength Jurisdiction Policy Files 8	Download and install from the Oracle website.

2. Obtain the following configuration settings from your managed PKI instance:

Setting	Comment
Verizon SSP CA Path	Distinguished name to directory instance supplied by Verizon
Verizon SSP Enrollment Agent	Distinguished name for the Registration Authority supplied by Verizon
Verizon SSP Service Point	Universal Resource Indicator end point of the Verizon SSP web service supplied by Verizon
Verizon SSP Registration Authority Operator Public Key Cryptography Standards (PKCS)#12	Credentials are supplied by Verizon SSP.
Verizon SSP Registration Authority Operator PKCS#12 Password	

3. Create a CA configuration by using the following procedures:
   a. In **MyID Desktop,** select the **Configuration** category.
   b. Select **Certificate Authorities** from the **Configuration** menu.
   c. Select **New** from the **Select a CA** drop-down menu.

d. From the **CA Type** drop-down menu, select **Entrust JTK**. A form with a setting specifically for the Entrust Datacard CA will appear.
e. Fill in the **Certificate Authority** form with the following settings from Step 2:

CA Name	Enter a short name to identify the Verizon SSP.
CA Description	Optional long description
CA Type	Leave this setting UniCERT.
Retry Delays	Leave the defaults.
CA Path	Retrieve setting from Step 2.
Service Point	Retrieve setting from Step 2.
Enrollment Agent	Retrieve setting from Step 2.
Directory	Select the Entrust directory configured from Step 2.2.1.2
Certificate Store	Retrieve setting from Step 2–enter fully qualified file path.
Certificate Password	Retrieve setting from Step 2.
Enable CA	Select this option.

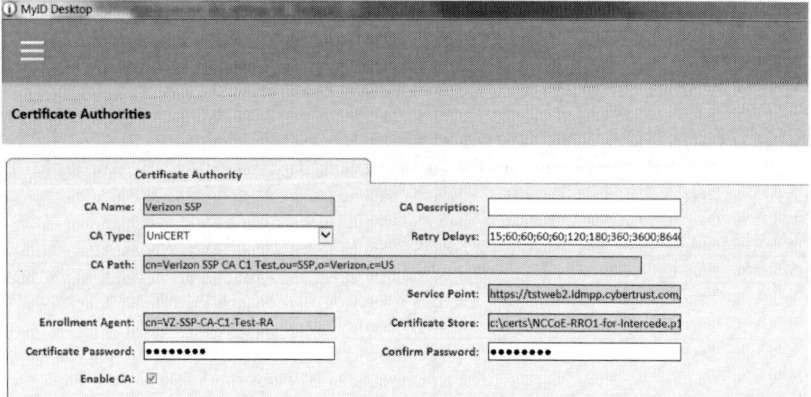

f. Click **Save**.

4. Enable Verizon SSP CA policies by using the following procedures.
   a. Within **MyID Desktop,** click the **Configuration** category and choose **Certificate Authorities.**
   b. From the **CA Name** drop-down, select the **Verizon SSP CA** configured in Step 3.
   c. Click **Edit**.
   d. In the **Available Certificates** list, select **PIV-SSP-Derived-Auth-sw-1yr-v3** to enable it for DPC issuance.

Derived Personal Identity Verification (PIV) Credentials   115

    e. Click the **Enabled (Allow Issuance)** checkbox.
    f. Set the following options for the policy.

Setting	Value
Display Name	Arbitrary name for this policy
Description	Optional description for this policy
Allow Identity Mapping	Unchecked
Reverse DN	Checked
Archive Keys	Unchecked
Certificate Lifetime	365
Automatic Renewal	Unchecked
Certificate Storage	Both
Recovery Storage	Both
Cryptographic Service Provider Name	Microsoft Enhanced Cryptographic Provider 1.0
Requires Validation	Unchecked
Private Key Exportable	Unchecked
User Protected	Unchecked
Key Algorithm	RSA 2048
Key Purpose	Signature

    g. Click **Edit Attributes** and set the following values:

Attribute	Type	Value
NACI Indicator	Dynamic	NACI Status
Subject Alt Microsoft UPN	Dynamic	User Principal Name
Subject Alt Uniform Resource Identifier	Dynamic	Universal Unique Identifier

5. Repeat Step 4 for the **PIV-Auth-1-yr-v2, PIV-CardAuth-1yr-v1,** and **PIV-Sig-1yr-v1** certificate profiles.

2.2.1.3. Configuration for DPC

Detailed instructions to configure an instance of the MyID CMS for DPC are in Intercede's *Derived Credentials Installation and Configuration Guide*. Here, we document the specific configurations used within our builds. Before you begin, you need the *Test Federal Common Policy CA* root certificate file, which can be downloaded from the Federal PKI test repository. Also obtain the intermediate certificates for the Verizon SSP certificate chain (Verizon SSP CA A2 Test and Verizon SSP CA C1 Test) from the Verizon certificate test repositories.

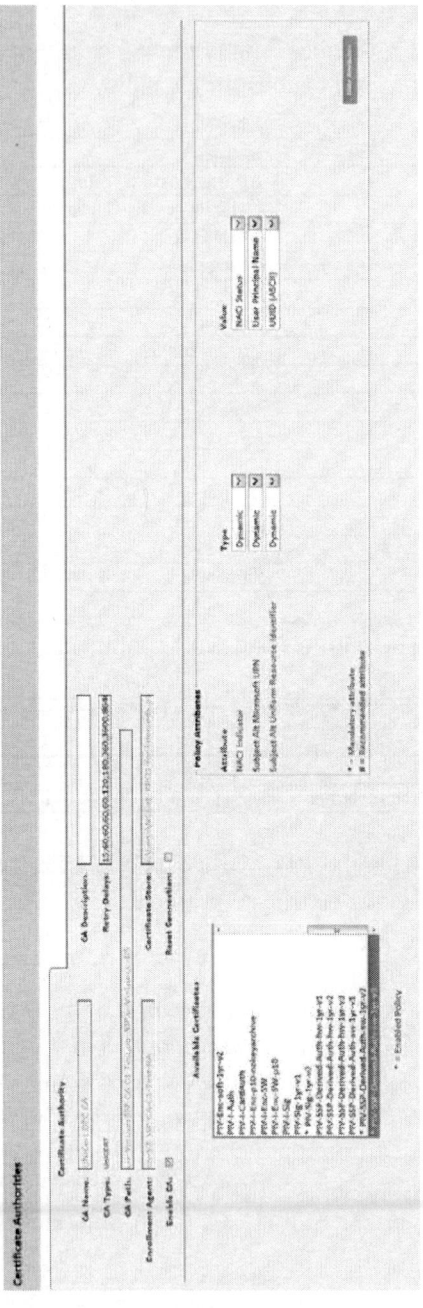

Figure 2-6. Certificate profile attributes.

The first step in configuration is to create a content signing certificate that is used to sign data stored on the DPC mobile container. This certificate (and associated private key) must be made available to MyID through the Windows Cryptographic Application Interface store on the same server where the MyID server is installed. There are various ways to generate a certificate; in our environment we chose to create a certificate authority on a separate instance of Windows Server 2012.

1. Install Microsoft Certificate Services. There are a few online resources that can assist in the in-stallation process. We suggest the Adding Active Directory Certificate Services to a Lab Environ-ment tutorial from the Microsoft Developer Network.
   Add a certificate template. For reference, we have exported the certificate template (PIVCon-tentSigning) that we used for the content signing certificate. The configuration file *(Certificate-Templates.xml)* is available for download from the NCCoE DPC Project website. A script to im-port the certificate template can be found at the Microsoft Script Center.
2. Request a content signing certificate from the MyID system by using the procedures noted in the "Request a Certificate" TechNet article.
3. Save the content signing certificate in binary format to the **Components** folder of the MyID in-stallation folder.
4. Edit the system registry with the following procedures:
   a. From the **Start** menu:
      - Select **Run.**
      - Type regedit in the dialogue displayed.
      - Click **OK.**
   b. Navigate to **HKEY_LOCAL_MACHINE\SOFTWARE\wow6432Node\Intercede\Edefice\ContentSigning.**
   c. Check that the value of the following string is set:
      Active–set to **WebService.**
   d. Set the value of the following string to the full path of the certificate on the application server:
      For example: *C:\Program Files (x86)\Intercede\MyID\Components\contentcert.cer*

5. Set the location of the MyID web service that allows a mobile device to collect the DPC by using the following procedures within MyID Desktop:
   a. From the **Configuration** category, select the **Operation Settings** workflow.
   b. Click the **Certificates** tab.
   c. Set the **Mobile Certificate Recovery Service URL** option to the location of the MyID Pro-cess Driver web service host.
      For example: https://<replace-with-your-hostname>
   d. Click **Save Changes**.
6. Set which PIV Cards are available for DPC by using the following procedures within MyID Desk-top:
   a. From the **Configuration** category, select the **Operation Settings** workflow.
   b. Click the **Certificates** tab.
   c. To allow eligibility for all PIV Federal Agency Smart Card Number values, set **Cards al-lowed for derivation** to **.+** (dot plus).
   d. Click **Save Changes**.
7. Configure the system to check the revocation status of the PIV Authentication certificate to seven days by using the following procedures within MyID Desktop:
   a. From the **Configuration** category, select **Operation Settings.**
   b. On the **Certificates** tab, set **Derived credential revocation check offset** to **7.**
   c. Click **Save Changes**.
8. Grant access to the following workflows by using the MyID Desktop: Request Derived Creden-tials, Cancel Credential, Enable/Disable ID, Request Replacement ID, Unlock Credential, Collect My Updates.
   a. From the **Configuration** category, select the **Edit Roles** workflow.
   b. Select the checkbox for each of the roles to which you want to grant access. In our envi-ronment, **Startup User** was selected for all workflows.
   c. Click **Save Changes**.
9. Edit the workflows from Step 8 with the appropriate permissions.
   a. From the **Configuration** category, select the **Edit Roles** workflow.
   b. Click **Show/Hide Roles**.

Derived Personal Identity Verification (PIV) Credentials 119

    c. Select the checkboxes for **Mobile User, Derived Credential Owner,** and **PIV Applicant.**
    d. Click **Close.**
    e. Select the corresponding roles:

Role	Permission
Mobile User	Console Logon, Request Derived Credentials (part 1), Mobile Certificate Recovery, Collect My Updates, Issue Device
Derived Credential Owner	Console Logon, Request Derived Credentials (part 2), Collect My Updates, Issue Device
PIV Applicant	Request Derived Credentials (part 2), Collect My Updates

10. Import the Test Federal Common Policy CA certificate into the MyID application server by using the following command as an administrator. This enables the administrator to control the PKI hierarchy that is trusted when verifying PIV Cards:

certutil -addstore -f -Enterprise DerivedCredentialTrustedRoots RootCA .cer

11. Configure the MyID system with the PIV Authentication and Digital Signature certificate policy Object Identifiers (OIDs) by using the following procedures. The values shown below are produc-tion values, so they may need to be changed for your organization:
    a. From the MyID Desktop **Configuration** category, select **Operation Settings.**
    b. On the **Certificates** tab, set the following values:

Setting	Value
Derived credential certificate OID	2.16.840.1.101.3.2.1.3.13
Derived credential signing certificate OID	2.16.840.1.101.3.2.1.3.6; 2.16.840.1.101.3.2.1.3.7; 2.16.840.1.101.3.2.1.3.16

12. Create an Identity Agent credential profile for the DPC by using the following procedures:
    a. From the MyID Desktop **Configuration** category, select **Credential Profiles.**
    b. Click **New.**
    c. In the **Name** field, enter a descriptive name for the profile.

d. In **Card Encoding,** select **Identity Agent (Only)** and **Derived Credential.**
e. In **Services,** leave default selections **MyID Logon** and **MyID Encryption.**
f. In **Issuance Settings,** in the **Mobile Device Restrictions** drop-down, select **Any.**
g. In **Issuance Settings, Require Facial Biometrics,** select **Never Required.**
h. In **PIN Settings,** configure the following settings:

Setting	Value
Authentication Mode	PIN
Maximum PIN Length	12
Minimum PIN Length	6
Repeated Characters Allowed	1
Sequential Characters Allowed	1
Logon Attempts	5
PIN Inactivity Time	180
PIN History	0
Issue With	User specified PIN (default)
Email PIN	Unselect
Length	0

i. In **Device Profiles,** select **PIVDerivedCredential.xml** from the **Card Format** drop-down.
j. Click **Next.**
k. In the **Select Certificates** tab, check **PIV-SSP-Derived-Auth-sw-1yr-v3** along with **Signing** under **Certificate Policy Description.** Choose **Authentication Certificate** in the **Container** drop-down.
l. Click **Next.**
m. Select the roles that receive, issue, and validate DPCs. **All** was chosen in this example.
n. Click **Next.**
o. Select **PIV_CON** in the **Select Card Layout** tab.
p. Click **Next.**
q. Enter text into the **Comments** and click **Next,** then **Finish.**

2.2.2. Intercede MyID Identity Agent

The MyID Identity Agent runs as an application and interfaces with the MyID CMS and supports a wide range of mobile devices and credential stores, including the device native keystore, software keystore, and microSD. The MyID Identity Agent mobile application is required to issue and manage DPCs. No special configuration is necessary after installing the application; scanning the QR code during the initial enrollment directs the Identity Agent to your instance of MyID CMS. MyID Identity Agent is supported for both iOS and Android platforms.

2.2.2.1. Installation
MyID Identity Agent is available on the Google Play Store and the Apple App Store. Detailed installation procedures are found on the Google Play Store and Apple App Store support sites.

2.2.3. Intercede Desktop Client
The Intercede Desktop component of this example solution serves as the main point of administration of the MyID CMS. It was installed on a Dell Latitude E6540 laptop running Windows 7. The procedures below are adapted from the *Installation and Configuration Guide Version 10.8,* Section 7.4.

2.2.3.1. Installation
Before installation, have available the host name and the distinguished name (DN) of the issuer of the Transport Layer Security (TLS) certificate used to communicate with the MyID application server.

1. Run the provided *.msi* file as an administrator.
2. Select the destination location, then click **Next**.
3. Select the desired shortcuts to be installed.
4. Click **Next**.
5. In the **MyID Desktop InstallShield Wizard:**
   a. In the **Server URL** field, enter the **URL** for your instance of MyID Server.
   b. In the **SSL Certificate Issuer DN** field, leave empty as this prompt is applicable only when mutual TLS is implemented.
   c. Click **Next**.
   d. Click **Install**.

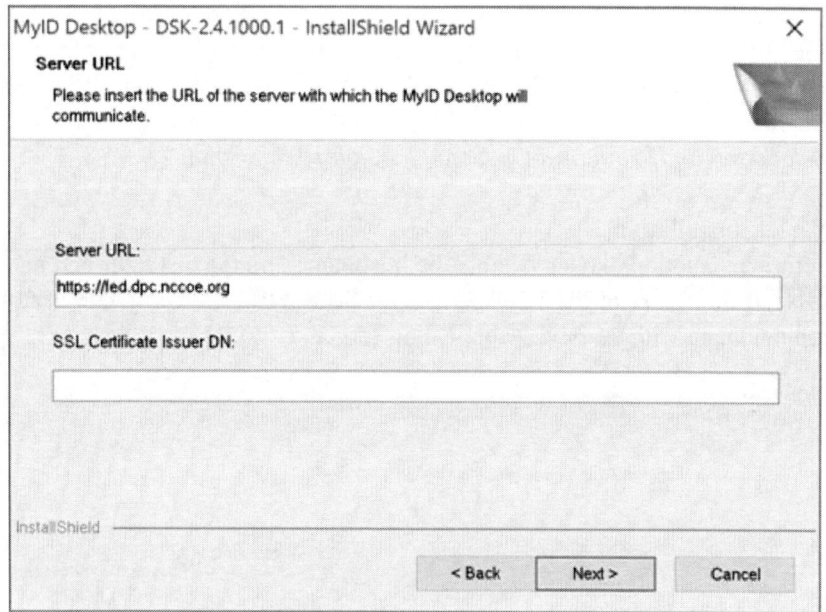

2.2.4. Intercede Self-Service Kiosk

The MyID Self-Service Kiosk serves as a DPC issuance station for eligible PIV holders. While the software is designed to run on a shared Windows system as a kiosk in public space, in this example it is installed on a Dell Latitude E6540 laptop running Windows 7. The procedures below are adapted from *Self-Service Kiosk Installation and Configuration* and *Derived Credentials Installation and Configuration Guide*.

2.2.4.1. Installation

Before installation, have available the host name and the issuer distinguished name of the TLS certificate used to communicate with the MyID application server.

1. Click **Next**.
2. Accept default and click **Next**.
3. In the **MyID Self-Service Kiosk InstallShield Wizard:**
    a. In the **Server URL** field, enter the **URL** of your instance of MyID Server.
    b. In the **SSL Certificate Issuer DN** field, leave empty as this prompt is applicable only when mutual TLS is implemented.
    c. Select **Next**.
    d. Select **Install**.
    e. Select **Finish**.

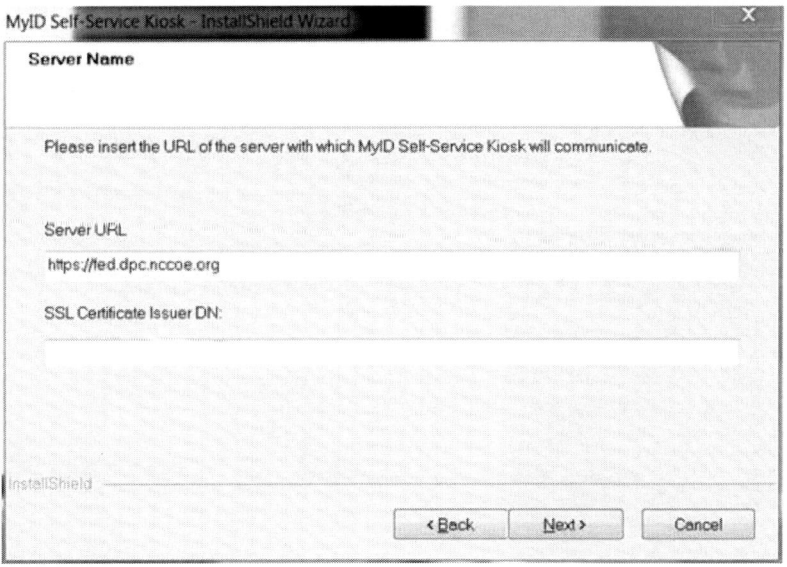

2.2.4.2. Configuration

Use the following procedures to configure the MyID Self-Service Kiosk for DPC issuance:

1. Set the time-out for the PIN entry screen by using the following procedures:

a. Open C:\Program Files (x86)\Intercede\MyIDSelfServiceKiosk\ MyIDKiosk.exe.config by using a text editor.
b. Edit the **value** parameter in the following line:

<add key="DerivedCredentialsPageTimeoutSeconds" value="120"/>

c. Edit the **value** parameter in the following line with the MyID application server address:

<add key="Server" value="http://myserver.example.com/"></add>

d. Save changes to the file.

2.2.5. Windows Client Installation for MyID and Intel Authenticate

The *Intel Authenticate Integration Guide for Active Directory Policy Objects* provides instructions on how to set up Group Policy Objects for various functions of the Intel Authenticate installation process. The following instructions are primarily repurposed from the *Intel Authenticate Integration Guide.*

2.2.5.1. Installing the MyID Self-Service Application

1. Run **SSP-2.3.1000.1_E.msi** on the client computer.
2. Click **Next.**

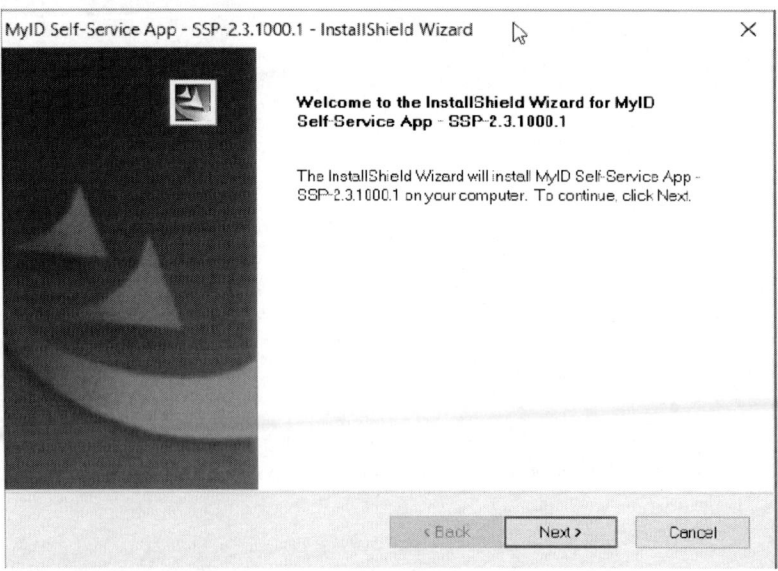

Derived Personal Identity Verification (PIV) Credentials 125

3. Click **Next**.

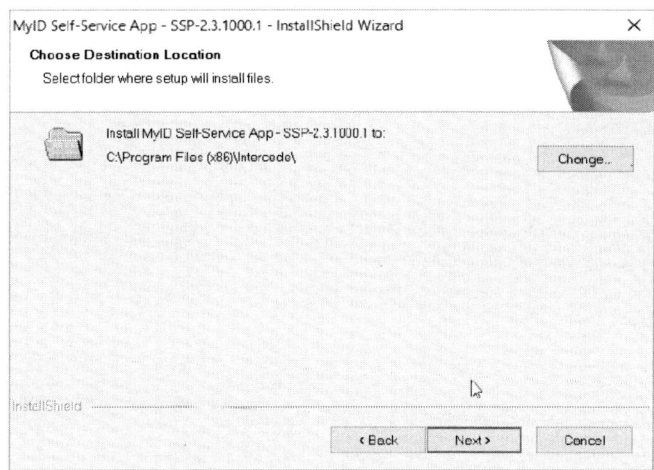

4. Enter the **Server URL** for your organization's MyID server. Leave the **SSL Certificate Issuer DN** field empty, as this prompt is applicable only when mutual TLS is implemented.
5. Click **Next**.

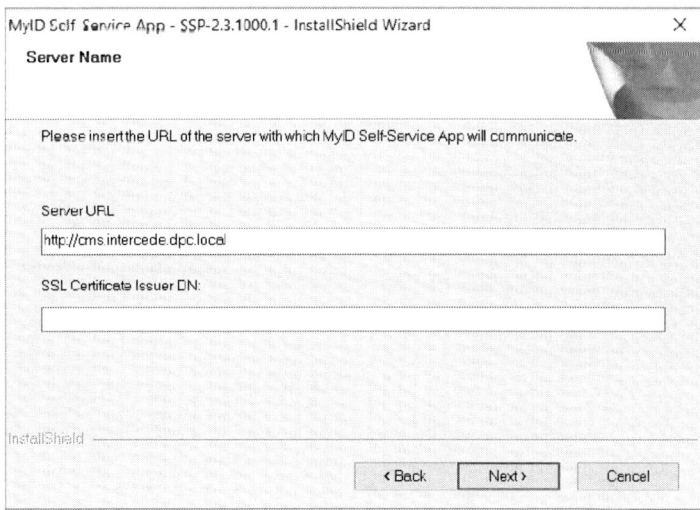

6. Click **Install**.

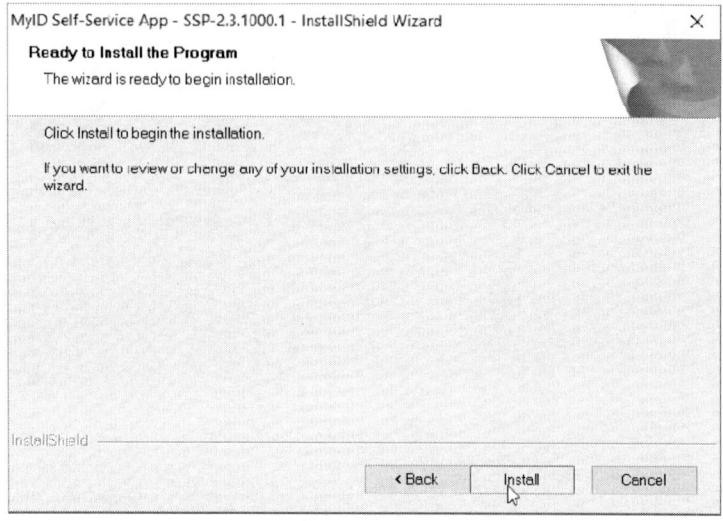

7. Click **Finish**

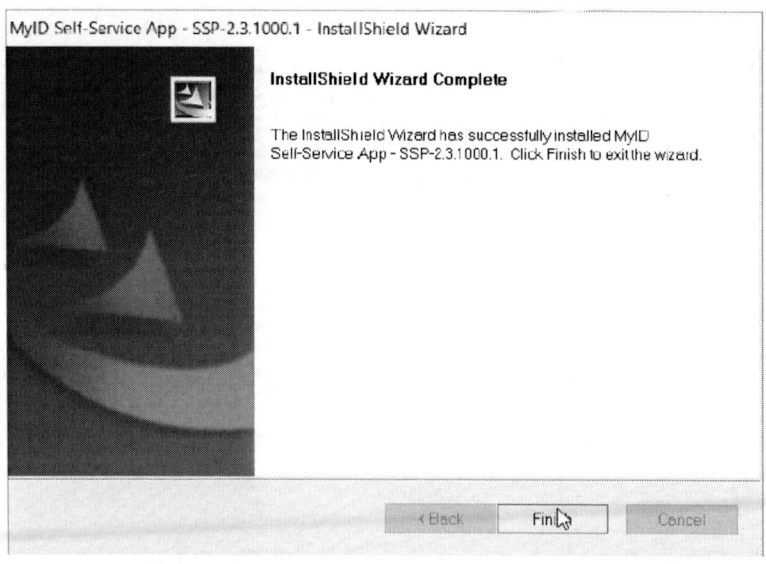

2.2.5.2. Installing the WSVC Service

1. Run **WSVC-1.6.1000.1_B.msi.**
2. Click **Next.**

Derived Personal Identity Verification (PIV) Credentials 127

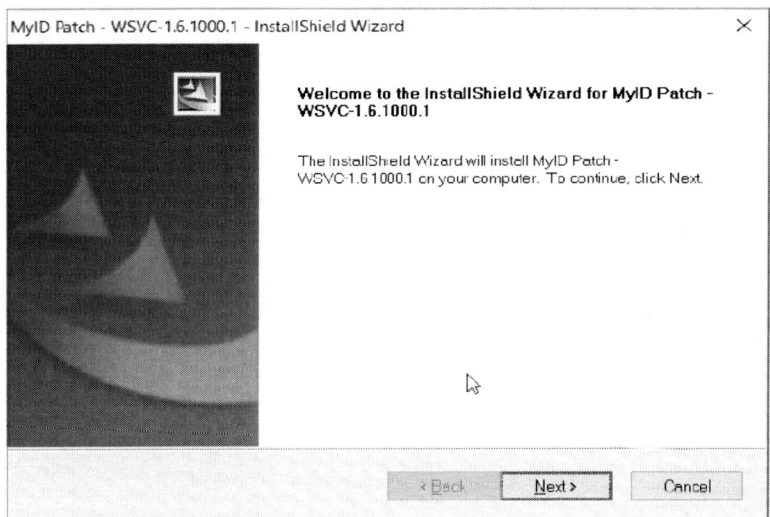

3. Enter the username and password for the account that will install the service.
4. Click **Next**.

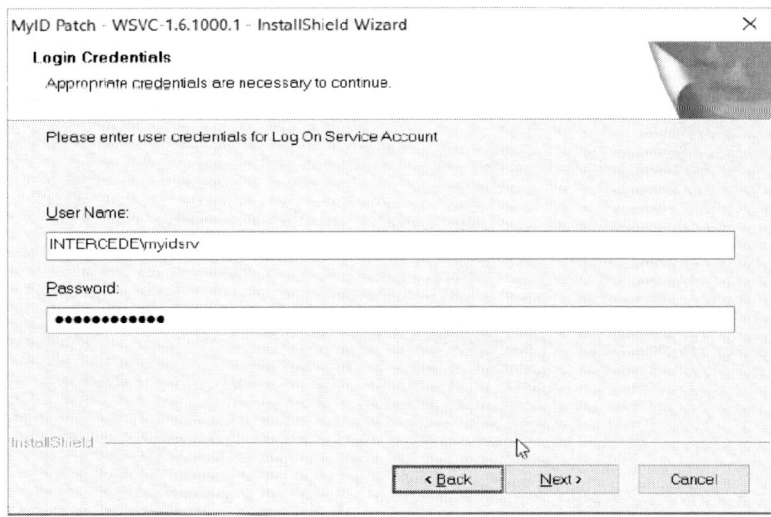

5. Click **Next**.

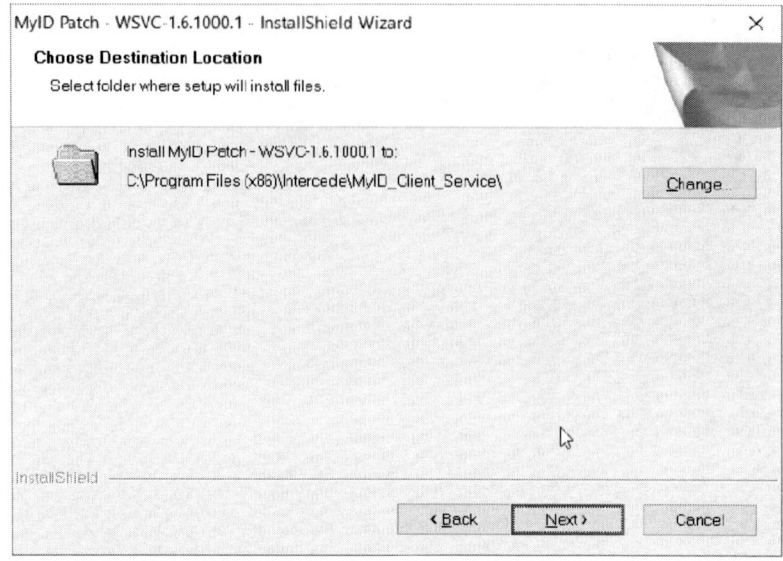

6. Click **Install**.

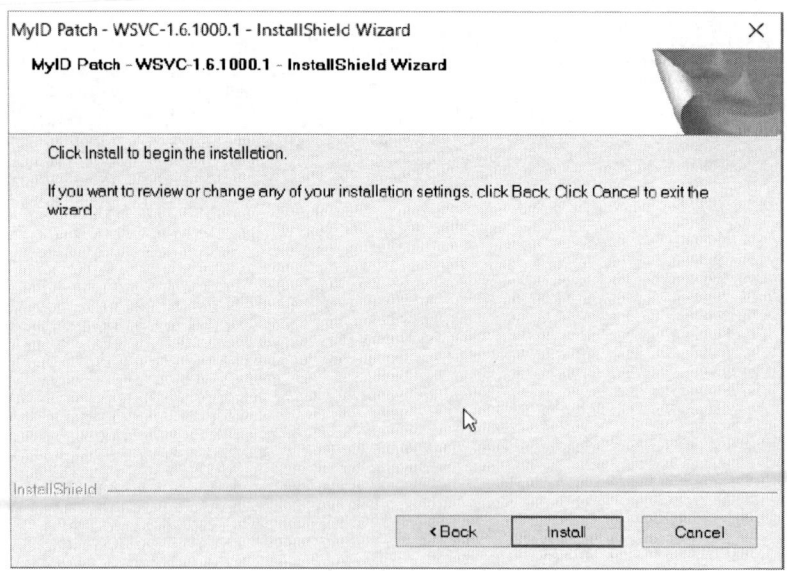

7. Click **Finish**.

Derived Personal Identity Verification (PIV) Credentials 129

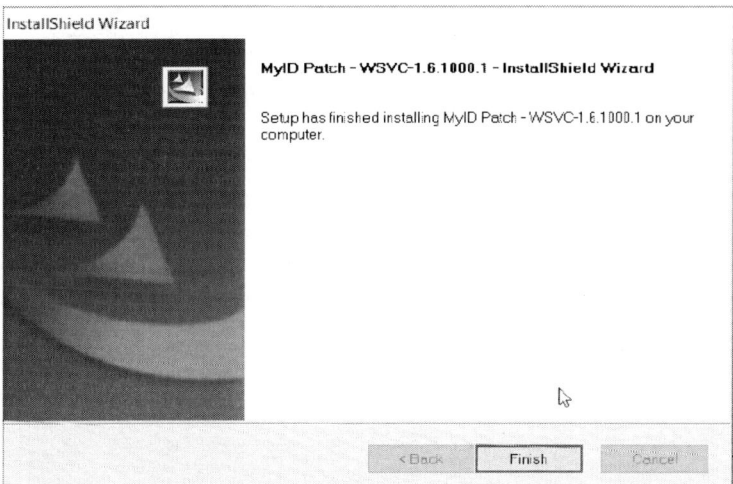

2.2.5.3. Installing Prerequisites for Intel Authenticate

This process may differ depending on the client system. Primarily, it is important that the Intel Management Engine is installed and that any Intel drivers are up to date so that the Intel Authenticate Precheck is successful.

1. Run *n1cra26w.exe.* (The name may differ based on your system—this is the Intel Management Engine.)
2. Click **Next.**

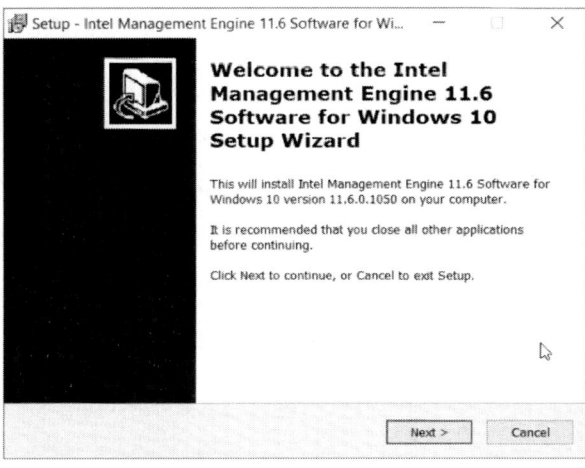

3. Select **I accept the agreement.**

4. Click **Next**.

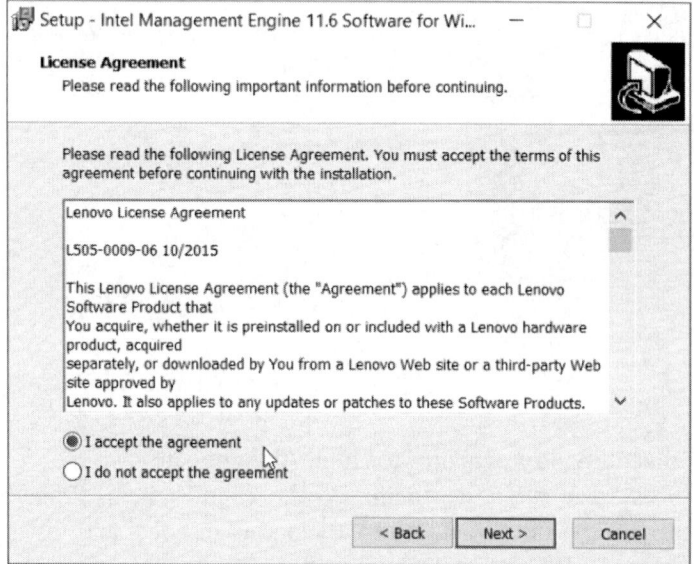

5. Click **Next**.

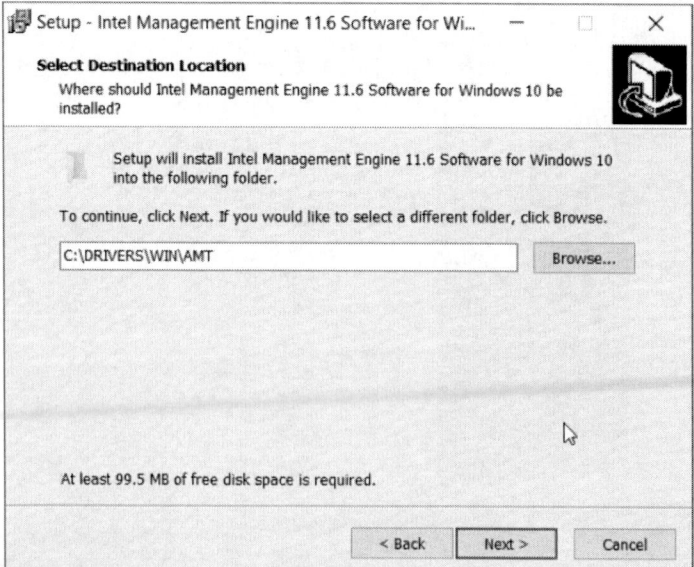

Derived Personal Identity Verification (PIV) Credentials   131

6. Click **Install**.

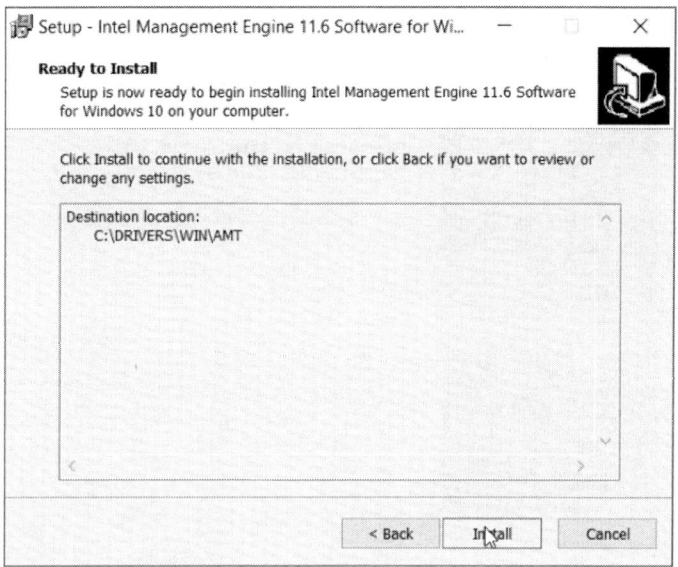

7. Check the box next to **Install Intel Management Engine 11.6 Software for Windows 10 now**.
8. Click **Finish**.

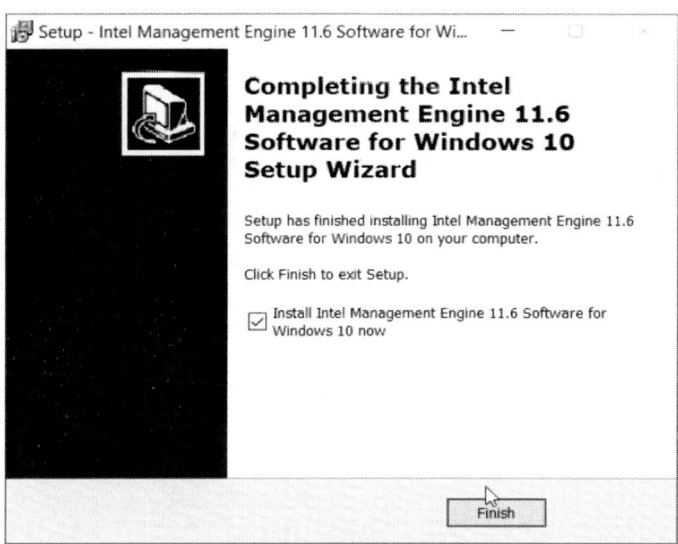

9. Run *u2vdo22us14avc.exe*. (The name may differ based on your system—this is the graphics driver update.)
10. Click **Next**.

11. Select **I accept the agreement.**
12. Click **Next**.

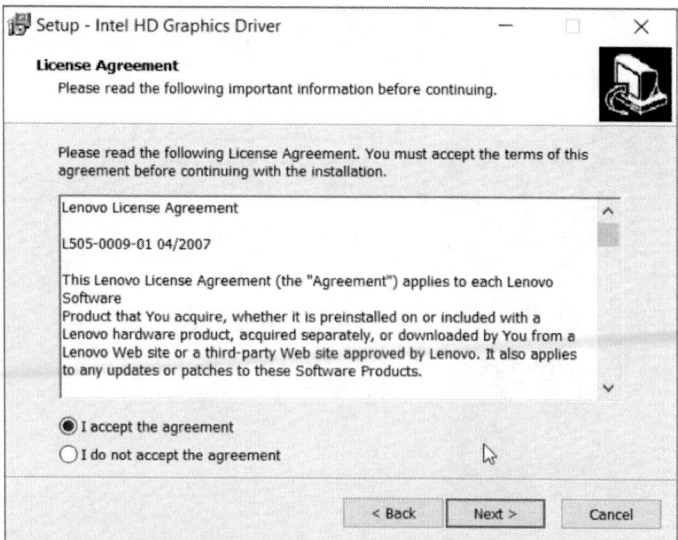

Derived Personal Identity Verification (PIV) Credentials 133

13. Click **Next**.

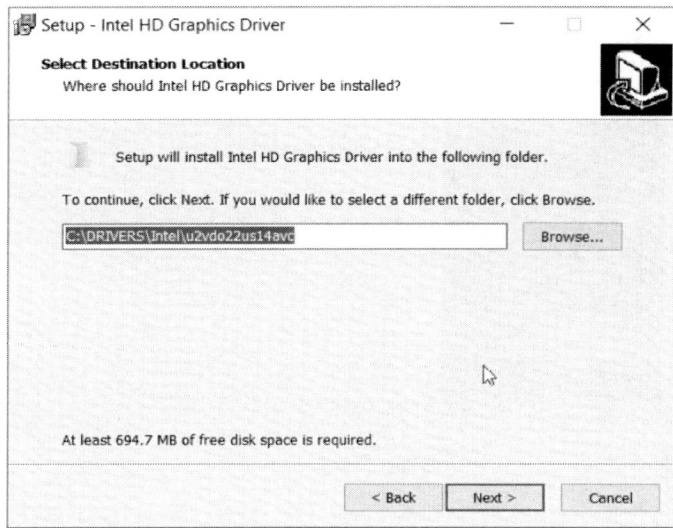

14. Click **Install**.

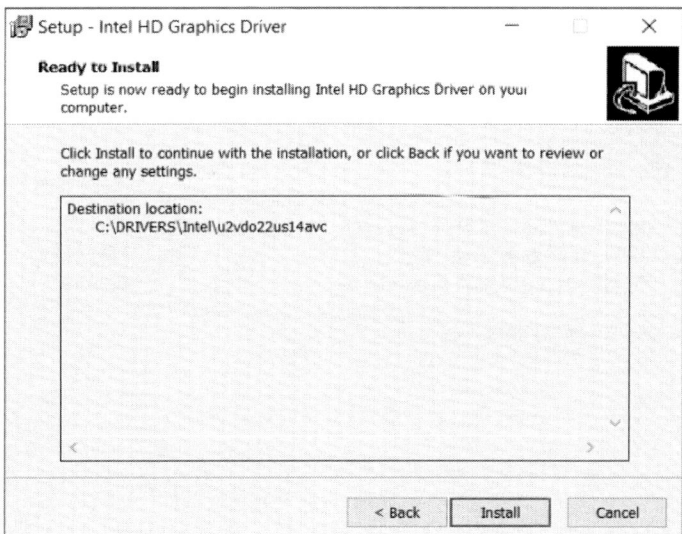

15. Check the box next to **Install Intel HD Graphics Driver now**.
16. Click **Finish**.

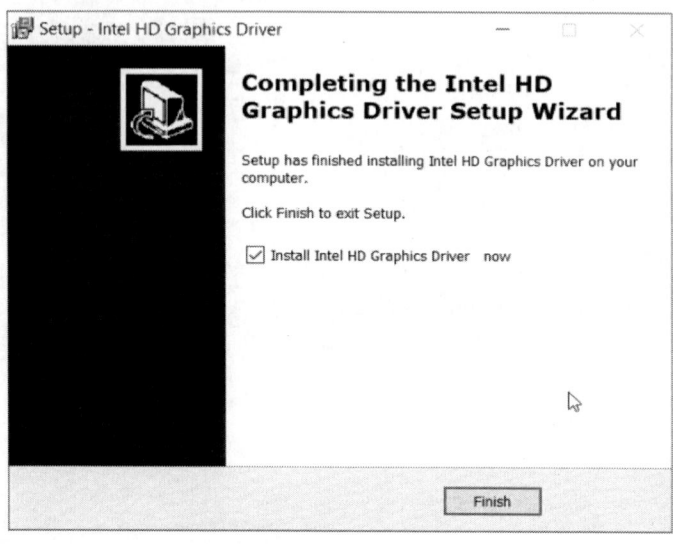

2.2.5.4. Installing the Intel Authenticate Client

The Intel Authenticate Client should be installed automatically by the Group Policy Object (GPO), but it can also be installed manually by running IAx64-2.5.0.68.msi.

1. Run **IAx64-2.5.0.68.msi.**
2. Click **Next.**

Derived Personal Identity Verification (PIV) Credentials   135

3. Select **I accept the terms in the License Agreement.**
4. Click **Next.**

5. Click **Install.**

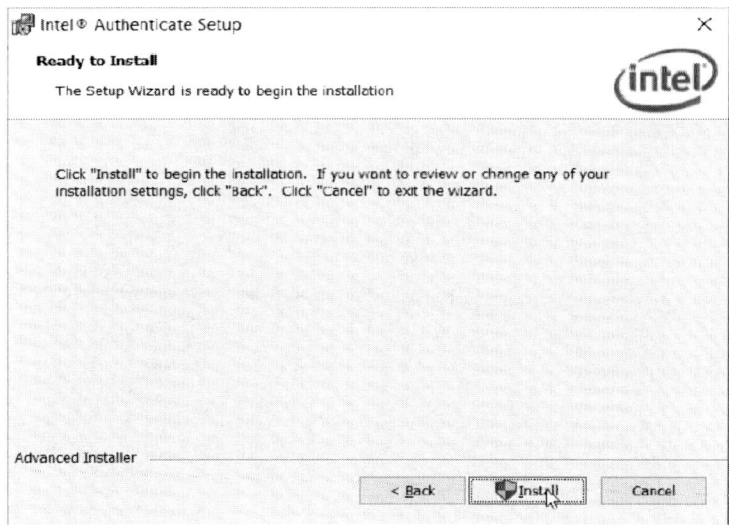

6. Click **Finish.**

2.2.5.5. Configuring Intel Authenticate

1. Once the Enforce Policy GPO is run, the window for configuring Intel Authenticate will open on the client machine. You can also open this manually by searching for Intel Authenticate in the Start Menu.
2. Click the **right arrow button.**

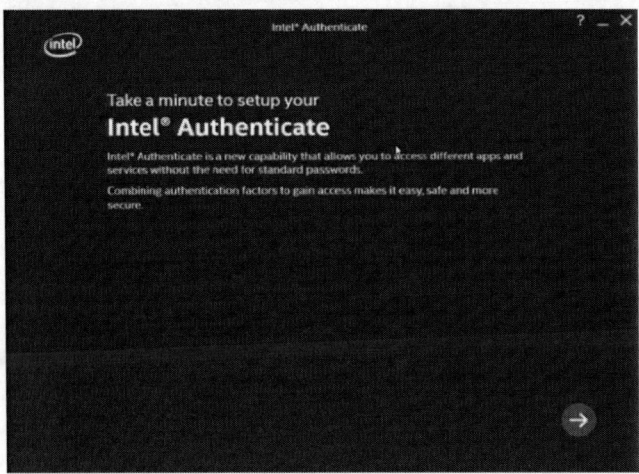

3. Click the **right arrow button.**

Derived Personal Identity Verification (PIV) Credentials 137

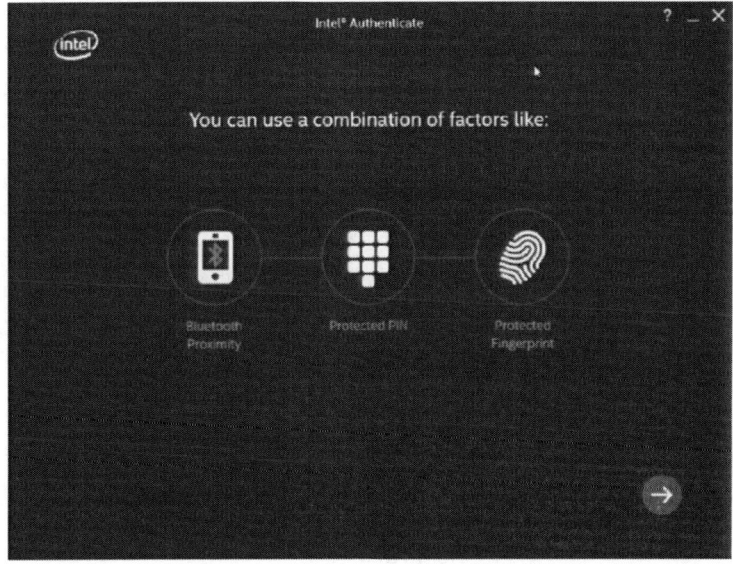

4. Click **Enroll Factor.**

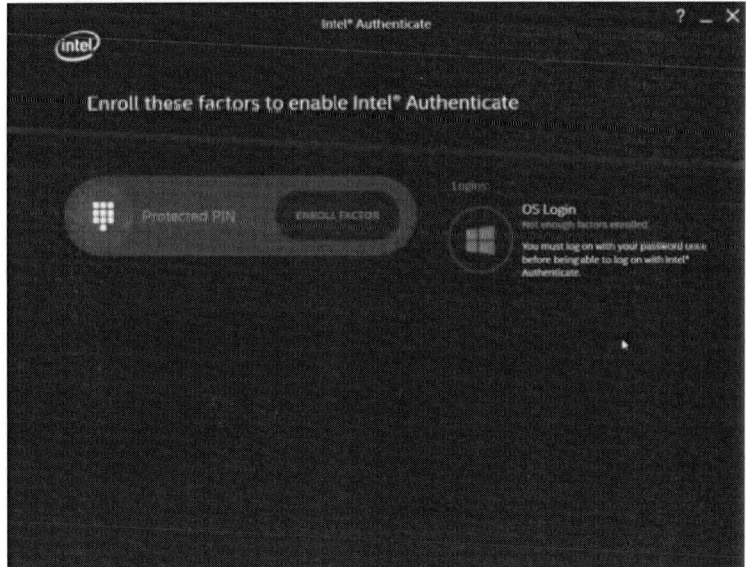

5. Click **Proceed.**

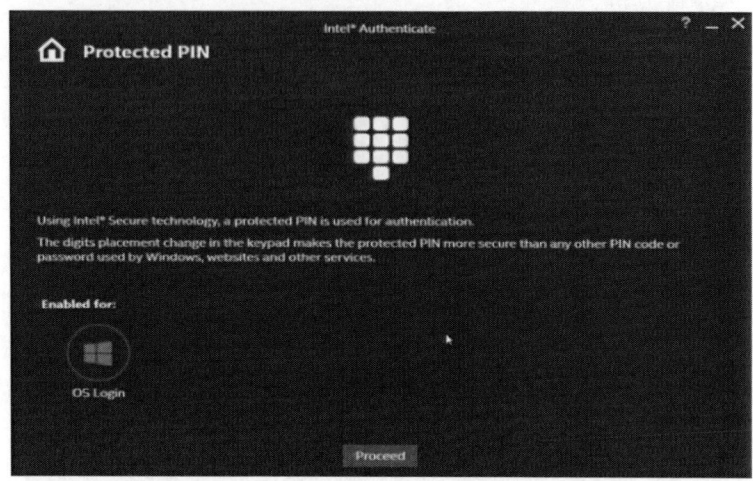

6. Enter a PIN for Intel Authenticate, which will be used for any certificates issued to the device.
7. Reenter the PIN.
8. Click **Return to home**.

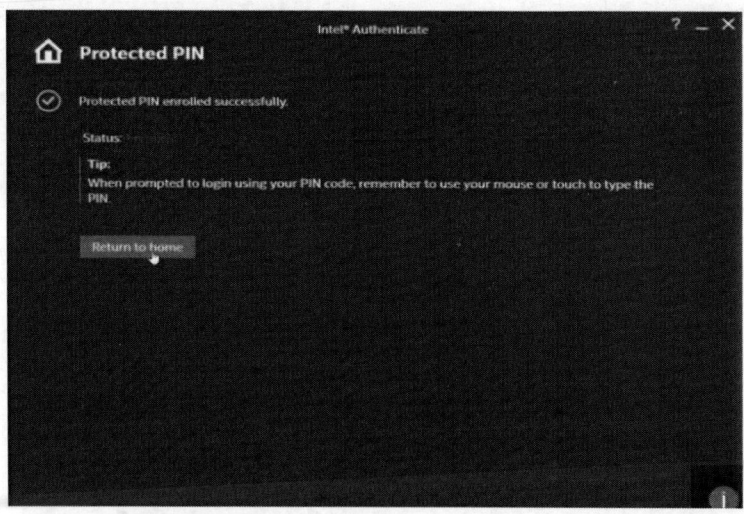

Derived Personal Identity Verification (PIV) Credentials 139

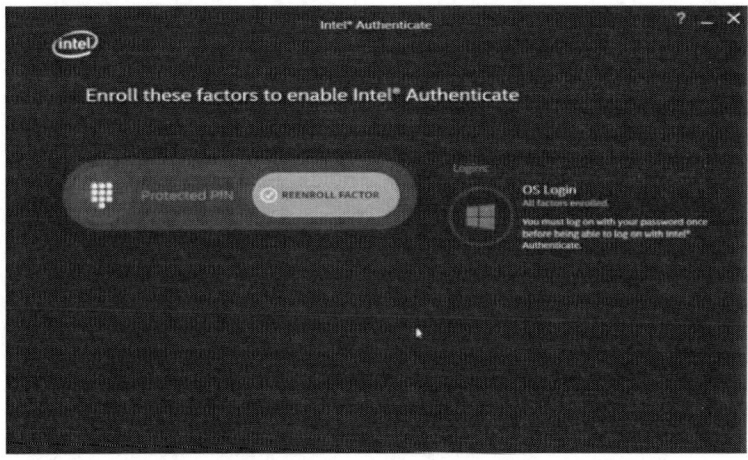

2.2.6. Intel Authenticate GPO

The *Intel Authenticate Integration Guide for Active Directory Policy Objects* provides instructions on how to set up GPOs for various functions of the Intel Authenticate installation process. The following instructions are primarily repurposed from the *Intel Authenticate Integration Guide*.

2.2.6.1. Preparing a Digital Signing Certificate

1. In a new PowerShell window, generate a new self-signed certificate to sign the Intel Policy. Enter the command:

New-SelfSignedCertificate –Subject "CN=TestCert" –KeyUsage Property All –KeyAl-gorithm RSA –KeyLength 2048 –KeyUsage DigitalSignature –Provider "Microsoft En-hanced RSA and AES Cryptographic Provider" –CertStoreLocation "Cert:\Curren-tUser\My"

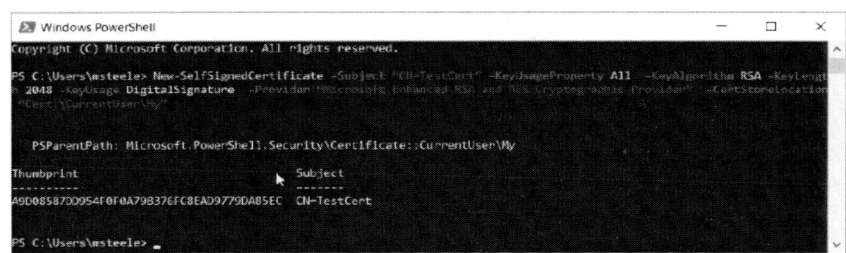

2. Run *mmc.exe* from the Start menu to open the **Microsoft Management Console** window.

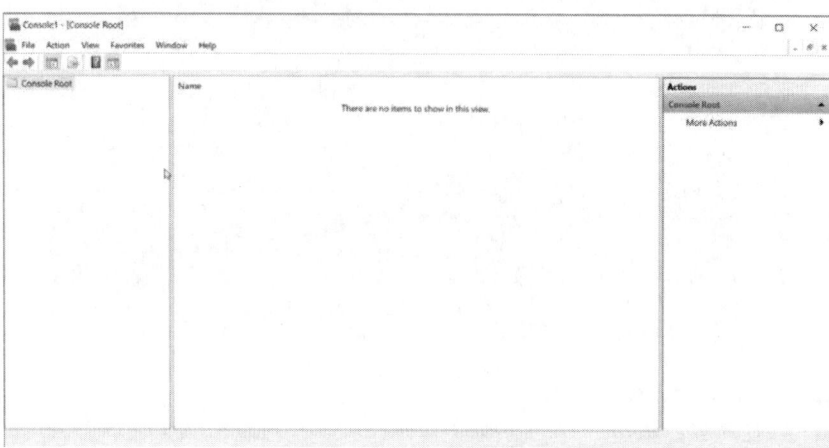

3. Select **File > Add/Remove Snap-In.** Add the **Certificates** snap-in.

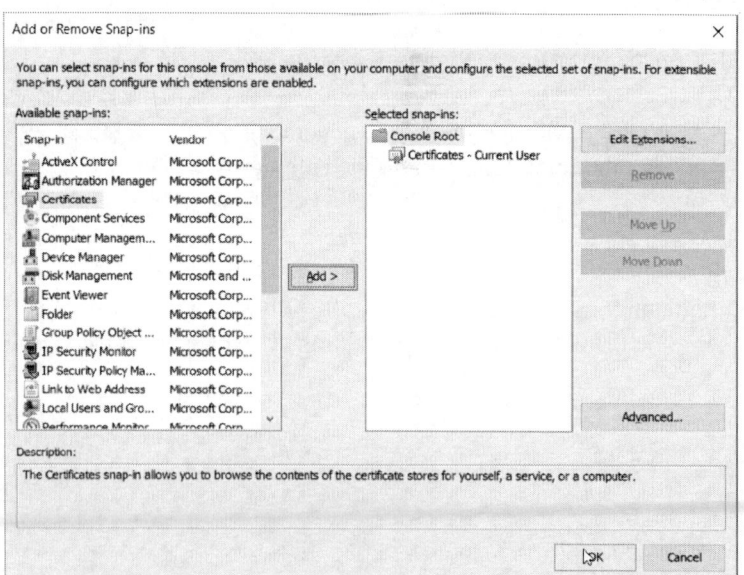

4. The newly created certificate should be in the **Certificates – Current User > Personal > Certifi-cates** store.

Derived Personal Identity Verification (PIV) Credentials 141

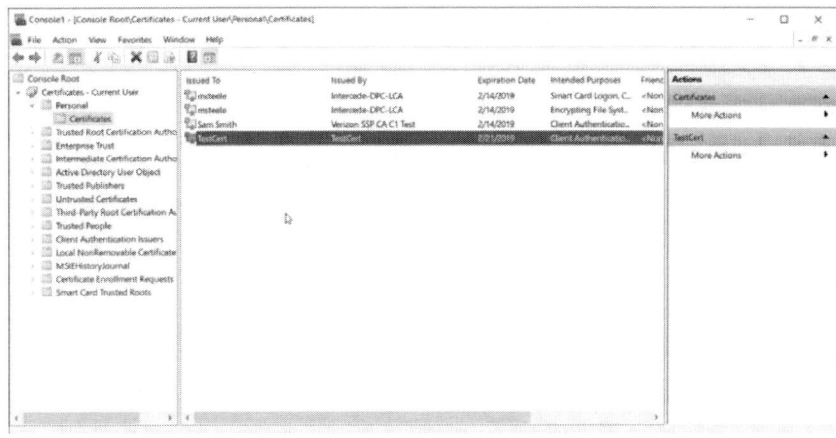

5. Right-click the newly created certificate and select **Copy**.
6. Navigate to **Certificates – Current User > Trusted Root Certification Authorities > Certificates** and paste the certificate there.
7. Click **Yes** when a warning message appears.

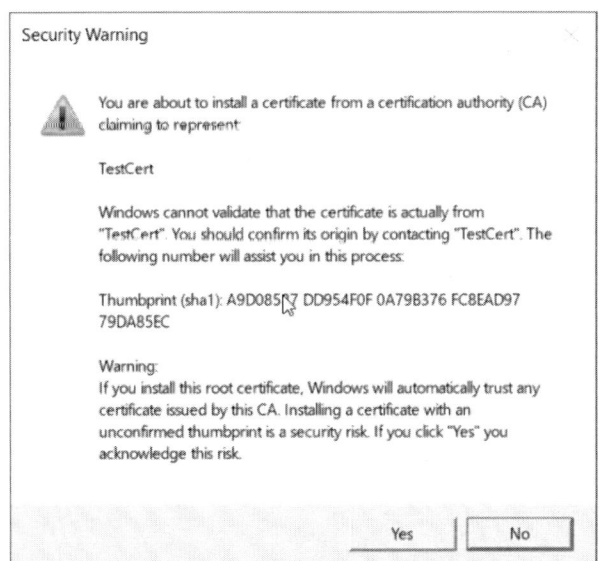

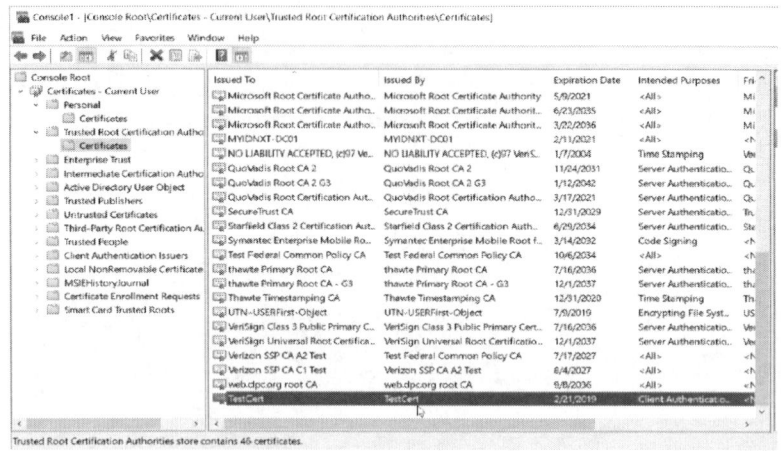

2.2.6.2. Creating a Profile

1. Run the ***ProfileEditor.exe*** file as an administrator.

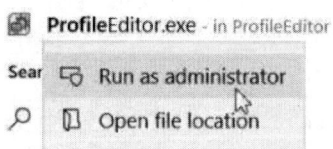

2. Click **Create a New Profile....**

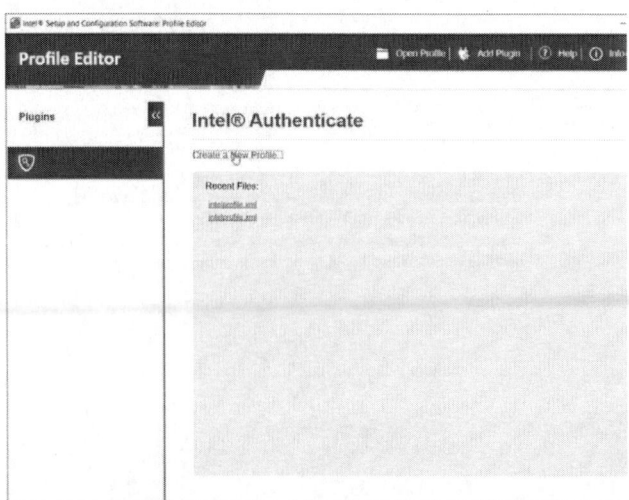

Derived Personal Identity Verification (PIV) Credentials 143

3. Click **Select Signing Certificate.**

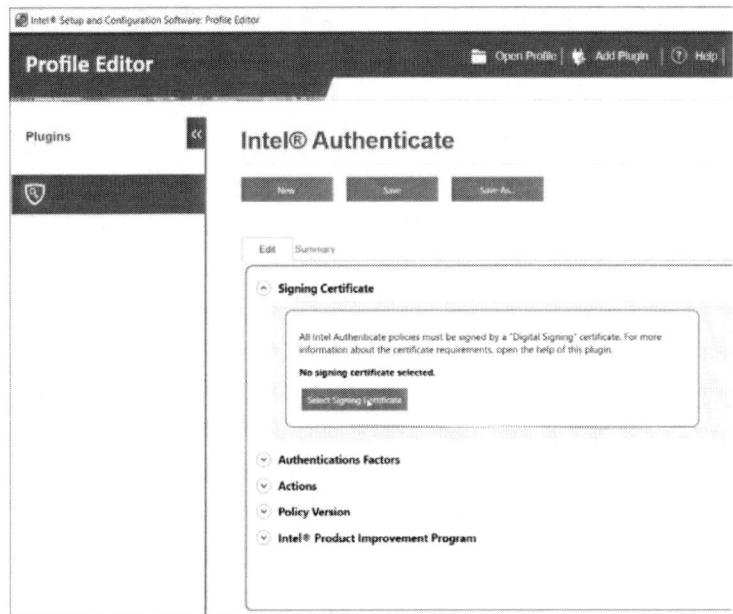

4. Select the newly created certificate and click **Select.**

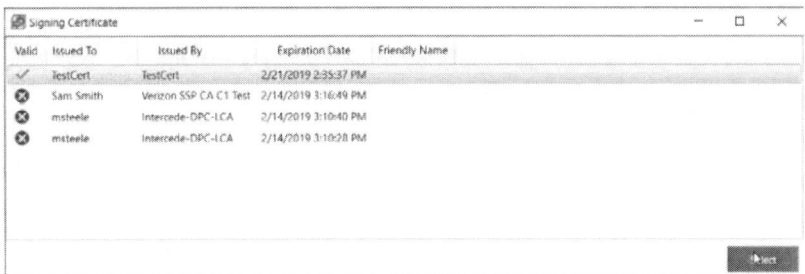

5. Under **Authentications Factors**, check the box next to **Protected PIN.**
6. Click the **Edit** button.

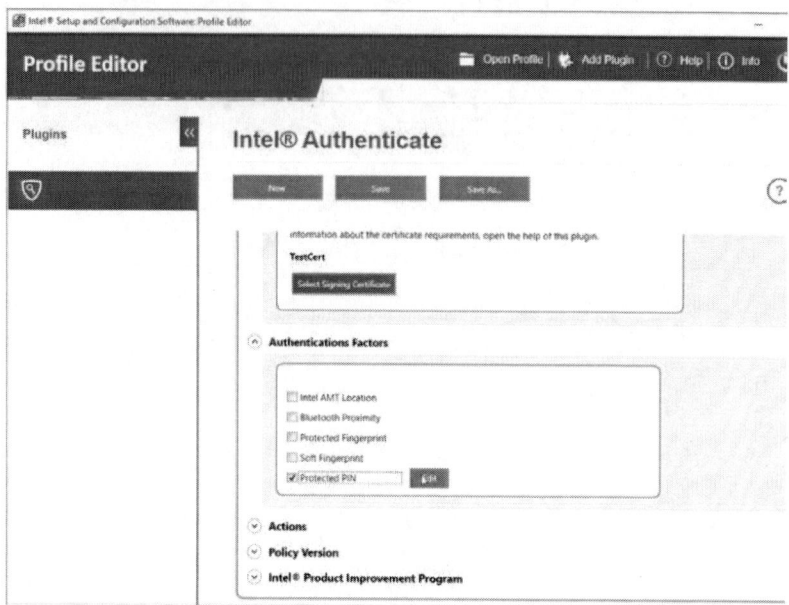

7. Set the PIN length and the minimum number of unique digits.
8. Click **Close**.

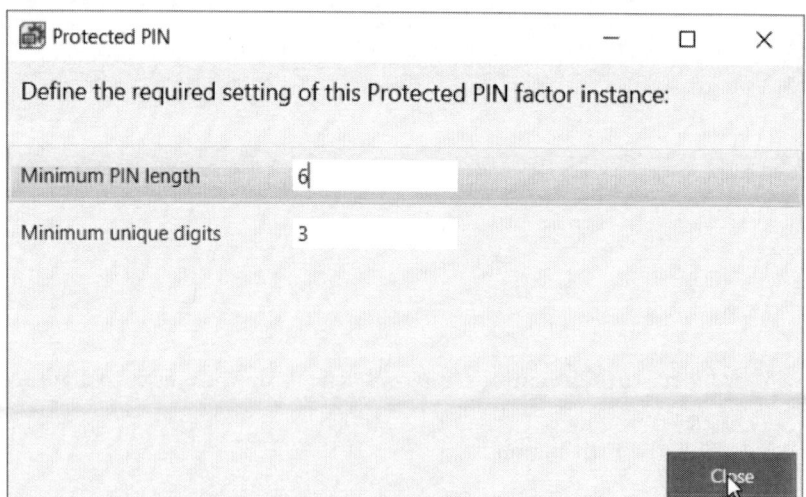

9. Under **Actions > OS Login,** check the box next to **Enable OS Login.**
10. Check the box next to **Protected PIN.**

11. Click **Advanced Settings.**

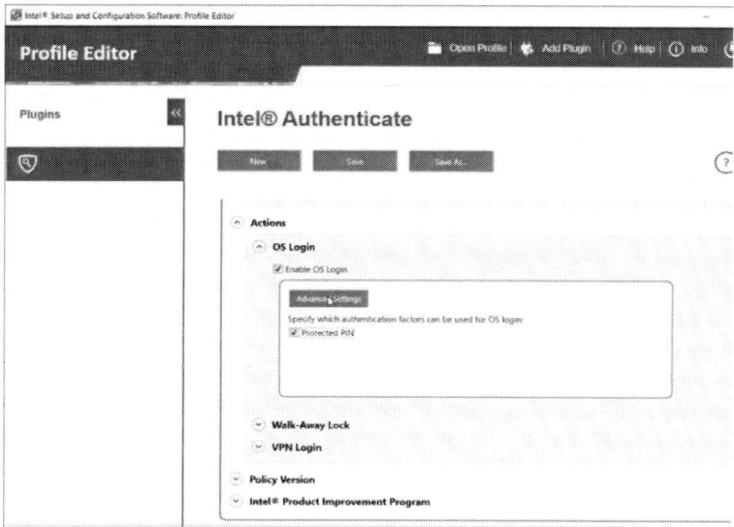

12. Uncheck the box next to **Require the system drive to be encrypted.**
13. Click **Close.**

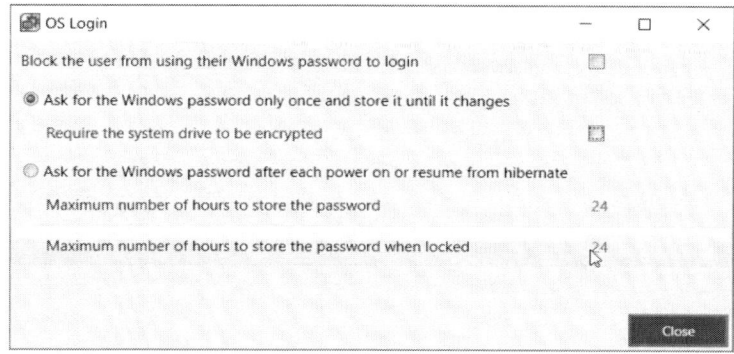

14. Click the **Save As...** button and save the profile.

2.2.6.3. Creating a Shared Folder

1. Create a new folder on the network.
2. Give it a name such as *shared-gpo-folder*.

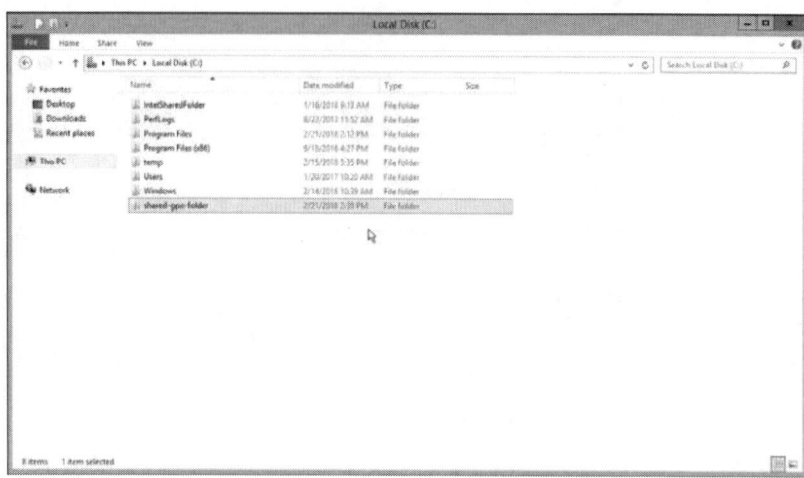

3. Right-click the folder and select **Properties**.
4. Go to the **Security** Tab.
5. Click **Edit**.

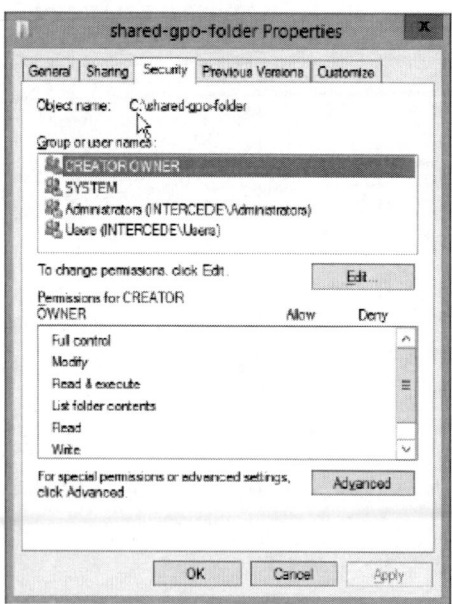

6. Click **Add**.

Derived Personal Identity Verification (PIV) Credentials 147

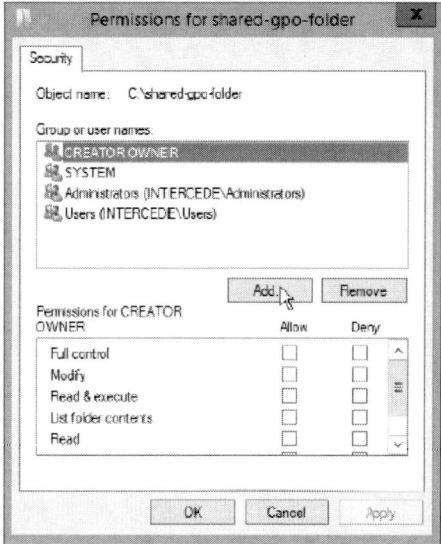

7. Enter **Domain Computers** in the text box.
8. Click **OK.**

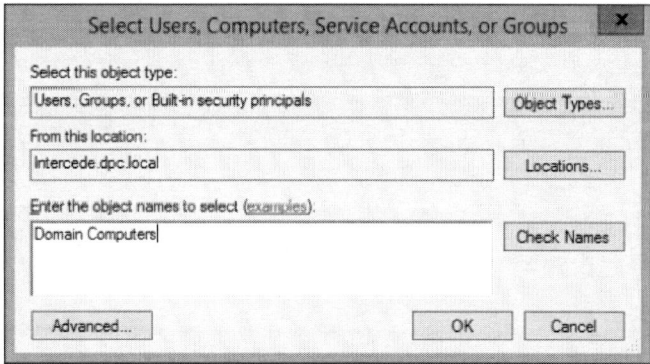

9. Ensure that the Domain Computers have read permissions on this folder.
10. Click **OK.**

11. Click **OK**.
12. Copy all the files from the HostFiles folder, as well as the Intel Profile you created, into this shared folder.

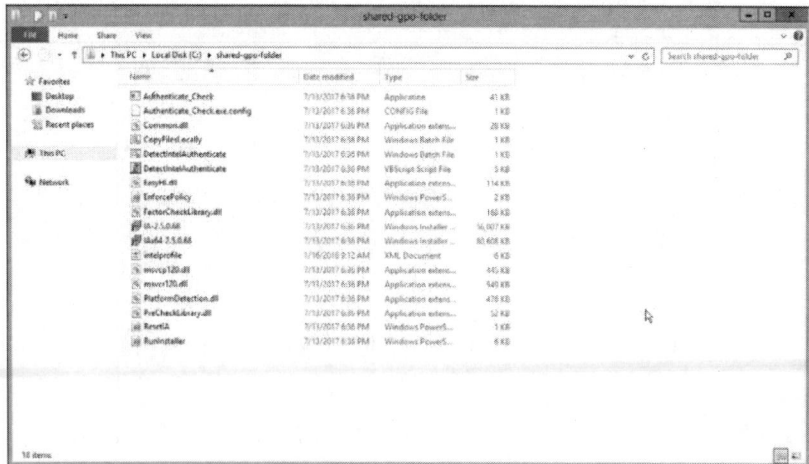

Derived Personal Identity Verification (PIV) Credentials 149

2.2.6.4. Creating Windows Management Instrumentation (WMI) Filters for the GPOs

1. Open the **Group Policy Management** window by running **gpmc.msc** from the **Start** menu.
2. Right-click **WMI Filters** and select **New….**

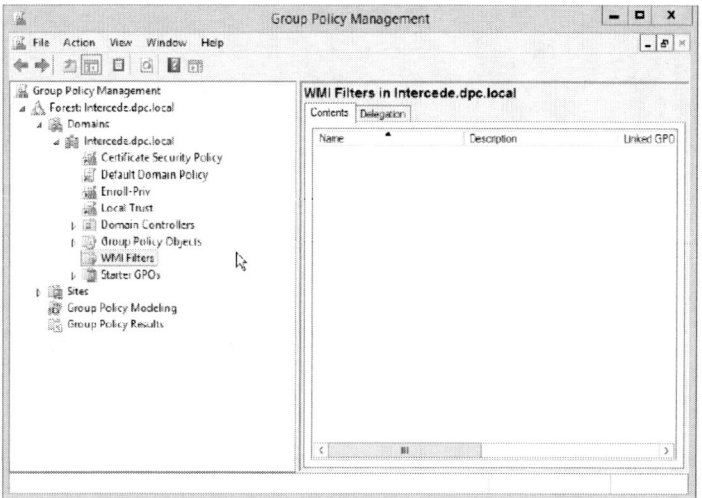

3. Enter a name such as *Is Intel Authenticate Supported* and click **Add.**

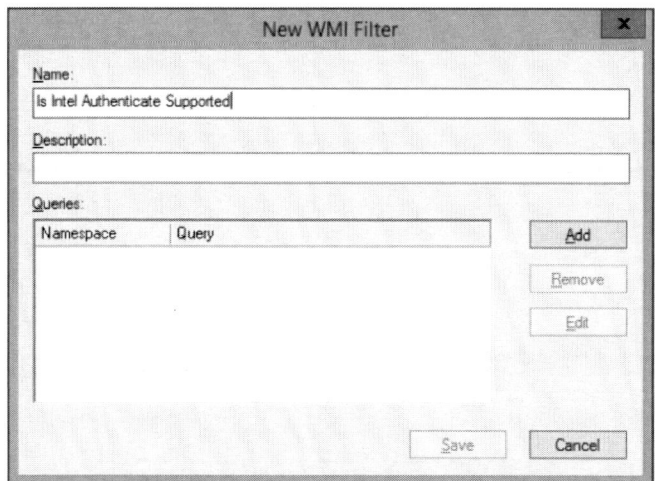

4. In the **Query** field, enter *SELECT * FROM Intel_Authenticate WHERE Supported="true"*.
5. Click **OK**.

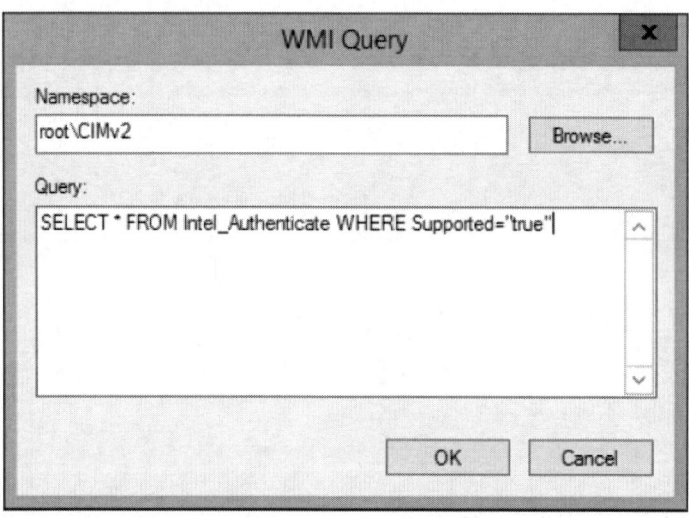

6. Click **Save**.

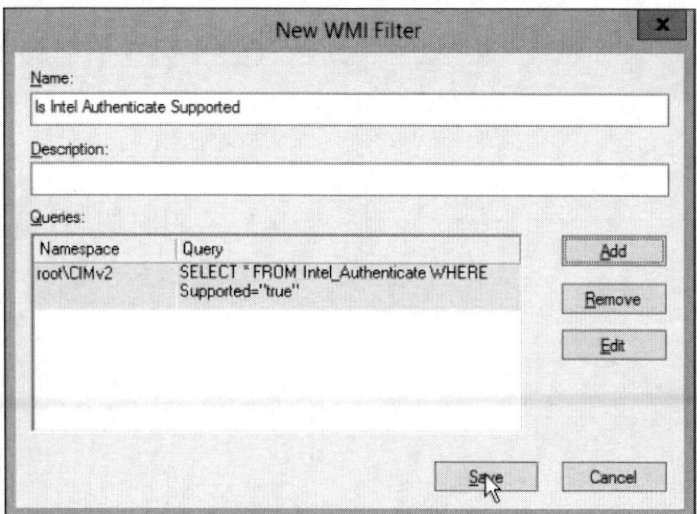

7. Right-click **WMI Filters** and select **New…**.

Derived Personal Identity Verification (PIV) Credentials 151

8. Enter a name such as *Is Intel Authenticate Installed* and click **Add**.

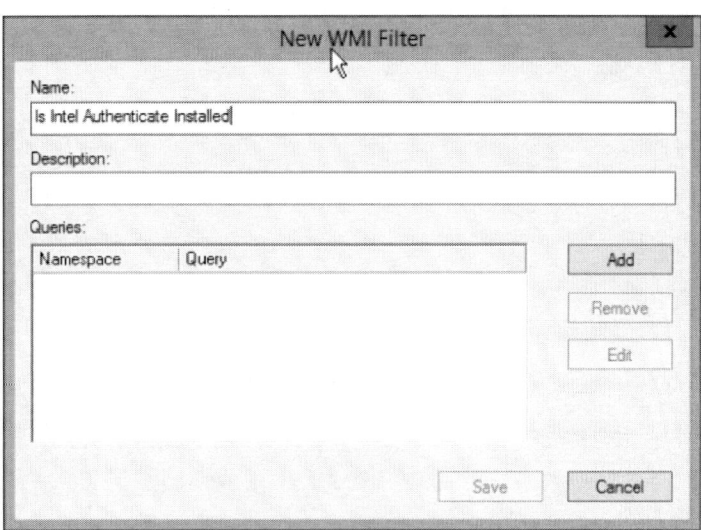

9. In the **Query** field, enter *SELECT * FROM Intel_Authenticate WHERE isClientInstalled="true" AND isEngineInstalled="true"*.
10. Click **OK**.

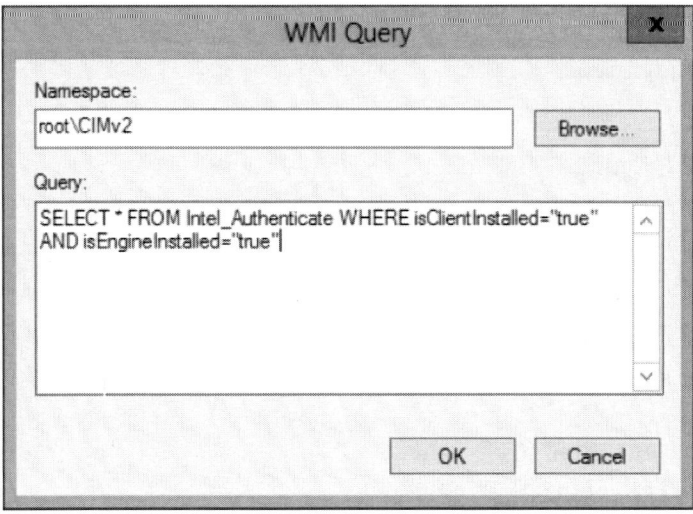

11. Click **Save**.

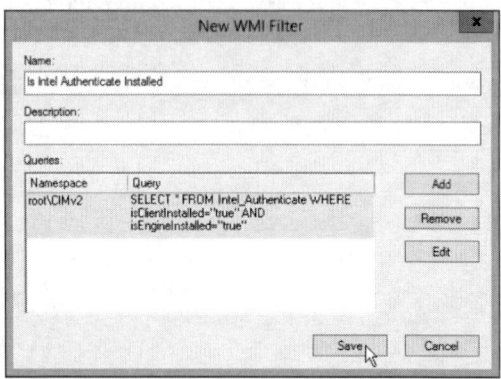

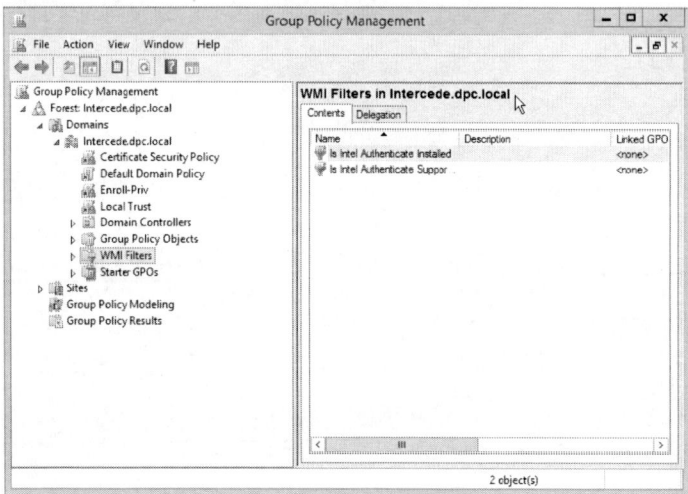

2.2.6.5. Creating a GPO to Discover Intel Authenticate

1. Open **Group Policy Management.**
2. In the Group Policy Management tree, right-click the domain and select **Create a GPO in the do-main and Link it here.**
3. Enter a **name** for this GPO.
4. Right-click the GPO just created and select **Edit.**
5. Right-click **Computer Configuration > Preferences > Control Panel Settings > Scheduled Tasks** and select **New > Scheduled Task (At least Windows 7).**

Derived Personal Identity Verification (PIV) Credentials

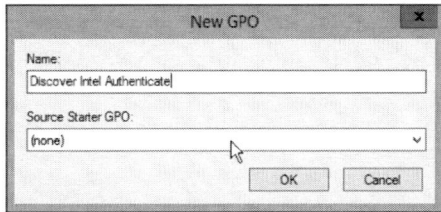

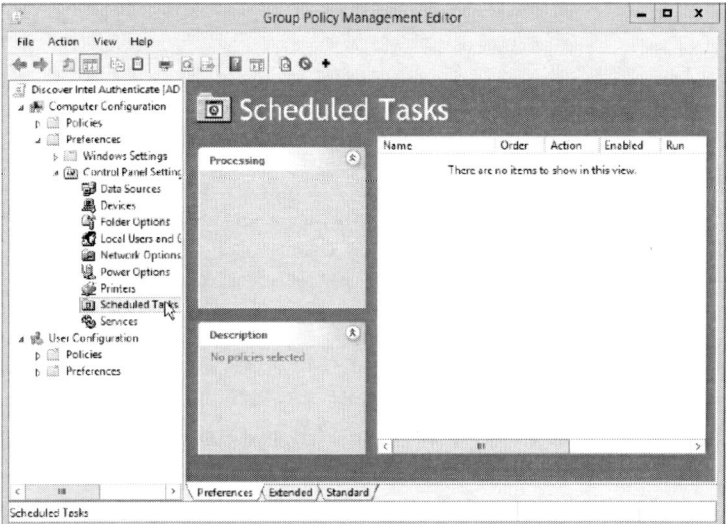

6. Select **Replace** from the drop-down list for **Action**.
7. Enter a descriptive name.
8. Click **Change User or Group**.
9. Enter *SYSTEM* and click **OK**.

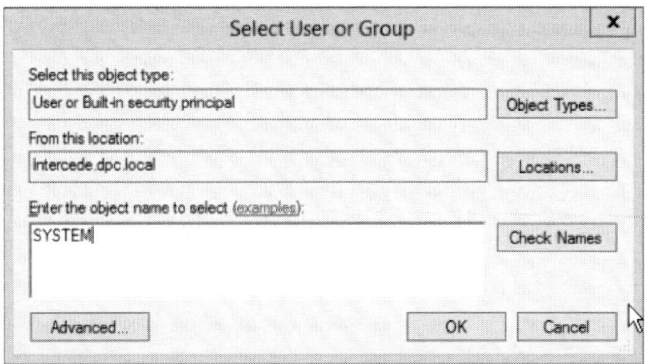

10. Check the box next to **Run whether user is logged on or not.**
11. A window will open asking for a password. Click **Cancel.**

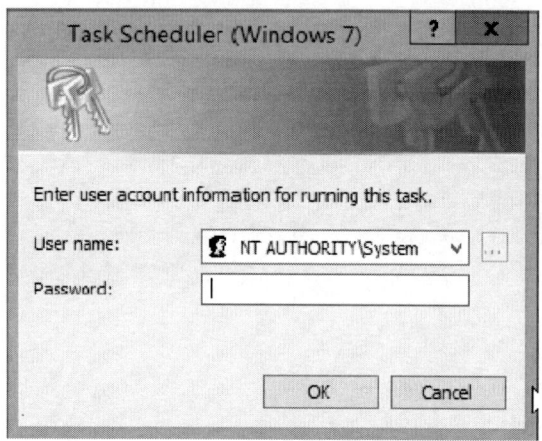

12. Check the box next to **Do not store password. The task will only have access to local resources.**
13. Check the box next to **Run with highest privileges.**

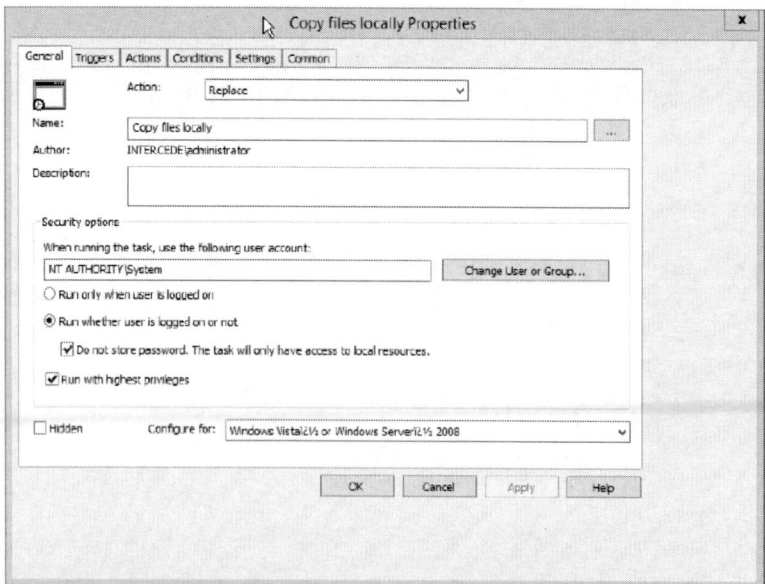

14. Select the **Triggers** tab.
15. Click **New....**

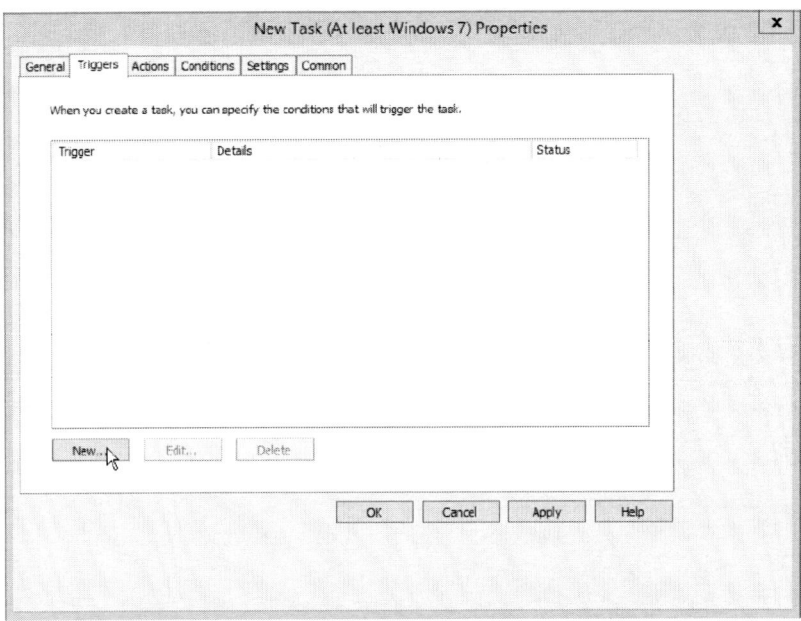

16. Select **At task creation/modification** for **Begin the task.**
17. Click **OK.**

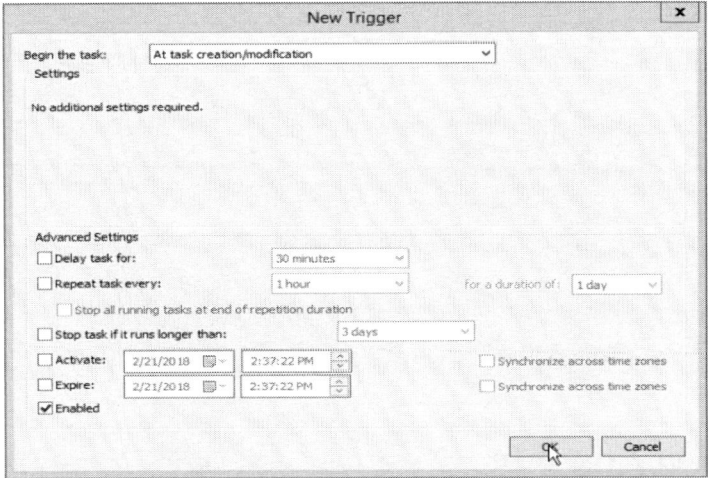

18. Select the **Actions** tab.
19. Click **New....**

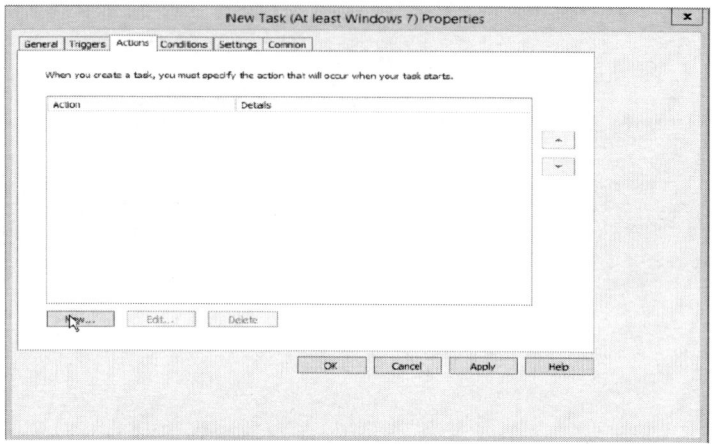

20. Select **Start a program.**
21. For **Program/script,** enter the network location of the *CopyFilesLocally.bat* file.
22. Click **OK.**

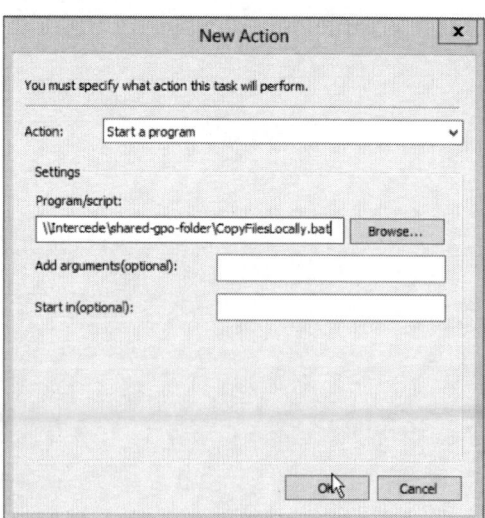

23. Click **OK.**

Derived Personal Identity Verification (PIV) Credentials 157

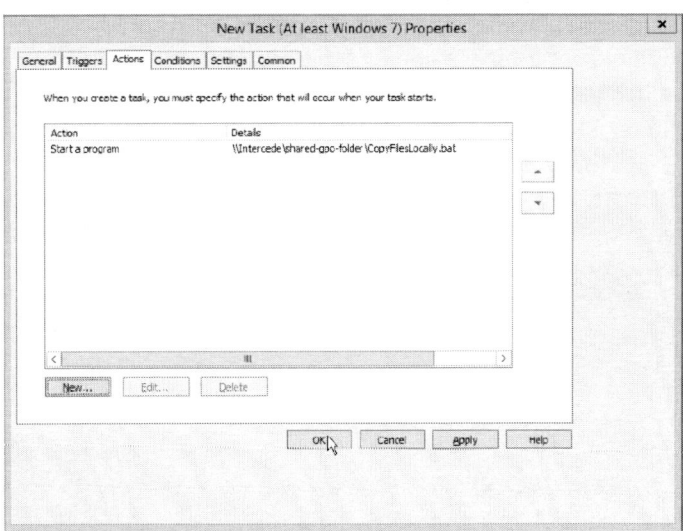

24. Right-click **Computer Configuration > Preferences > Control Panel Settings > Scheduled Tasks** and select **New > Scheduled Task (At least Windows 7)**.

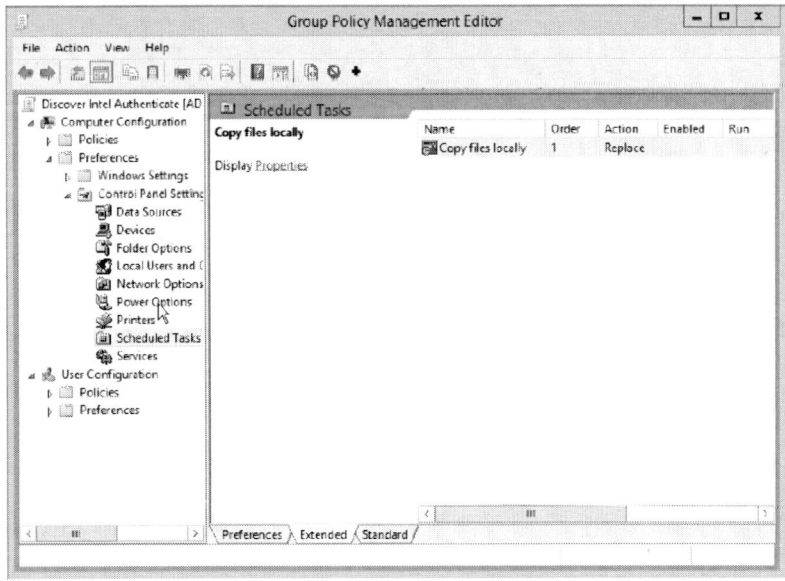

25. Select **Replace** from the drop-down list for **Action**.
26. Enter a descriptive name.
27. Click **Change User or Group**.
28. Enter *SYSTEM* and click **OK**.

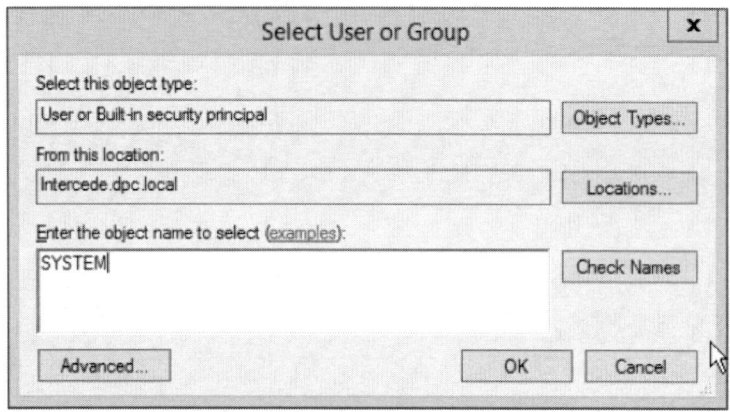

29. Check the box next to **Run whether user is logged on or not**.
30. A window will open asking for a password. Click **Cancel**.

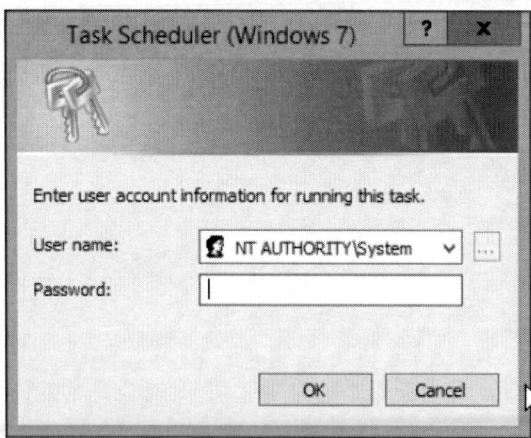

31. Check the box next to **Do not store password. The task will only have access to local resources**.
32. Check the box next to **Run with highest privileges**.

Derived Personal Identity Verification (PIV) Credentials

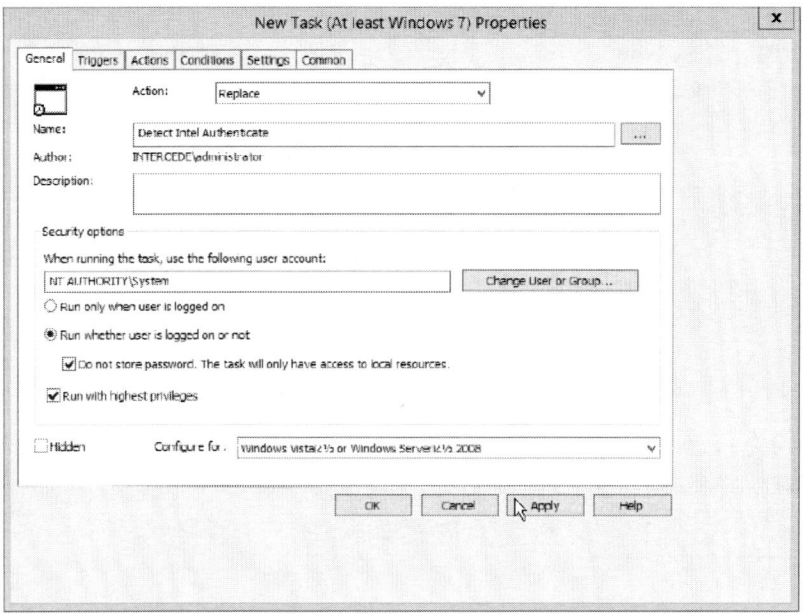

33. Select the **Triggers** tab.
34. Click **New…**.
35. Select **At task creation/modification** for **Begin the task**.
36. Click **OK**.

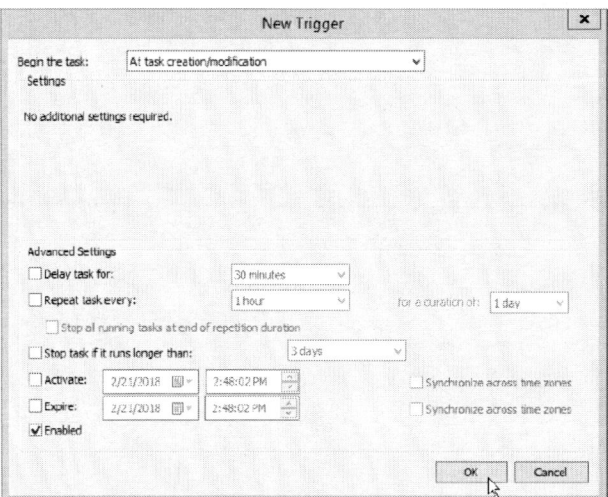

37. Select the **Actions** tab.
38. Click **New….**
39. Select **Start a program.**

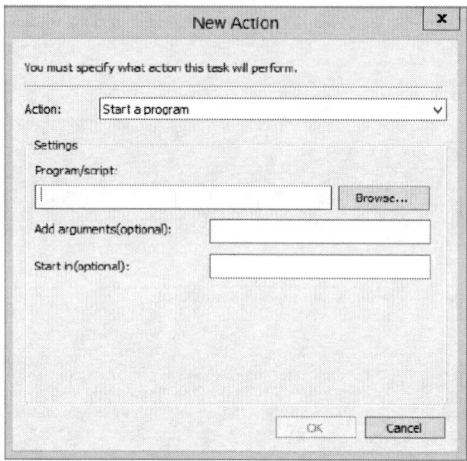

40. For **Program/script**, enter *C:\Temp\DetectIntelAuthenticate.bat*.
41. For **Start In,** enter *C:\Temp*.
42. Click **OK.**

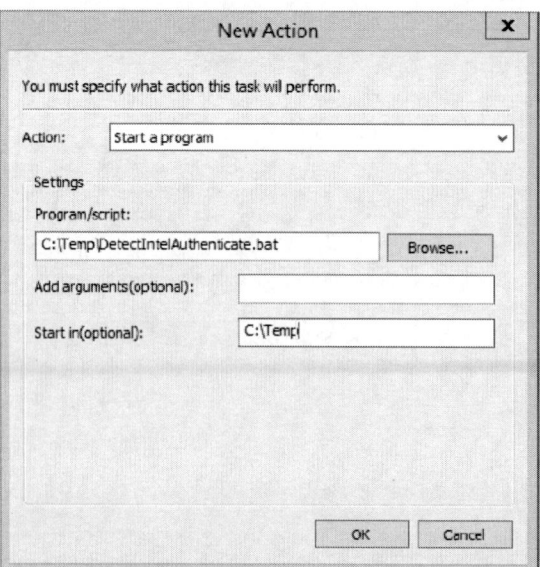

43. Click **OK**.

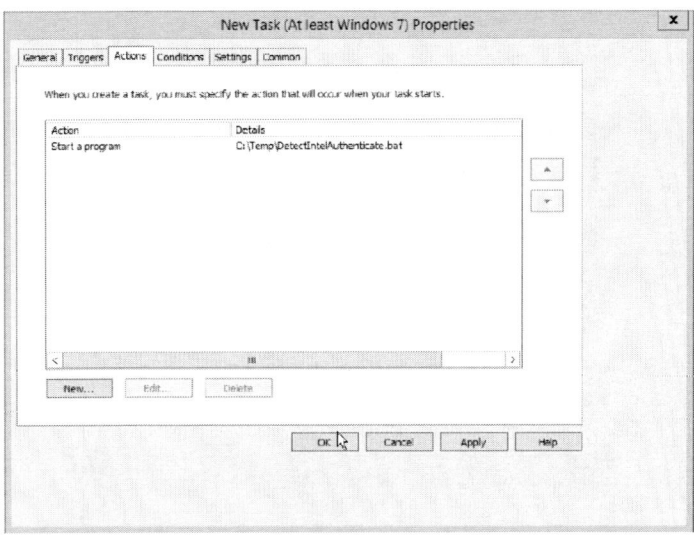

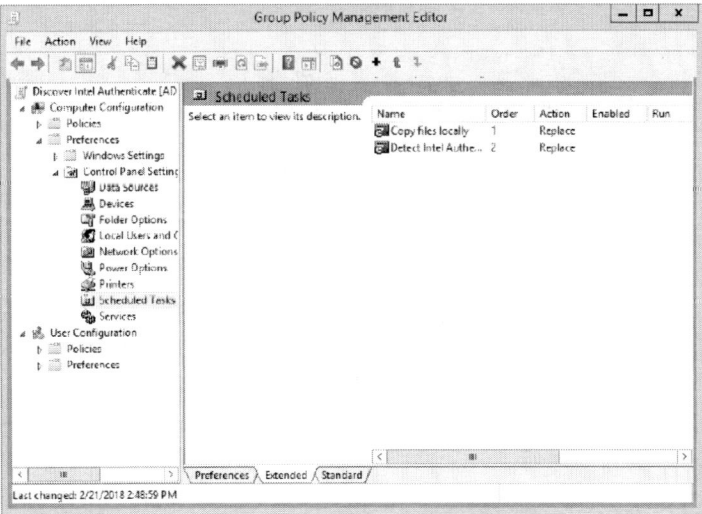

2.2.6.6. Creating a GPO to Install Intel Authenticate

1. Open **Group Policy Management.**
2. In the Group Policy Management tree, right-click the domain and select **Create a GPO in the do-main and Link it here.**

3. Enter a **name** for this GPO.
4. Click **OK**.

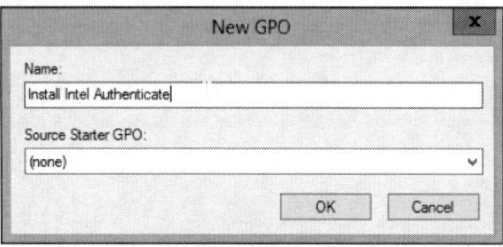

5. Select the GPO you just created and select **Is Intel Authenticate Supported** in the **WMI Filtering** section.
6. Click **Yes**.

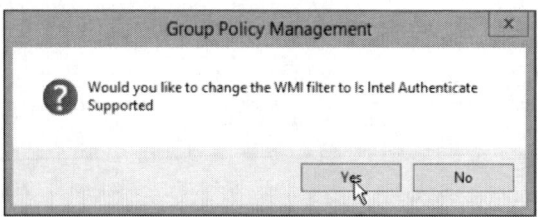

7. Right-click the GPO just created and select **Edit**.

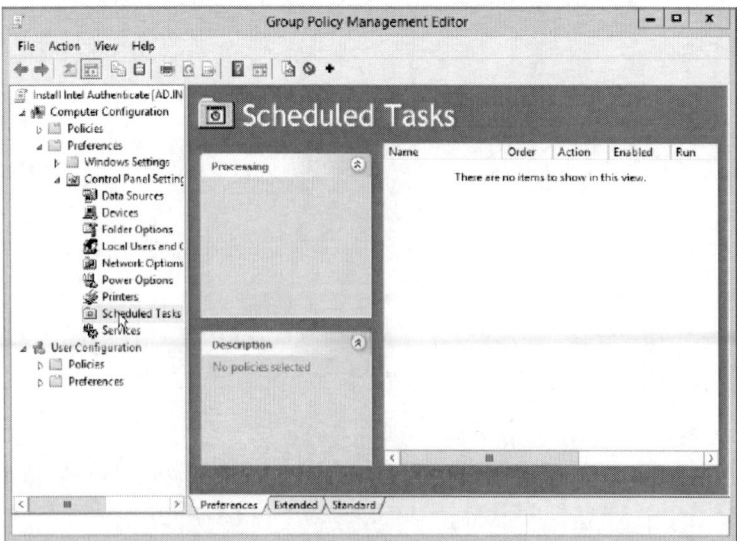

Derived Personal Identity Verification (PIV) Credentials   163

8. Right-click **Computer Configuration > Preferences > Control Panel Settings > Scheduled Tasks** and select **New > Scheduled Task (At least Windows 7)**.
9. Select **Replace** from the drop-down list for **Action**.
10. Enter a descriptive name.
11. Click **Change User or Group**.
12. Enter *SYSTEM* and click **OK**.

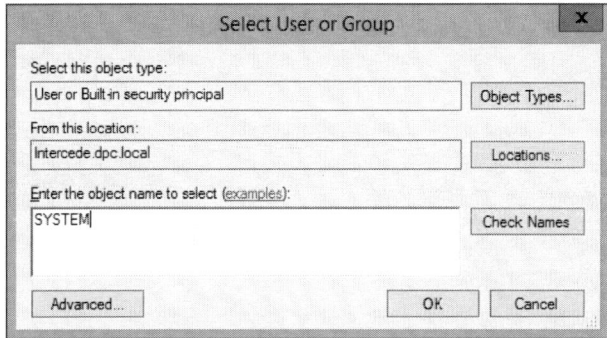

13. Check the box next to **Run whether user is logged on or not**.
14. A window will open asking for a password. Click **Cancel**.

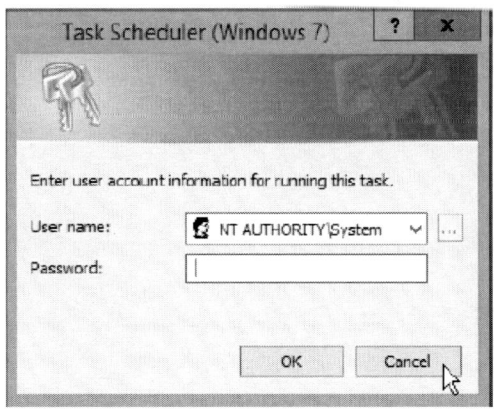

15. Check the box next to **Do not store password. The task will only have access to local resources.**
16. Check the box next to **Run with highest privileges**.

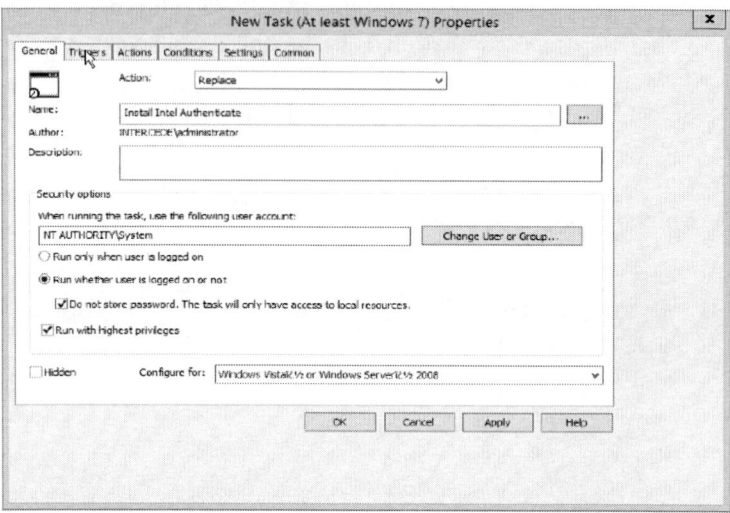

17. Select the **Triggers** tab.
18. Click **New....**
19. Select **At task creation/modification** for **Begin the task.**
20. Check the box next to **Delay task for.**
21. Select **30 minutes.**
22. Ensure **Enabled** is selected and click **OK.**

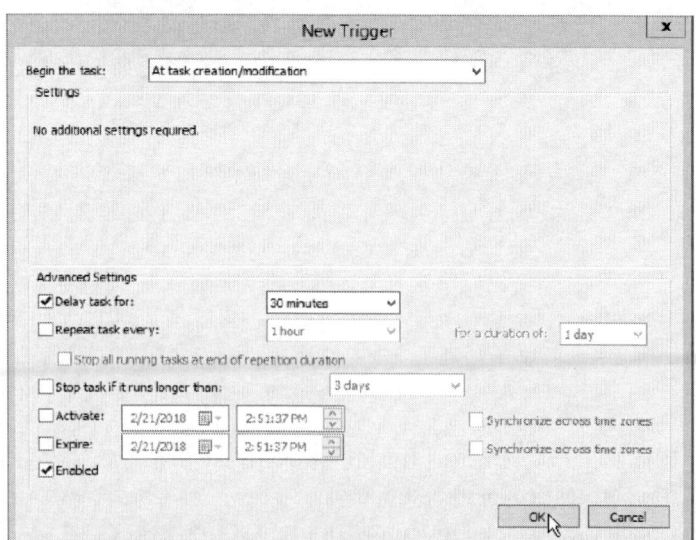

Derived Personal Identity Verification (PIV) Credentials   165

23. Select the **Actions** tab.
24. Click **New....**
25. Select **Start a program.**
26. For **Program/script,** enter *C:\Windows\System32\WindowsPower Shell\v1.0\powershell.exe.*
27. For **Add arguments,** enter-*executionpolicy unrestricted C:\Temp\ RunInstaller.ps1.*
28. For **Start In,** enter *C:\Temp.*
29. Click **OK.**

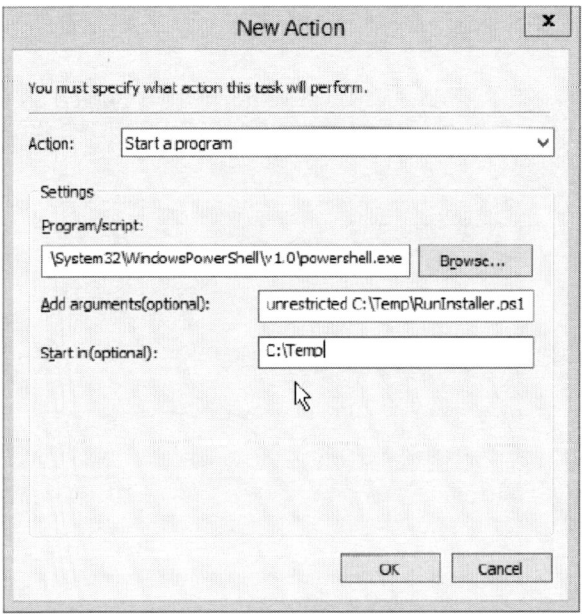

30. Click **OK.**
31. Right-click **Computer Configuration > Preferences > Control Panel Settings > Scheduled Tasks** and select **New > Scheduled Task (At least Windows 7).**
32. Select **Replace** from the drop-down list for **Action.**
33. Enter a descriptive name.
34. Click **Change User or Group.**
35. Enter *SYSTEM* and click **OK.**

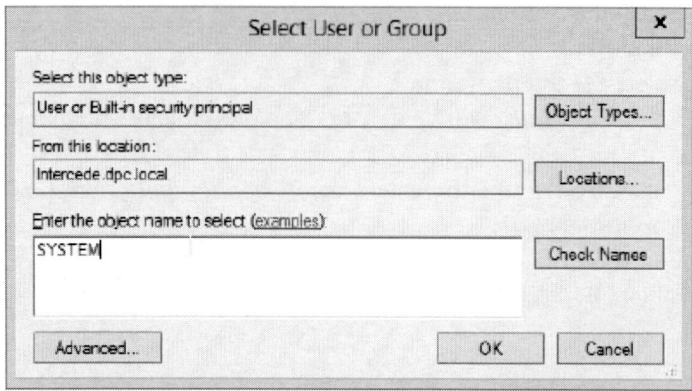

36. Check the box next to **Run whether user is logged on or not**.
37. A window will open asking for a password. Click **Cancel**.

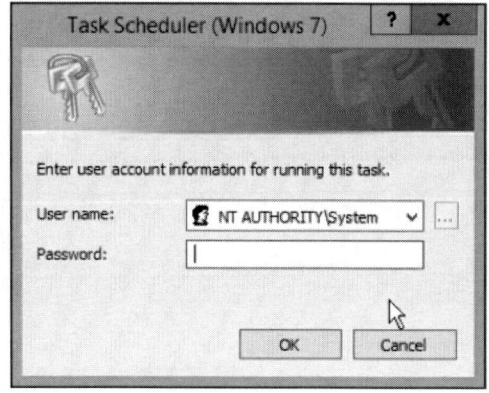

38. Check the box next to **Do not store password. The task will only have access to local resources.**
39. Check the box next to **Run with highest privileges**.
40. Select the **Triggers** tab.
41. Click **New....**
42. Select **At task creation/modification** for **Begin the task.**
43. Check the box next to **Delay task for.**
44. Select **30 minutes.**
45. Ensure **Enabled** is selected and click **OK**

Derived Personal Identity Verification (PIV) Credentials

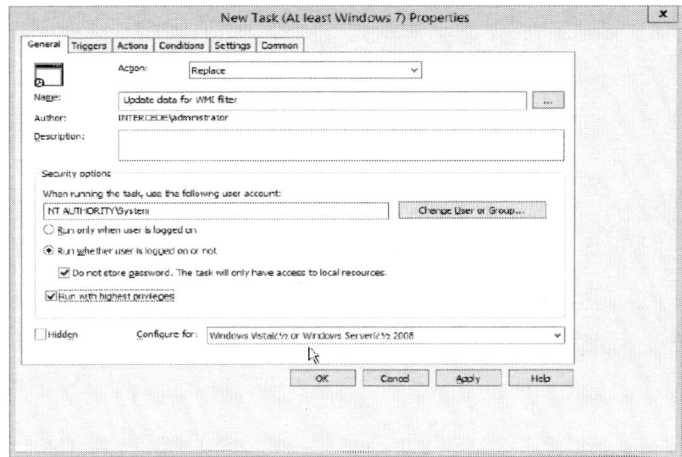

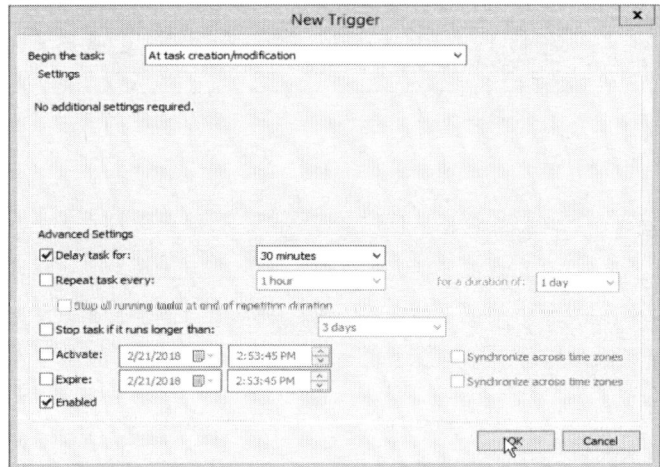

46. Select the **Actions** tab.
47. Click **New…**.
48. Select **Start a program.**
49. For **Program/script,** enter *C:\Temp\DetectIntelAuthenticate.bat*.
50. For **Start In,** enter *C:\Temp*.
51. Click **OK.**

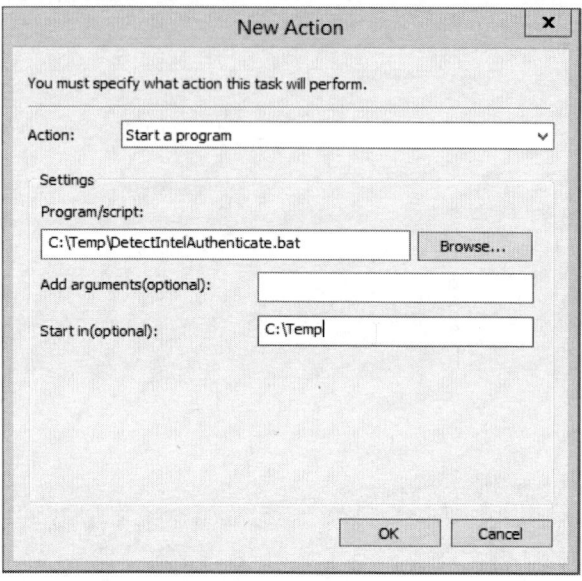

52. Click **OK**.

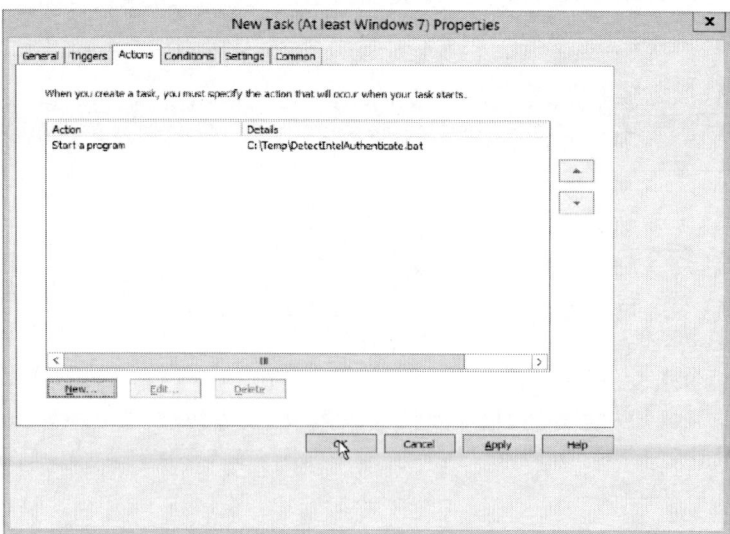

Derived Personal Identity Verification (PIV) Credentials 169

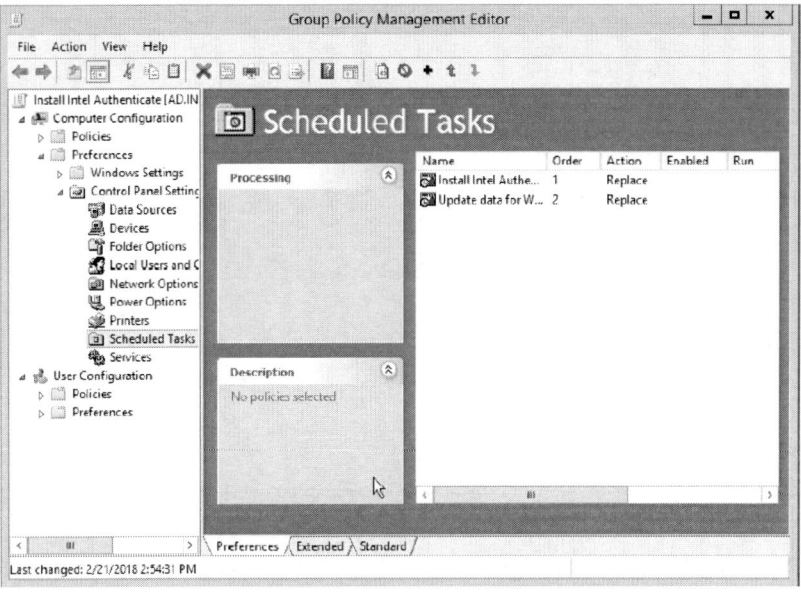

2.2.6.7. Creating a GPO to Enforce the Policy

1. Open **Group Policy Management.**
2. In the Group Policy Management tree, right-click the domain and select **Create a GPO in the do-main and Link it here.**
3. Enter a name for this GPO.
4. Click **OK.**

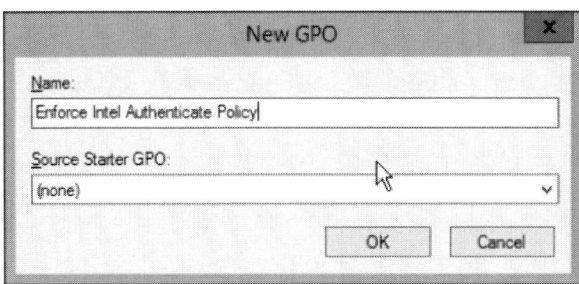

5. Select the GPO you just created and select **Is Intel Authenticate Installed** in the **WMI Filtering** section.
6. Click **Yes.**

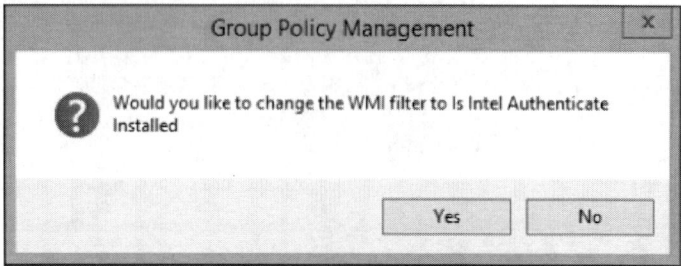

7. Right-click the GPO just created and select **Edit**.

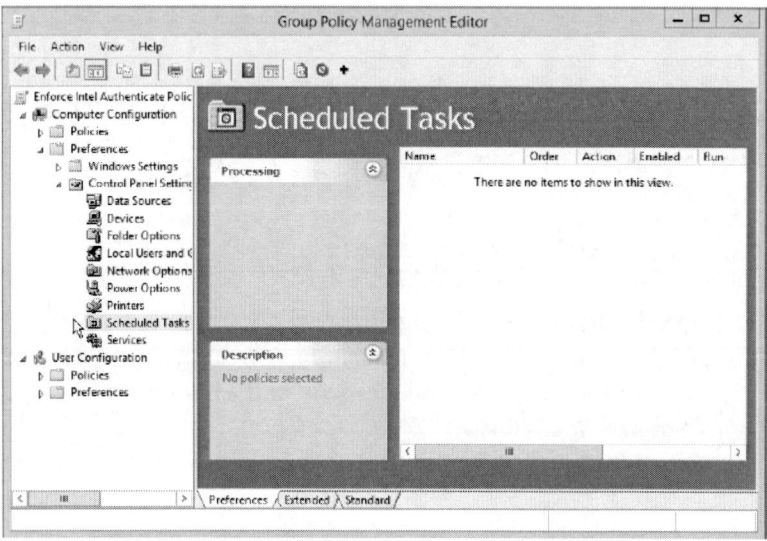

8. Right-click **Computer Configuration** > **Preferences** > **Control Panel Settings** > **Scheduled Tasks** and select **New** > **Scheduled Task (At least Windows 7)**.
9. Select **Replace** from the drop-down list for **Action**.
10. Enter a descriptive name.
11. Click **Change User or Group**.
12. Enter *SYSTEM* and click **OK**.

Derived Personal Identity Verification (PIV) Credentials 171

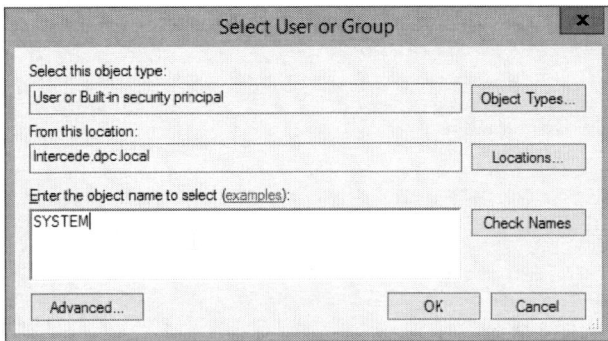

13. Check the box next to **Run whether user is logged on or not**.
14. A window will open asking for a password. Click **Cancel**.

15. Check the box next to **Do not store password. The task will only have access to local resources**.
16. Check the box next to **Run with highest privileges**.
17. Select the **Triggers** tab.
18. Click **New…**.
19. Select **On a schedule** for **Begin the task**.
20. Select **Daily**.
21. Check the box next to **Delay task for**.
22. Select **30 minutes**.
23. Ensure **Enabled** is selected and click **OK**.

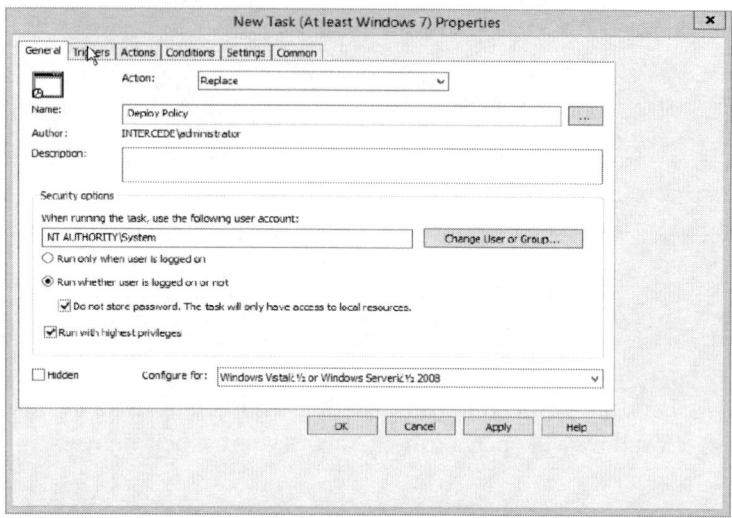

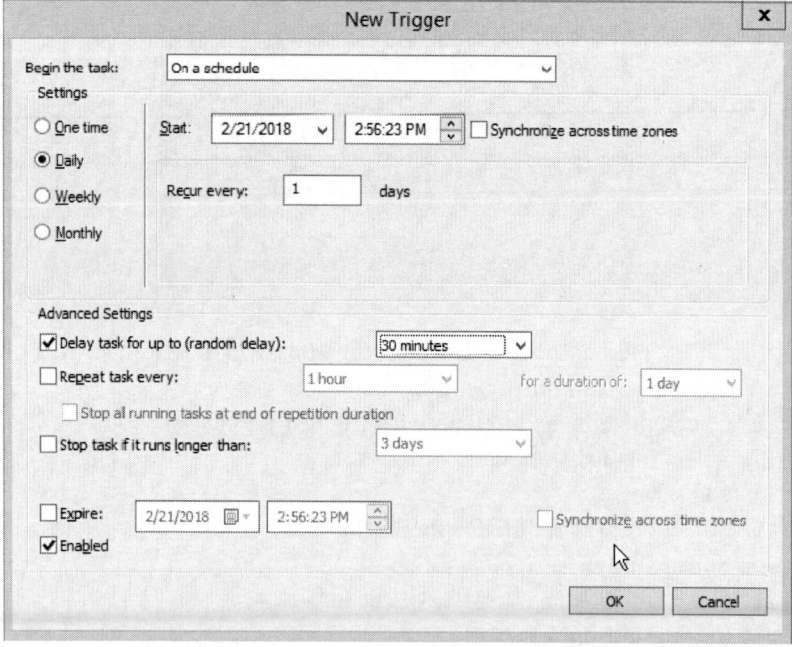

24. Select the **Actions** tab.
25. Click **New....**
26. Select **Start a program.**

27. For **Program/script,** enter *C:\Windows\System32\WindowsPowerShell\v1.0\powershell.exe.*
28. For **Add arguments,** enter *-executionpolicy unrestricted "C:\Temp\EnforcePolicy.ps1" "C:\Temp\intelprofile.xml".*
29. For **Start In,** enter *C:\Temp.*
30. Click **OK.**

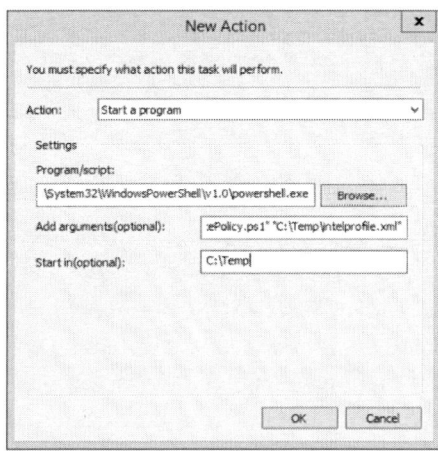

31. Click **OK.**

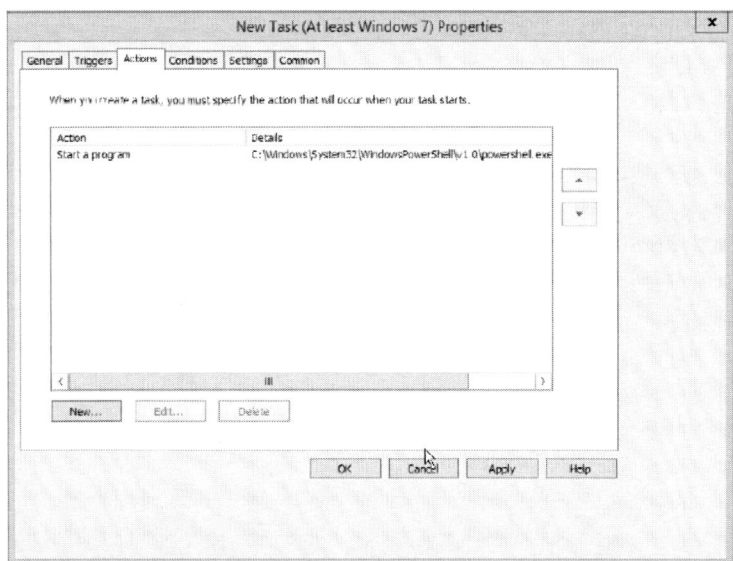

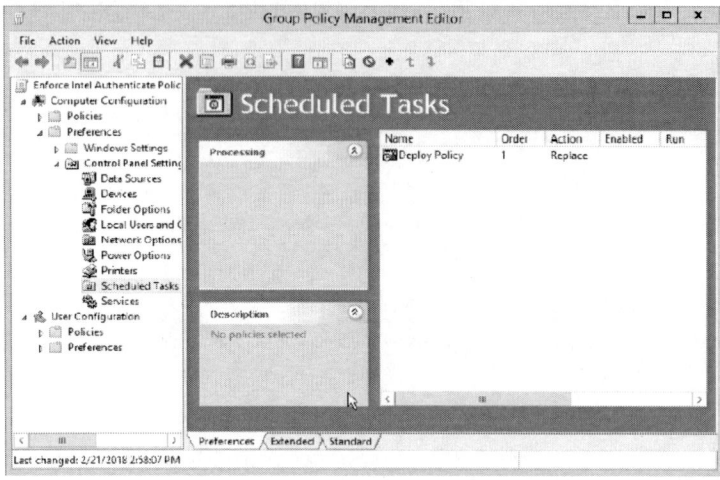

2.2.7. Intel Virtual Smart Card (VSC) Configuration

The *Intel Authenticate Integration Guide for Active Directory Policy Objects* provides instructions on how to set up GPOs for various functions of the Intel Authenticate installation process. The following instructions are primarily repurposed from the *Intel Authenticate Integration Guide*.

2.2.7.1. Configuring MyID for Intel VSC

1. Open **MyID Desktop**.
2. Click **New Action**.
3. Click **Configuration > Operation Settings**.

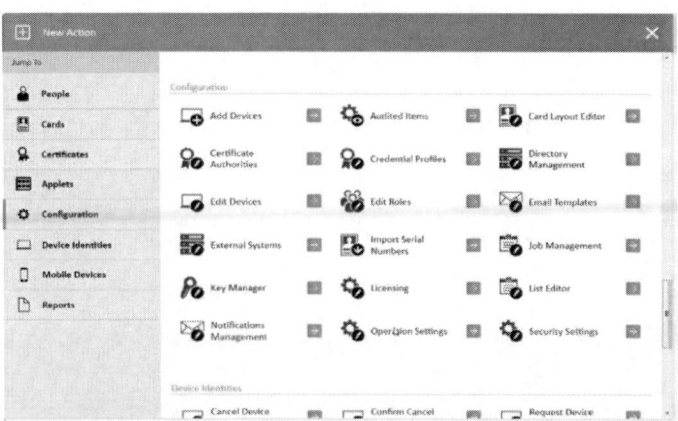

Derived Personal Identity Verification (PIV) Credentials   175

4. Go to the **Devices** tab.
5. Delete the value in **Default Card Data Model**.
6. Set **Enable Intel Virtual Smart Card support** to **Yes**.
7. Click **Save changes**.

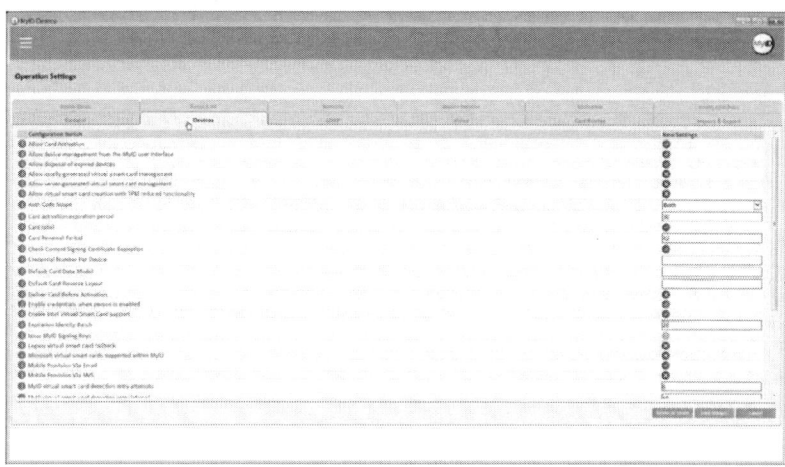

2.2.7.2. Setting up a PIN Protection Key

1. Click **New Action**.
2. Click **Configuration > Key Manager**.

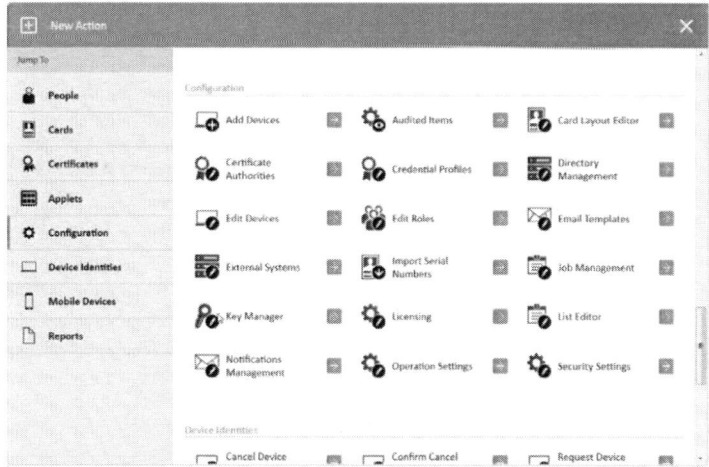

3. For **Select Key Type to Manage**, select **PIN Generation Key**.
4. Click **Next**.

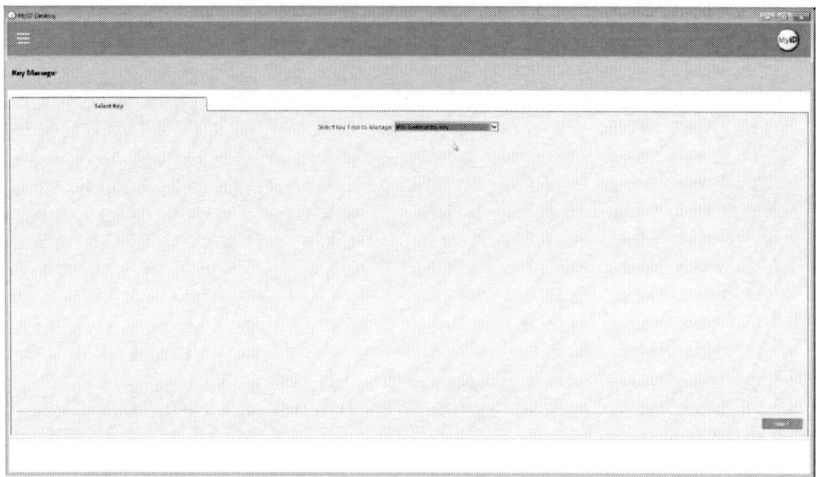

5. Click **Add New Key**.

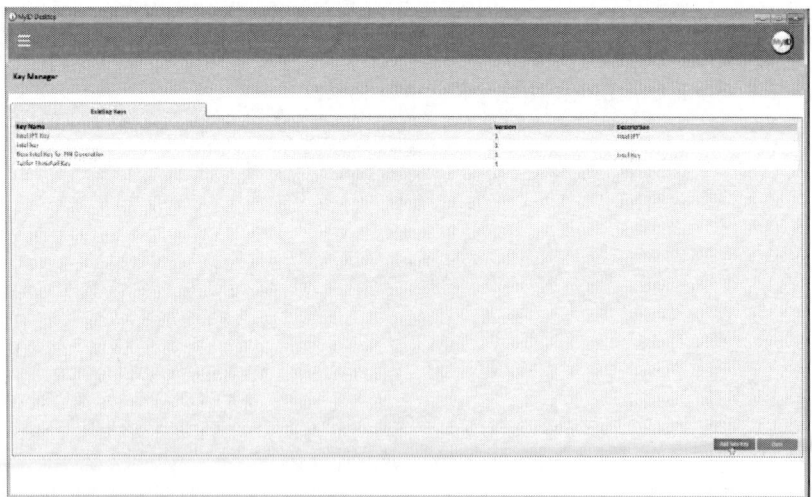

6. Enter a **name** and a **description**.
7. For **Encryption Type**, select **3DES**.

Derived Personal Identity Verification (PIV) Credentials 177

8. Select **Automatically Generate Encryption Key in Software and Store on Database.**
9. Click **Save.**

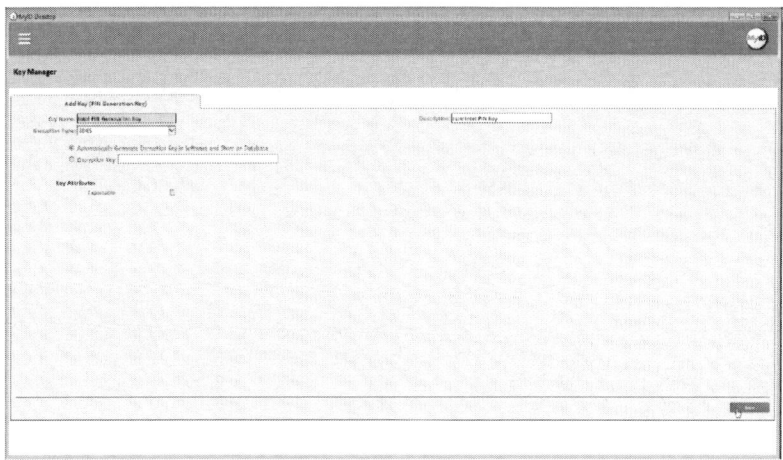

2.2.7.3. Creating a Credential Profile

1. Click **New Action.**
2. Click **Configuration > Credential Profiles.**
3. Click **New.**

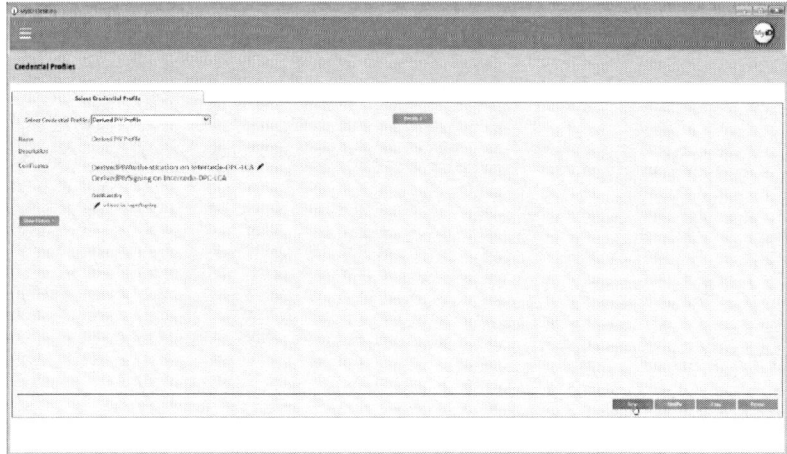

4. Enter a name and a description.
5. Check the box next to **Derived Credential.**
6. Check the box next to **Intel Virtual Smart Card (Only).**

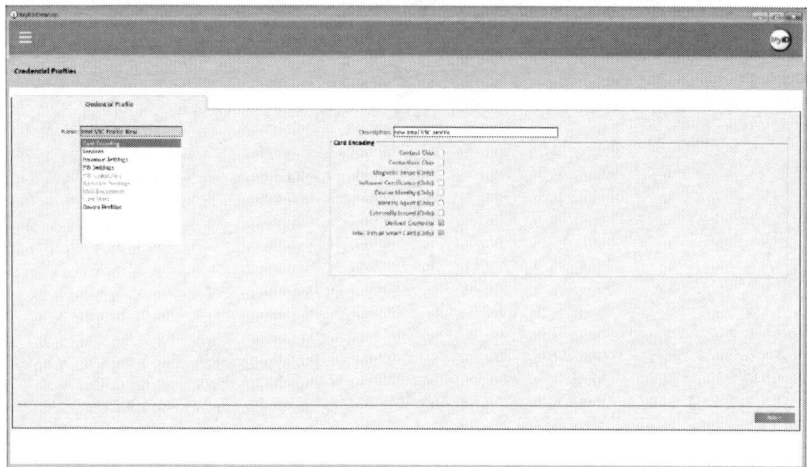

7. Select the **Services** tab.
8. Check the box next to **MyID Logon.**
9. Check the box next to **MyID Encryption.**

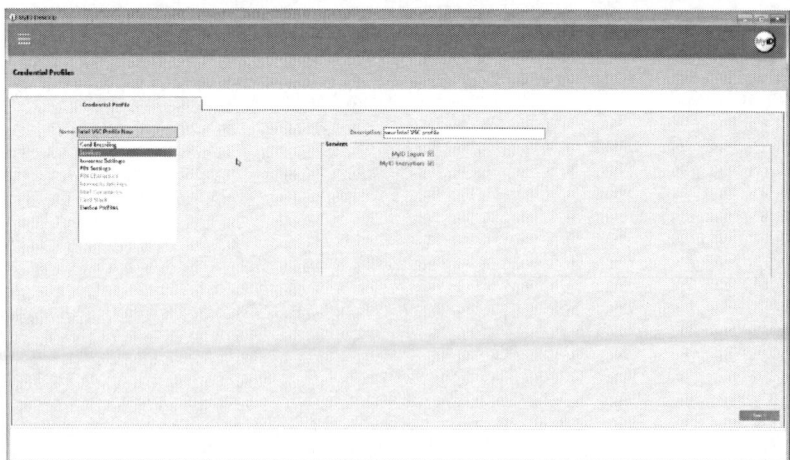

Derived Personal Identity Verification (PIV) Credentials

10. Select the **Issuance Settings** tab.
11. Set **Require Activation** to **No**.
12. Set **Pre-encode Card** to **None**.
13. Set **Require Fingerprints at Issuance** to **Never Required**.
14. Set **Require Facial Biometrics** to **Never Required**.
15. Set **Additional Authentication** to **None**.
16. Set **Terms and Conditions** to **None**.
17. Set **Proximity Card Check** to **None**.
18. Set **Notification Scheme** to **None**.
19. Uncheck all boxes.
20. Set **Mobile Device Restrictions** to **Any**.
21. Set **Generate Logon Code** to **Simple**.

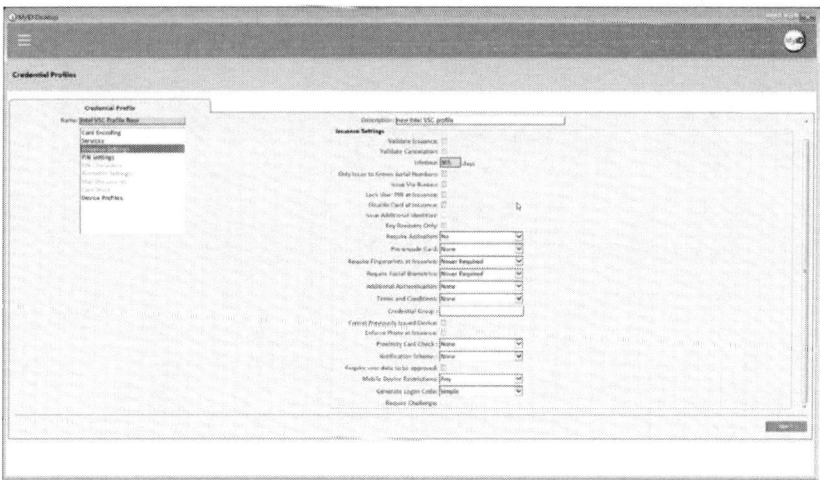

22. Select the **PIN Settings** tab.
23. For **PIN Algorithm,** select **EdeficePinGenerator**.
24. For **Protected Key,** select the PIN generation key created earlier.
25. Select the **Device Profiles** tab.
26. For **Card Format,** select **PIVDerivedCredential.xml**.
27. Click **Next**.

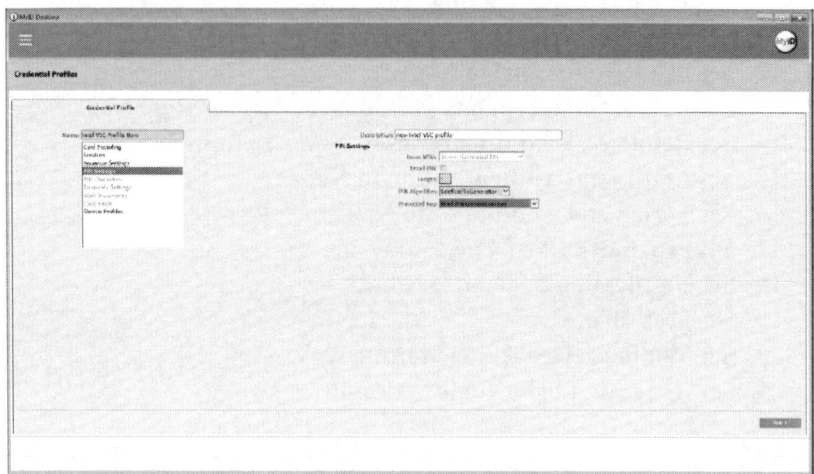

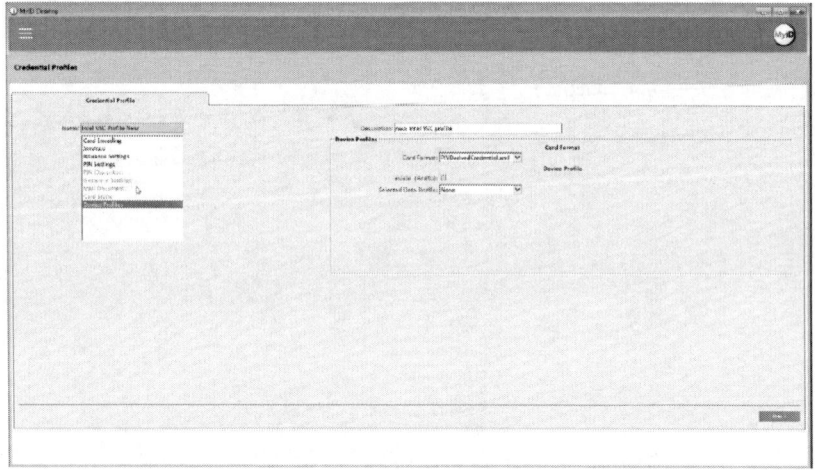

28. Select the certificates to be issued with the VSC.
29. Click **Next**.
30. Select the roles that are allowed to use this profile.
31. Click **Next**.
32. Enter a description and click **Next**.

Derived Personal Identity Verification (PIV) Credentials

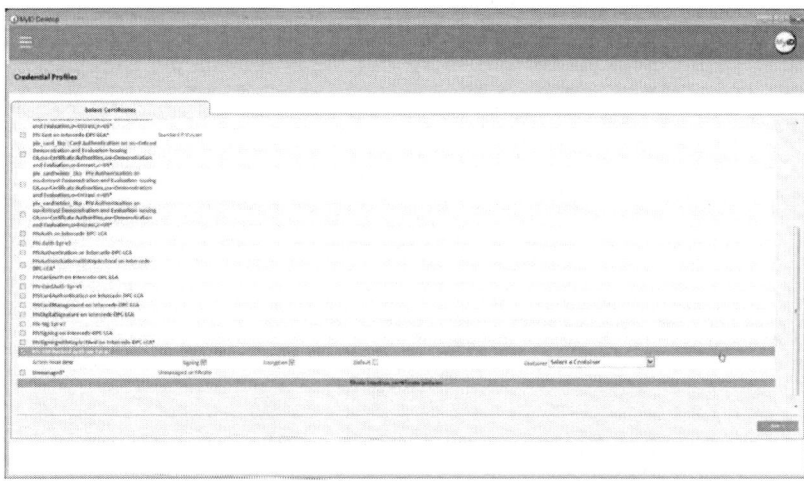

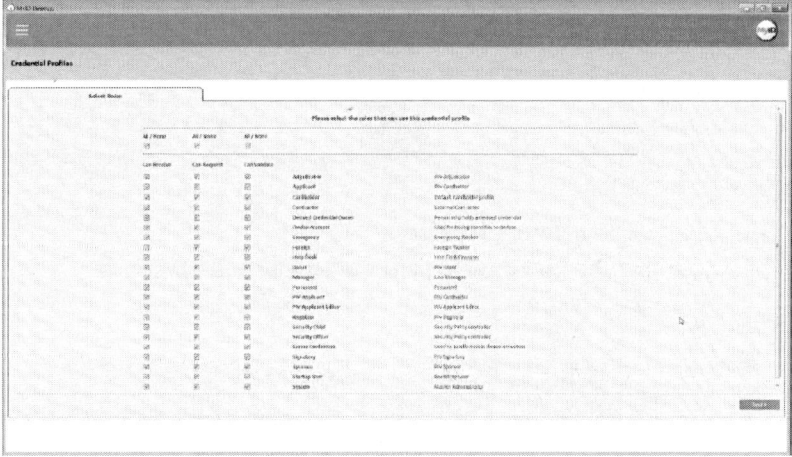

2.2.8. DPC Life-Cycle Workflows

This section details the steps to perform issuance and termination of the DPC by using the MyID CMS. Issuance is started from the MyID Self-Service Kiosk application, while termination uses the MyID Desktop administration application.

2.2.8.1. Mobile Device Issuance Workflow

The following steps are performed by the DPC Applicant by using the MyID Self-Service Kiosk and the MyID Identity Agent application on the target mobile device.

1. At the Welcome screen of the MyID Self-Service Kiosk, insert your PIV Card into the card reader.

2. On the **Enter your PIN** screen:
   a. Enter the PIN used to activate the inserted PIV Card.
   b. Select **Next**.

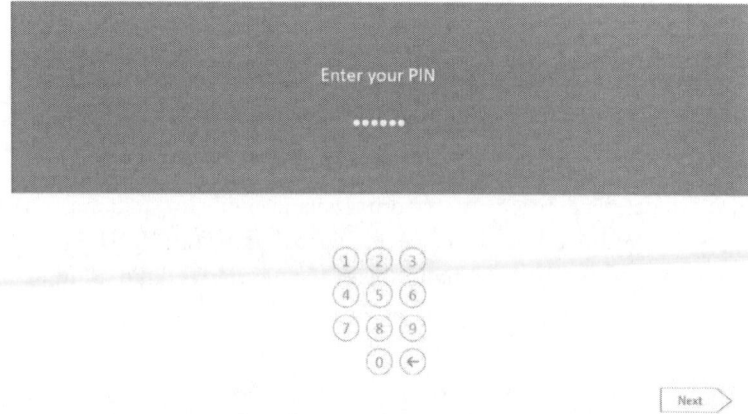

Derived Personal Identity Verification (PIV) Credentials   183

3. On the **Select Credential Profile** screen:
   a. To provision the DPC to the MyID software token, select **Derived PIV Profile.**
   b. To provision the DPC to the iOS Secure Enclave hardware-backed token, select **DPC for Native iOS Keystore.**

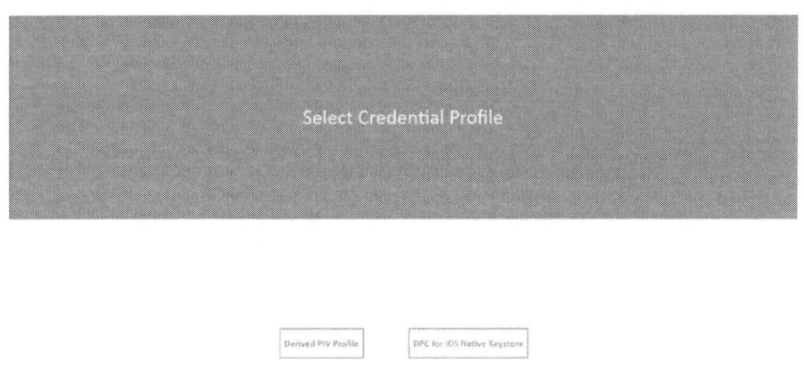

   c. The MyID Self-Service Kiosk will display a QR code; the remaining steps are completed by using the MyID Identity Agent application on the target mobile device.

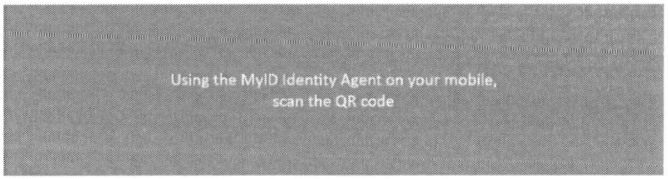

4. Launch MyID Identity Agent.
5. On the initial screen, under **Actions,** tap **Scan QR Code.**
6. Use the device camera to capture the QR code displayed by the MyID Self-Service Kiosk.

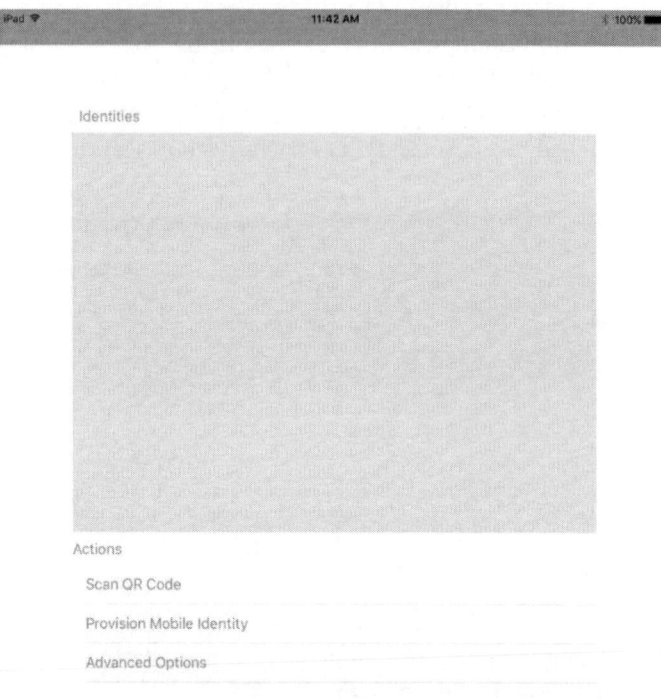
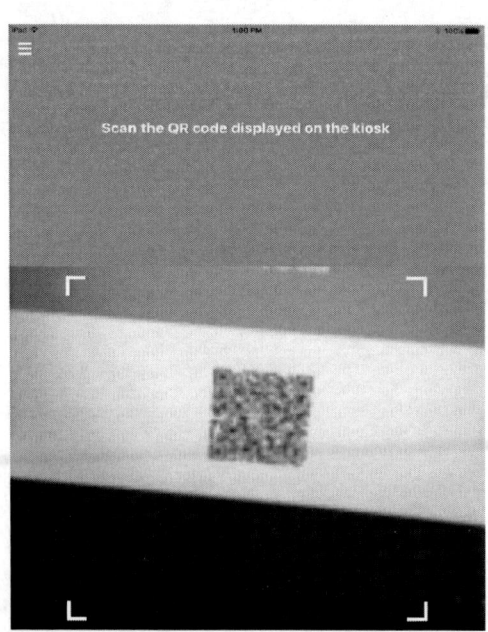

Derived Personal Identity Verification (PIV) Credentials 185

7. On the **Set PIN** screen:
   a. In the **Enter PIN** field, enter a numeric PIN that will be used to activate the DPC.
   b. In the **Confirm PIN** field, enter the same numeric PIN.

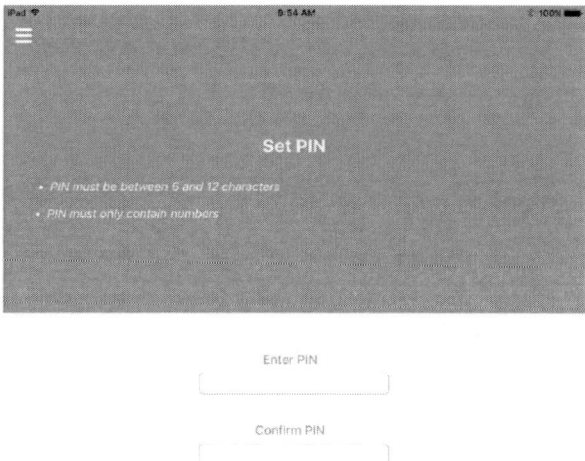

8. If DPC provisioning was successful, the Identities screen will provide a visual representation of information for the DPC subscriber's linked PIV Card.

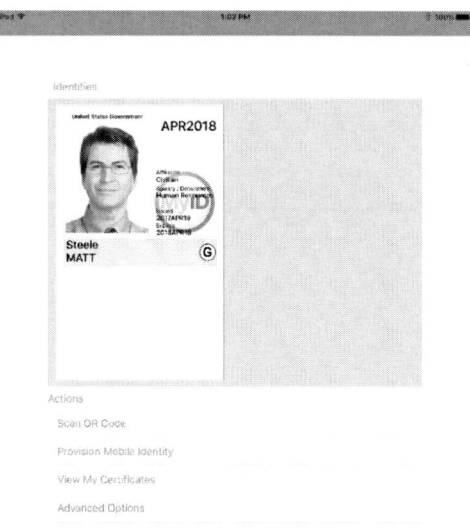

2.2.8.2. Intel Authenticate Issuance Workflow

2.2.8.2.1. Requesting a DPC for Intel VSC

1. Go to a **MyID Kiosk**.

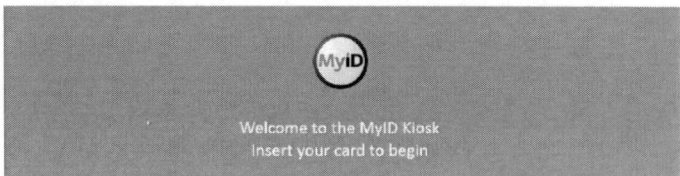

2. Insert a PIV Card.
3. Enter the PIN for the PIV Card.

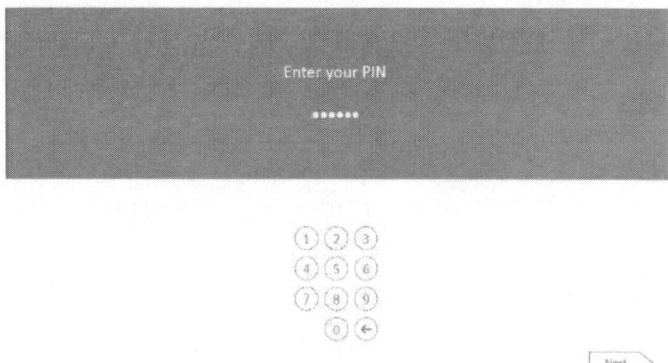

4. Select the profile created for Derived PIV. An email will be sent to the user with a onetime code for collection.

Derived Personal Identity Verification (PIV) Credentials   187

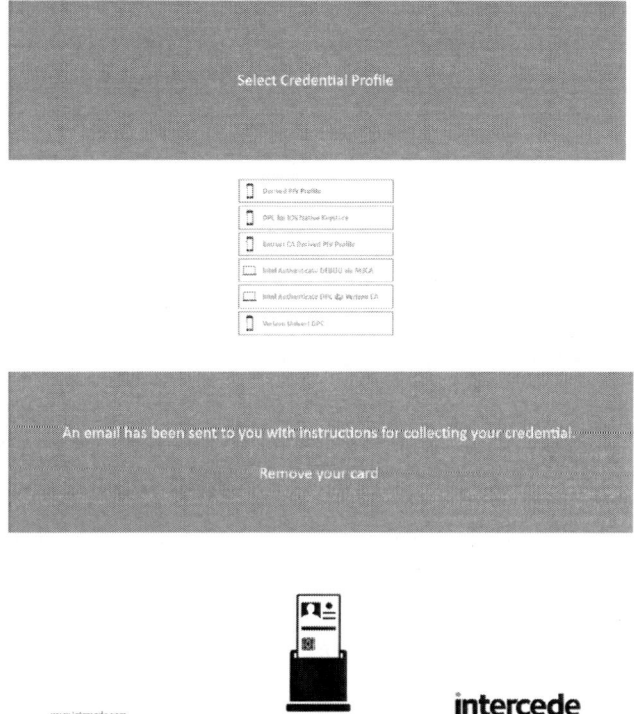

2.2.8.2.2. Collecting the DPC

The following procedures will request and install the DPC in the Intel Authenticate protected token. Note that the DPC will be protected by the enrollment factors set in Section 2.2.5.5.

1. On the client machine, open the MyID Self-Service Application with the parameters:
   /nopopup and /iptonly. $ MyIDApp.exe /nopopup /iptonly
2. Click **Continue.**
3. Enter the **Logon Code** from the email.
4. Click continue.
5. Click **Finish** after the certificates are successfully collected.

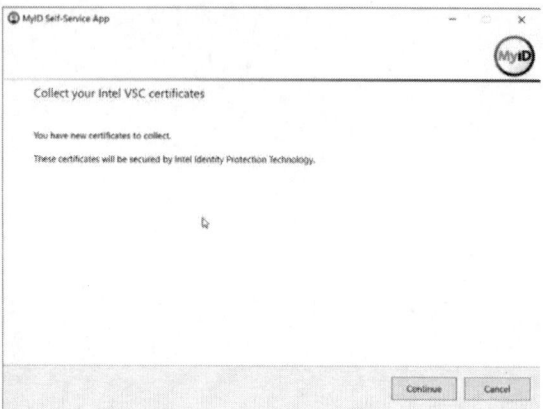

3. Enter the **Logon Code** from the email.
4. Click **Continue.**

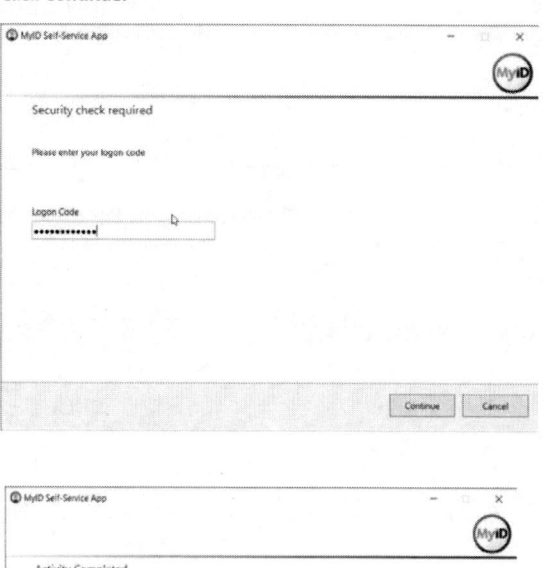

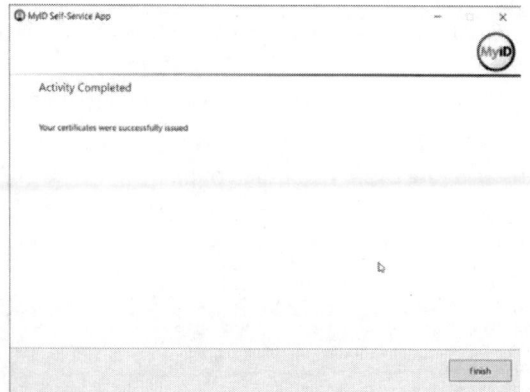

2.2.8.3. Maintenance Workflow

Changes to a DPC subscriber's PIV Card that would result in a rekey or reissuance (e.g., official name change) require the subscriber to repeat the initial issuance workflow as described in the previous section. The issued DPC will replace any existing DPC in the Identity Agent container.

2.2.8.4. Termination Workflow

1. Select the target device associated with the DPC subscriber that will be terminated.

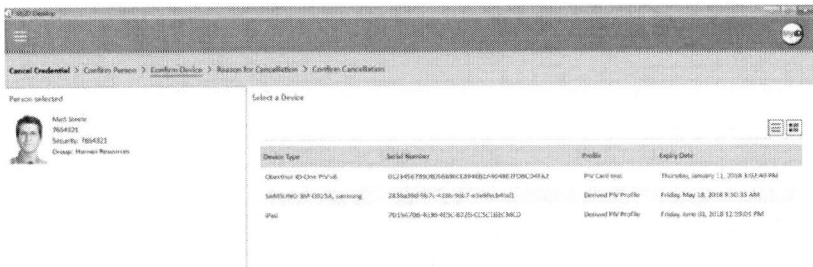

2. Select a reason for termination, and enter any other required information for policy compliance.

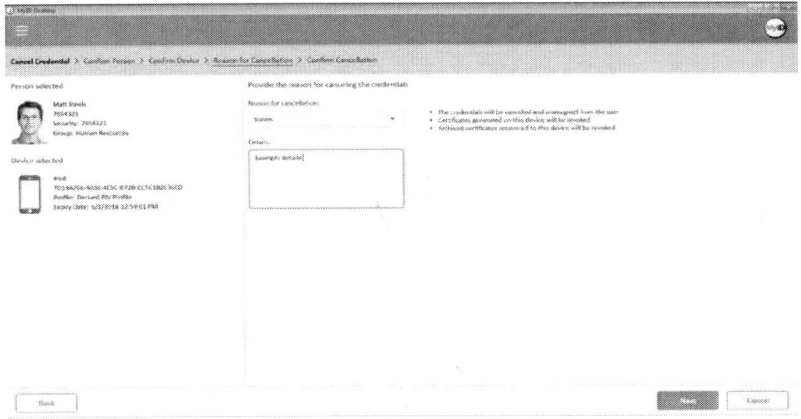

3. Click **Next**.
4. Confirm the termination of the DPC.

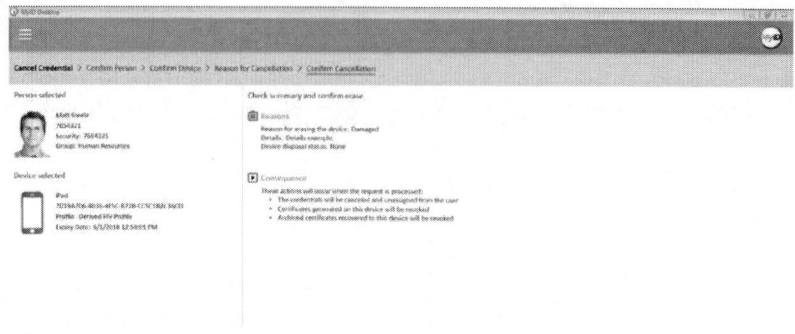

Appendix A. List of Acronyms

AD	Active Directory
ADFS	Active Directory Federation Services
CA	Certificate Authority
CMS	Credential Management System
DMZ	Demilitarized Zone
DN	Distinguished Name
DPC	Derived PIV Credential
EMM	Enterprise Mobility Management
GPO	Group Policy Object
IDAM	Identity and Access Management
IDG	Identity Guard
IDMS	Identity Management System
IIS	Internet Information Services
IT	Information Technology
JTK	Java Tool Kit
LDAP	Lightweight Directory Access Protocol
NACI	National Agency Check with Inquiries
NCCoE	National Cybersecurity Center of Excellence
NIST	National Institute of Standards and Technology
OFW	Outer Firewall
OID	Object Identifier
OS	Operating System
OU	Organizational Unit
PIN	Personal Identification Number

PIV	Personal Identity Verification
PKCS	Public Key Cryptography Standards
PKI	Public Key Infrastructure
QR	Quick Response (code)
RSA	Rivest-Shamir-Adleman
SCEP	Simple Certificate Enrollment Protocol
SP	Special Publication
SQL	Structured Query Language
SSL	Secure Sockets Layer
SSP	Shared Service Provider
TLS	Transport Layer Security
UPI	UniCERT Programmatic Interface
UPN	User Principal Name
URL	Universal Resource Locator
VLAN	Virtual Local Area Network
VSC	Virtual Smart Card
WAN	Wide Area Network
WMI	Windows Management Instrumentation
WSVC	World Wide Web Publishing Service

Chapter 2

Digital Identity Guidelines: Enrollment and Identity Proofing[*]

Paul A. Grassi
James L. Fenton
Naomi B. Lefkovitz
Jamie M. Danker
Yee-Yin Choong
Kristen K. Greene
and Mary F. Theofanos

Abstract

These guidelines provide technical requirements for federal agencies implementing digital identity services and are not intended to constrain the development or use of standards outside of this purpose. This guideline focuses on the enrollment and verification of an identity for use in digital authentication. Central to this is a process known as identity proofing in which an applicant provides evidence to a credential service provider (CSP) reliably identifying themselves, thereby allowing the CSP to assert that identification at a useful identity assurance level. This document defines technical requirements for each of three identity assurance levels. This publication supersedes corresponding sections of NIST Special Publication (SP) 800-63-2.

---

[*] This is an edited, reformatted and augmented version of National Institute of Standards and Technology Special Publication 800-63A, dated June 2017.

In: Guidelines for Digital Identity Verification
Editor: Damon Solis
ISBN: 979-8-88697-838-4
© 2023 Nova Science Publishers, Inc.

Keywords: authentication, credential service provider, electronic authentication, digital authentication, electronic credentials, digital credentials, identity proofing, federation

1. Purpose

This chapter provides requirements for enrollment and identity proofing of applicants that wish to gain access to resources at each Identity Assurance Level (IAL). The requirements detail the acceptability, validation, and verification of identity evidence that will be presented by a subscriber to support their claim of identity. This chapter also details the responsibilities of Credential Service Providers (CSPs) with respect to establishing and maintaining enrollment records and binding authenticators (either CSP-issued or subscriber-provided) to the enrollment record.

2. Introduction

One of the challenges associated with digital identity is the association of a set of online activities with a single specific entity. While there are situations where this is not required or is even undesirable (e.g., use cases where anonymity or pseudonymity are required), there are others where it is important to reliably establish an association with a real-life subject. Examples include obtaining health care and executing financial transactions. There are also situations where the association is required for regulatory reasons (e.g., the financial industry's 'Know Your Customer' requirements, established in the implementation of the USA PATRIOT Act of 2001) or to establish accountability for high-risk actions (e.g., changing the release rate of water from a dam).

There are also instances where it is desirable for a relying party (RP) to know something about a subscriber executing a transaction, but not know their real-life identity. For example, it may be desirable to only know a subscriber's home ZIP code for purposes of census-taking or petitioning an elected official. In both instances, the ZIP code is sufficient to deliver the service; it is not necessary or desirable to know the underlying identity of the person.

The following table states which sections of this document are normative and which are informative.

Digital Identity Guidelines

Table 2-1. Normative and informative sections of SP 800-63A

Section Name	Normative/Informative
1. Purpose	Informative
2. Introduction	Informative
3. Definitions and Abbreviations	Informative
4. Identity Assurance Level Requirements	Normative
5. Identity Resolution, Validation, and Verification	Normative
6. Derived Credentials	Informative
7. Threats and Security Considerations	Informative
8. Privacy Considerations	Informative
9. Usability Considerations	Informative
10. References	Informative

2.1. Expected Outcomes of Identity Proofing

When a subject is identity proofed, the expected outcomes are:

- Resolve a claimed identity to a single, unique identity within the context of the population of users the CSP serves.
- Validate that all supplied evidence is correct and genuine (e.g., not counterfeit or misappropriated).
- Validate that the claimed identity exists in the real world.
- Verify that the claimed identity is associated with the real person supplying the identity evidence.

2.2. Identity Assurance Levels

Assurance in a subscriber's identity is described using one of three IALs:

IAL1: There is no requirement to link the applicant to a specific real-life identity. Any attributes provided in conjunction with the subject's activities are self-asserted or should be treated as self- asserted (including attributes a CSP asserts to an RP). Self-asserted attributes are neither validated nor verified.

IAL2: Evidence supports the real-world existence of the claimed identity and verifies that the applicant is appropriately associated with this real-world identity. IAL2 introduces the need for either remote or physically-present identity proofing. Attributes could be asserted by CSPs to RPs in support of pseudonymous identity with verified attributes. A CSP that supports IAL2 can support IAL1 transactions if the user consents.

IAL3: Physical presence is required for identity proofing. Identifying attributes must be verified by an authorized and trained CSP representative. As with IAL2, attributes could be asserted by CSPs to RPs in support of pseudonymous identity with verified attributes. A CSP that supports IAL3 can support IAL1 and IAL2 identity attributes if the user consents.

At IAL2 and IAL3, pseudonymity in federated environments is enabled by limiting the number of attributes sent from the CSP to the RP, or the way they are presented. For example, if a RP needs a valid birthdate but no other personal details, the RP should leverage a CSP to request just the birthdate of the subscriber. Wherever possible, the RP should ask the CSP for an attribute reference. For example, if a RP needs to know if a claimant is older than 18 they should request a 196oolean value, not the entire birthdate, to evaluate age. Conversely, it may be beneficial to the user that uses a high assurance CSP for transactions at lower assurance levels. For example, a user may maintain an IAL3 identity, yet should be able to use their CSP for IAL2 and IAL1 transactions.

Since the individual will have undergone an identity proofing process at enrollment, transactions with respect to individual interactions with the CSP may not necessarily be pseudonymous.

Detailed requirements for each of the IALs are given in *Section 4* and *Section 5*.

3. Definitions and Abbreviations

See *SP 800-63*, Appendix A for a complete set of definitions and abbreviations.

4. Identity Assurance Level Requirements

This document describes the common pattern in which an applicant undergoes an identity proofing and enrollment process whereby their identity evidence

Digital Identity Guidelines

and attributes are collected, uniquely resolved to a single identity within a given population or context, then validated and verified. See *SP 800-63-3* Section 6.1 for details on how to choose the most appropriate IAL. A CSP may then bind these attributes to an authenticator (described in *SP 800-63B*).

Identity proofing's sole objective is to ensure the applicant is who they claim to be to a stated level of certitude. This includes presentation, validation, and verification of the minimum attributes necessary to accomplish identity proofing. There may be many different sets that suffice as the minimum, so CSPs should choose this set to balance privacy and the user's usability needs, as well as the likely attributes needed in future uses of the digital identity. For example, such attributes — to the extent they are the minimum necessary — could include:

1. Full name
2. Date of birth
3. Home Address

This document also provides requirements for CSPs collecting additional information used for purposes other than identity proofing.

4.1. Process Flow

Figure 4-1. outlines the basic flow for identity proofing and enrollment.

The following provides a sample of how a CSP and an applicant interact during the identity proofing process:

1) Resolution
   a) The CSP collects PII from the applicant, such as name, address, date of birth, email, and phone number.
   b) The CSP also collects two forms of identity evidence, such as a driver's license and a passport. For example, using the camera of a laptop, the CSP can capture a photo of both sides of both pieces of identity evidence.
2) Validation
   a) The CSP validates the information supplied in 1a by checking an authoritative source. The CSP determines the information supplied by the applicant matches their records.

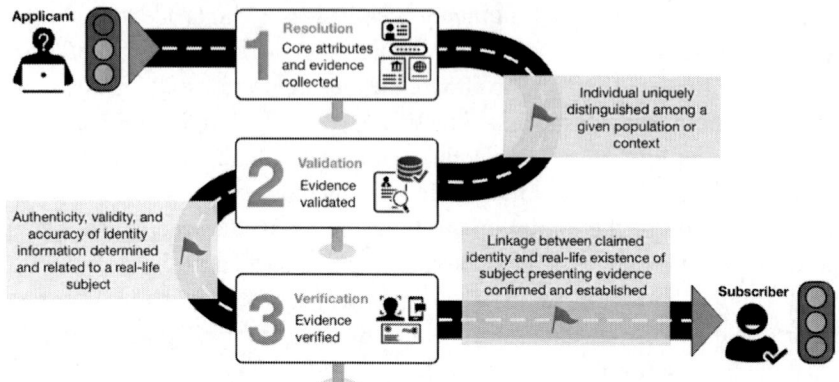

Figure 4-1. The identity proofing user journey.

    b) The CSP checks the images of the license and the passport, determines there are no alterations, the data encoded in the QR codes matches the plain-text information, the identification numbers follow standard formats, and that the physical and digital security features are valid.

    c) The CSP queries the issuing sources for the license and passport and validates the information matches.

3) Verification

    a) The CSP asks the applicant to take a photo of themselves, with liveness checks, to match the license and passport.

    b) The CSP matches the pictures on the license and the passport to the applicant picture and determines they match.

    c) The CSP sends an enrollment code to the validated phone number of the applicant, the user provides the enrollment code to the CSP, and the CSP confirms they match, verifying the user is in possession and control of the validated phone number.

    d) The applicant has been successfully proofed.

Note: The identity proofing process can be delivered by multiple service providers. It is possible, but not expected, that a single organization, process, technique, or technology will fulfill these process steps.

4.2. General Requirements

The following requirements apply to any CSP performing identity proofing at IAL2 or IAL3:

1) Identity proofing SHALL NOT be performed to determine suitability or entitlement to gain access to services or benefits.
2) Collection of PII SHALL be limited to the minimum necessary to validate the existence of the claimed identity and associate the claimed identity with the applicant providing identity evidence for appropriate identity resolution, validation, and verification. This MAY include attributes that correlate identity evidence to authoritative sources and to provide RPs with attributes used to make authorization decisions.
3) The CSP SHALL provide explicit notice to the applicant at the time of collection regarding the purpose for collecting and maintaining a record of the attributes necessary for identity proofing, including whether such attributes are voluntary or mandatory to complete the identity proofing process, and the consequences for not providing the attributes.
4) If CSPs process attributes for purposes other than identity proofing, authentication, or attribute assertions (collectively "identity service"), related fraud mitigation, or to comply with law or legal process, CSPs SHALL implement measures to maintain predictability and manageability commensurate with the privacy risk arising from the additional processing. Measures MAY include providing clear notice, obtaining subscriber consent, or enabling selective use or disclosure of attributes. When CSPs use consent measures, CSPs SHALL NOT make consent for the additional processing a condition of the identity service.
5) The CSP SHALL provide mechanisms for redress of applicant complaints or problems arising from the identity proofing. These mechanisms SHALL be easy for applicants to find and use. The CSP SHALL assess the mechanisms for their efficacy in achieving resolution of complaints or problems.
6) The identity proofing and enrollment processes SHALL be performed according to an applicable written policy or *practice statement* that specifies the particular steps taken to verify identities. The *practice statement* SHALL include control information detailing how the

CSP handles proofing errors that result in an applicant not being successfully enrolled. For example, the number of retries allowed, proofing alternatives (e.g., in-person if remote fails), or fraud countermeasures when anomalies are detected.

7) The CSP SHALL maintain a record, including audit logs, of all steps taken to verify the identity of the applicant and SHALL record the types of identity evidence presented in the proofing process. The CSP SHALL conduct a risk management process, including assessments of privacy and security risks to determine:
   a) Any steps that it will take to verify the identity of the applicant beyond any mandatory requirements specified herein;
   b) The PII, including any biometrics, images, scans, or other copies of the identity evidence that the CSP will maintain as a record of identity proofing (Note: Specific federal requirements may apply.); and
   c) The schedule of retention for these records (Note: CSPs may be subject to specific retention policies in accordance with applicable laws, regulations, or policies, including any National Archives and Records Administration (NARA) records retention schedules that may apply).
8) All PII collected as part of the enrollment process SHALL be protected to ensure confidentiality, integrity, and attribution of the information source.
9) The entire proofing transaction, including transactions that involve a third party, SHALL occur over an authenticated protected channel.
10) The CSP SHOULD obtain additional confidence in identity proofing using fraud mitigation measures (e.g., inspecting geolocation, examining the device characteristics of the applicant, evaluating behavioral characteristics, checking vital statistic repositories such as the Death Master File [DMF], so long as any additional mitigations do not substitute for the mandatory requirements contained herein. In the event the CSP uses fraud mitigation measures, the CSP SHALL conduct a privacy risk assessment for these mitigation measures. Such assessments SHALL include any privacy risk mitigations (e.g., risk acceptance or transfer, limited retention, use limitations, notice) or other technological mitigations (e.g., cryptography), and be documented per requirement 4.2(7) above.
11) In the event a CSP ceases to conduct identity proofing and enrollment processes, the CSP SHALL be responsible for fully disposing of or

Digital Identity Guidelines 201

destroying any sensitive data including PII, or its protection from unauthorized access for the duration of retention.
12) Regardless of whether the CSP is an agency or private sector provider, the following requirements apply to the agency offering or using the proofing service:
   a) The agency SHALL consult with their Senior Agency Official for Privacy (SAOP) to conduct an analysis determining whether the collection of PII to conduct identity proofing triggers Privacy Act requirements.
   b) The agency SHALL publish a System of Records Notice (SORN) to cover such collection, as applicable.
   c) The agency SHALL consult with their SAOP to conduct an analysis determining whether the collection of PII to conduct identity proofing triggers E-Government Act of 2002 requirements.
   d) The agency SHALL publish a Privacy Impact Assessment (PIA) to cover such collection, as applicable.
13) The CSP SHOULD NOT collect the Social Security Number (SSN) unless it is necessary for performing identity resolution, and identity resolution cannot be accomplished by collection of another attribute or combination of attributes.

4.3. Identity Assurance Level 1

A CSP that supports only IAL1 SHALL NOT validate and verify attributes.

1) The CSP MAY request zero or more self-asserted attributes from the applicant to support their service offering.
2) An IAL2 or IAL3 CSP SHOULD support RPs that only require IAL1, if the user consents.

4.4. Identity Assurance Level 2

IAL2 allows for *remote or in-person* identity proofing. IAL2 supports a wide range of acceptable identity proofing techniques in order to increase user adoption, decrease false negatives (legitimate applicants that cannot successfully complete identity proofing), and detect to the best extent possible the presentation of fraudulent identities by a malicious applicant.

A CSP SHALL preferentially proof according to the requirements in *Section 4.4.1*. Depending on the population the CSP serves, the CSP MAY additionally implement identity proofing in accordance with *Section 4.4.2*.

4.4.1. IAL2 Conventional Proofing Requirements

The following sections provide requirements for resolution, evidence collection, validation, verification, and presence. They also explore biometric collection and security controls.

4.4.1.1. Resolution Requirements

Collection of PII SHALL be limited to the minimum necessary to resolve to a unique identity in a given context. This MAY include the collection of attributes that assist in data queries. See *Section 5.1* for general resolution requirements.

4.4.1.2. Evidence Collection Requirements

The CSP SHALL collect the following from the applicant:

1) One piece of SUPERIOR or STRONG evidence if the evidence's issuing source, during its identity proofing event, confirmed the claimed identity by collecting two or more forms of SUPERIOR or STRONG evidence and the CSP validates the evidence directly with the issuing source; OR
2) Two pieces of STRONG evidence; OR
3) One piece of STRONG evidence plus two pieces of FAIR evidence

See *Section 5.2.1* Identity Evidence Quality Requirements for more information on acceptable identity evidence.

4.4.1.3. Validation Requirements

The CSP SHALL validate each piece of evidence with a process that can achieve the same strength as the evidence presented. For example, if two forms of STRONG identity evidence are presented, each piece of evidence will be validated at a strength of STRONG.

See *Section 5.2.2* Validating Identity Evidence for more information on validating identity evidence.

4.4.1.4. Verification Requirements
The CSP SHALL verify identity evidence as follows:

1) At a minimum, the applicant's binding to identity evidence must be verified by a process that is able to achieve a strength of STRONG.
2) Knowledge-based verification (KBV) SHALL NOT be used for in-person (physical or supervised remote) identity verification.

See Section 5.3 Identity Verification for more information on acceptable identity evidence.

4.4.1.5. Presence Requirements
The CSP SHALL support in-person or remote identity proofing. The CSP SHOULD offer both in-person and remote proofing.

4.4.1.6. Address Confirmation

1) Valid records to confirm address SHALL be issuing source(s) or authoritative source(s).
2) The CSP SHALL confirm address of record. The CSP SHOULD confirm address of record through validation of the address contained on any supplied, valid piece of identity evidence. The CSP MAY confirm address of record by validating information supplied by the applicant that is not contained on any supplied piece of identity evidence.
3) Self-asserted address data that has not been confirmed in records SHALL NOT be used for confirmation.
4) If the CSP performs in-person proofing (physical or supervised remote):
    a) The CSP SHOULD send a notification of proofing to a confirmed address of record.
    b) The CSP MAY provide an enrollment code directly to the subscriber if binding to an authenticator will occur at a later time.
    c) The enrollment code SHALL be valid for a maximum of 7 days.
5) If the csp performs remote proofing (unsupervised):
    a) The CSP SHALL send an enrollment code to a confirmed address of record for the applicant.
    b) The applicant SHALL present a valid enrollment code to complete the identity proofing process.

c) The CSP SHOULD send the enrollment code to the postal address that has been validated in records. The CSP MAY send the enrollment code to a mobile telephone (SMS or voice), landline telephone, or email if it has been validated in records.
d) If the enrollment code is also intended to be an authentication factor, it SHALL be reset upon first use.
e) Enrollment codes SHALL have the following maximum validities:
    (i) 10 days, when sent to a postal address of record within the contiguous United States;
    (ii) 30 days, when sent to a postal address of record outside the contiguous United States;
    (iii) 10 minutes, when sent to a telephone of record (SMS or voice);
    (iv) 24 hours, when sent to an email address of record.
f) The CSP SHALL ensure the enrollment code and notification of proofing are sent to different addresses of record. For example, if the CSP sends an enrollment code to a phone number validated in records, a proofing notification will be sent to the postal address validated in records or obtained from validated and verified evidence, such as a driver's license.

Note: Postal address is the preferred method of sending any communications, including enrollment code and notifications, with the applicant. However, these guidelines support any confirmed address of record, whether physical or digital.

4.4.1.7. Biometric Collection

The CSP MAY collect biometrics for the purposes of non-repudiation and re-proofing. See *SP 800-63B,* Section 5.2.3 for more detail on biometric collection.

4.4.1.8. Security Controls

The CSP SHALL employ appropriately tailored security controls, to include control enhancements, from the moderate or high baseline of security controls defined in SP 800-53 or equivalent federal (e.g., FEDRAMP) or industry standard. The CSP SHALL ensure that the minimum assurance-related controls for moderate-impact systems or equivalent are satisfied.

Digital Identity Guidelines

4.4.2. IAL2 Trusted Referee Proofing Requirements
In instances where an individual cannot meet the identity evidence requirements specified in *Section 4.4.1*, the agency MAY use a trusted referee to assist in identity proofing the applicant. See Section *5.3.4* for more details.

4.5. Identity Assurance Level 3

IAL3 adds additional rigor to the steps required at IAL2, to include providing further evidence of superior strength, and is subject to additional and specific processes (including the use of biometrics) to further protect the identity and RP from impersonation, fraud, or other significantly harmful damages. Biometrics are used to detect fraudulent enrollments, duplicate enrollments, and as a mechanism to re-establish binding to a credential. In addition, identity proofing at IAL3 is performed in-person (to include supervised remote). See Section 5.3.3 for more details.

4.5.1. Resolution Requirements
Collection of PII SHALL be limited to the minimum necessary to resolve to a unique identity record. This MAY include the collection of attributes that assist in data queries. See Section 5.1 for general resolution requirements.

4.5.2. Evidence Collection Requirements
The CSP SHALL collect the following from the applicant:

1) Two pieces of SUPERIOR evidence; *OR*
2) One piece of SUPERIOR evidence and one piece of STRONG evidence *if* the issuing source of the STRONG evidence, during its identity proofing event, confirmed the claimed identity by collecting two or more forms of SUPERIOR or STRONG evidence *and* the CSP validates the evidence directly with the issuing source; *OR*
3) Two pieces of STRONG evidence plus one piece of FAIR evidence.

See *Section 5.2.1 Identity Evidence Quality Requirements* for more information on acceptable identity evidence.

4.5.3. Validation Requirements

The CSP SHALL validate identity evidence as follows:

Each piece of evidence must be validated with a process that is able to achieve the same strength as the evidence presented. For example, if two forms of STRONG identity evidence are presented, each piece of evidence will be validated at a strength of STRONG.

See *Section 5.2.2* Validating Identity Evidence for more information on validating identity evidence.

4.5.4. Verification Requirements

The CSP SHALL verify identity evidence as follows:

1) At a minimum, the applicant's binding to identity evidence must be verified by a process that is able to achieve a strength of SUPERIOR.
2) KBV SHALL NOT be used for in-person (physical or supervised remote) identity verification.

See *Section 5.3* Identity Verification for more information on acceptable identity evidence.

4.5.5. Presence Requirements

The CSP SHALL perform all identity proofing steps with the applicant in-person. See *Section 5.3.3* for more details.

4.5.6. Address Confirmation

1) The CSP SHALL confirm address of record. The CSP SHOULD confirm address of record through validation of the address contained on any supplied, valid piece of identity evidence. The CSP MAY confirm address of record by validating information supplied by the applicant, not contained on any supplied, valid piece of identity evidence.
2) Self-asserted address data SHALL NOT be used for confirmation.
3) A notification of proofing SHALL be sent to the confirmed address of record.
4) The CSP MAY provide an enrollment code directly to the subscriber if binding to an authenticator will occur at a later time. The enrollment code SHALL be valid for a maximum of 7 days.

4.5.7. Biometric Collection

The CSP SHALL collect and record a biometric sample at the time of proofing (e.g., facial image, fingerprints) for the purposes of non-repudiation and re-proofing. See Section 5.2.3 of SP 800-63B for more detail on biometric collection.

4.5.8. Security Controls

The CSP SHALL employ appropriately tailored security controls, to include control enhancements, from the high baseline of security controls defined in *SP 800-53* or an equivalent federal (e.g., *FEDRAMP*) or industry standard. The CSP SHALL ensure that the minimum assurance-related controls for *high-impact* systems or equivalent are satisfied.

4.6. Enrollment Code

An enrollment code allows the CSP to confirm that the applicant controls an address of record, as well as offering the applicant the ability to reestablish binding to their enrollment record.

Binding NEED NOT be completed in the same session as the original identity proofing transaction.

An enrollment code SHALL be comprised of one of the following:

1) Minimally, a random six character alphanumeric or equivalent entropy. For example, a code generated using an approved random number generator or a serial number for a physical hardware authenticator; OR
2) A machine-readable optical label, such as a QR Code, that contains data of similar or higher entropy as a random six character alphanumeric.

4.7. Summary of Requirements

Table 4-1 summarizes the requirements for each of the authenticator assurance levels.

Table 4-1. IAL Requirements summary

Requirement	IAL1	IAL2	IAL3
Presence	No Requirements	In-person and unsupervised remote.	In-person and supervised remote.
Resolution	No Requirements	The minimum attributes necessary to accomplish identity resolution. KBV may be used for added confidence.	Same as IAL2
Evidence	No identity evidence is collected.	One piece of SUPERIOR or STRONG evidence depending on strength of original proof and validation occurs with issuing source, OR Two pieces of STRONG evidence, OR	Two pieces of SUPERIOR evidence, OR One piece of SUPERIOR evidence and one piece of STRONG evidence depending on strength of original proof and validation occurs with issuing source, OR
		One piece of STRONG evidence plus two (2) pieces of FAIR evidence.	Two pieces of STRONG evidence plus one piece of FAIR evidence.
Validation	No validation	Each piece of evidence must be validated with a process that is able to achieve the same strength as the evidence presented.	Same as IAL2
Verification	No verification	Verified by a process that is able to achieve a strength of STRONG.	Verified by a process that is able to achieve a strength of SUPERIOR.
Address Confirmation	No requirements for address confirmation	Required. Enrollment code sent to any address of record. Notification sent by means different from enrollment code.	Required. Notification of proofing to postal address.
Biometric Collection	No	Optional	Mandatory
Security Controls	N/A	SP 800-53 Moderate Baseline (or equivalent federal or industry standard).	SP 800-53 High Baseline (or equivalent federal or industry standard).

Digital Identity Guidelines 209

5. Identity Resolution, Validation, and Verification

This section lists the requirements to resolve, validate, and verify an identity and any supplied identity evidence. The requirements are intended to ensure the claimed identity is the actual identity of the subject attempting to enroll with the CSP and that scalable attacks affecting a large population of enrolled individuals require greater time and cost than the value of the resources the system is protecting.

5.1. Identity Resolution

The goal of identity resolution is to uniquely distinguish an individual within a given population or context. Effective identity resolution uses the smallest set of attributes necessary to resolve a unique individual. It provides the CSP an important starting point in the overall identity proofing process, to include the initial detection of potential fraud, but in no way represents a complete and successful identity proofing transaction.

1) Exact matches of information used in the proofing process can be difficult to achieve. The CSP MAY employ appropriate matching algorithms to account for differences in personal information and other relevant proofing data across multiple forms of identity evidence, issuing sources, and authoritative sources. Matching algorithms and rules used SHOULD be available publicly or, at minimum, to the relevant community of interest. For example, they may be included as part of the written policy or *practice statement* referred to in *Section 4.2*.
2) KBV (sometimes referred to as knowledge-based authentication) has historically been used to verify a claimed identity by testing the knowledge of the applicant against information obtained from public databases. The CSP MAY use KBV to resolve to a unique, claimed identity.

5.2. Identity Evidence Collection and Validation

The goal of identity validation is to collect the most appropriate identity evidence (e.g., a passport or driver's license) from the applicant and determine its authenticity, validity, and accuracy. Identity validation is made up of three process steps: collecting the appropriate identity evidence, confirming the evidence is genuine and authentic, and confirming the data contained on the identity evidence is valid, current, and related to a real-life subject.

5.2.1. Identity Evidence Quality Requirements

This section provides quality requirements for identity evidence collected during identity proofing.

Table 5-1. Strengths of identity evidence

Strength	Qualities of Identity Evidence
Unacceptable	No acceptable identity evidence provided.
Weak	<ul><li>The issuing source of the evidence did not perform identity proofing.</li><li>The issuing process for the evidence means that it can reasonably be assumed to have been delivered into the possession of the applicant.</li><li>The evidence contains:<ul><li>At least one reference number that uniquely identifies itself or the person to whom it relates, *OR*</li><li>The issued identity evidence contains a photograph or biometric template (of any modality) of the person to whom it relates.</li></ul></li></ul>
Fair	<ul><li>The issuing source of the evidence confirmed the claimed identity through an identity proofing process.</li><li>The issuing process for the evidence means that it can reasonably be assumed to have been delivered into the possession of the person to whom it relates.</li><li>The evidence:<ul><li>Contains at least one reference number that uniquely identifies the person to whom it relates, *OR*</li><li>Contains a photograph or biometric template (any modality) of the person to whom it relates, *OR*</li><li>Can have ownership confirmed through KBV.</li></ul></li><li>Where the evidence includes digital information, that information is protected using approved cryptographic or proprietary methods, or both, and those methods ensure the integrity of the information and enable the authenticity of the claimed issuing source to be confirmed.</li><li>Where the evidence includes physical security features, it requires proprietary knowledge to be able to reproduce it.</li><li>The issued evidence is unexpired.</li></ul>

Strength	Qualities of Identity Evidence
Strong	- The issuing source of the evidence confirmed the claimed identity through written procedures designed to enable it to form a reasonable belief that it knows the real-life identity of the person. Such procedures are subject to recurring oversight by regulatory or publicly-accountable institutions. For example, the Customer Identification Program guidelines established in response to the USA PATRIOT Act of 2001 or the *Red Flags Rule*, under Section 114 of the Fair and Accurate Credit Transaction Act of 2003 (FACT Act).
- The issuing process for the evidence ensured that it was delivered into the possession of the subject to whom it relates.
- The issued evidence contains at least one reference number that uniquely identifies the person to whom it relates.
- The full name on the issued evidence must be the name that the person was officially known by at the time of issuance. Not permitted are pseudonyms, aliases, an initial for surname, or initials for all given names.
- The:
- Issued evidence contains a photograph or biometric template (of any modality) of the person to whom it relates, *OR*
- Applicant proves possession of an AAL2 authenticator, or equivalent, bound to an IAL2 identity, at a minimum.
- Where the issued evidence includes digital information, that information is protected using approved cryptographic or proprietary methods, or both, and those methods ensure the integrity of the information and enable the authenticity of the claimed issuing source to be confirmed.
- Where the issued evidence contains physical security features, it requires proprietary knowledge and proprietary technologies to be able to reproduce it.
- The evidence is unexpired.
Superior	- The issuing source of the evidence confirmed the claimed identity by following written procedures designed to enable it to have high confidence that the source knows the real-life identity of the subject. Such procedures are subject to recurring oversight by regulatory or publicly accountable institutions.
- The issuing source visually identified the applicant and performed further checks to confirm the existence of that person;.
- The issuing process for the evidence ensured that it was delivered into the possession of the person to whom it relates.
- The evidence contains at least one reference number that uniquely identifies the person to whom it relates.

Table 5-1. (Continued)

Strength	Qualities of Identity Evidence
	• The full name on the evidence must be the name that the person was officially known by at the time of issuance. Not permitted are pseudonyms, aliases, an initial for surname, or initials for all given names. • The evidence contains a photograph of the person to whom it relates. • The evidence contains a biometric template (of any modality) of the person to whom it relates. • The evidence includes digital information, the information is protected using approved cryptographic or proprietary methods, or both, and those methods ensure the integrity of the information and enable the authenticity of the issuing source to be confirmed. • The evidence includes physical security features that require proprietary knowledge and proprietary technologies to be able to reproduce it. • The evidence is unexpired.

Table 5-1 lists strengths, ranging from unacceptable to superior, of identity evidence that is collected to establish a valid identity. Unless otherwise noted, to achieve a given strength the evidence SHALL, at a minimum, meet all the qualities listed.

5.2.2. Validating Identity Evidence

Once the CSP obtains the identity evidence, the accuracy, authenticity, and integrity of the evidence and related information is checked against authoritative sources in order to determine that the presented evidence:

- Is genuine, authentic, and not a counterfeit, fake, or forgery;
- Contains information that is correct; and
- Contains information that relates to a real-life subject.

Table 5-2 lists strengths, ranging from unacceptable to superior, of identity validation performed by the CSP to validate the evidence presented for the current proofing session and the information contained therein.

Table 5-2. Validating identity evidence

Strength	Method(s) Performed by the CSP
Unacceptable	Evidence validation was not performed, or validation of the evidence failed.
Weak	All personal details from the evidence have been confirmed as valid by comparison with information held or published by an authoritative source.
Fair	Attributes contained in the evidence have been confirmed as valid by comparison with information held or published by the issuing source or authoritative source(s), OR The evidence has been confirmed as genuine using appropriate technologies, confirming the integrity of physical security features and that the evidence is not fraudulent or inappropriately modified, OR The evidence has been confirmed as genuine by trained personnel, OR The evidence has been confirmed as genuine by confirmation of the integrity of cryptographic security features.
Strong	The evidence has been confirmed as genuine: using appropriate technologies, confirming the integrity of physical security features and that the evidence is not fraudulent or inappropriately modified, OR by trained personnel and appropriate technologies, confirming the integrity of the physical security features and that the evidence is not fraudulent or inappropriately modified, OR by confirmation of the integrity of cryptographic security features. All personal details and evidence details have been confirmed as valid by comparison with information held or published by the issuing source or authoritative source(s).
Superior	The evidence has been confirmed as genuine by trained personnel and appropriate technologies including the integrity of any physical and cryptographic security features. All personal details and evidence details from the evidence have been confirmed as valid by comparison with information held or published by the issuing source or authoritative source(s).

Training requirements for personnel validating evidence SHALL be based on the policies, guidelines, or requirements of the CSP or RP.

5.3. Identity Verification

The goal of identity verification is to confirm and establish a linkage between the claimed identity and the real-life existence of the subject presenting the evidence.

5.3.1. Identity Verification Methods

Table 5-3 details the verification methods necessary to achieve a given identity verification strength. The CSP SHALL adhere to the requirements in Section 5.3.2 if KBV is used to verify an identity.

Table 5-3. Verifying identity evidence

Strength	Identity Verification Methods
Unacceptable	Evidence verification was not performed or verification of the evidence failed. Unable to confirm that the applicant is the owner of the claimed identity.
Weak	The applicant has been confirmed as having access to the evidence provided to support the claimed identity.
Fair	• The applicant's ownership of the claimed identity has been confirmed by: 　o KBV. See *Section 5.3.2.* for more details, OR 　o a physical comparison of the applicant to the strongest piece of identity evidence provided to support the claimed identity. Physical comparison performed remotely SHALL adhere to all requirements as specified in *SP 800-63B,* Section 5.2.3, OR 　o biometric comparison of the applicant to the identity evidence. Biometric comparison performed remotely SHALL adhere to all requirements as specified in *SP 800-63B,* Section 5.2.3.
Strong	• The applicant's ownership of the claimed identity has been confirmed by: 　o physical comparison, using appropriate technologies, to a photograph, to the strongest piece of identity evidence provided to support the claimed identity. Physical comparison performed remotely SHALL adhere to all requirements as specified in *SP 800-63B,* Section 5.2.3, OR 　o biometric comparison, using appropriate technologies, of the applicant to the strongest piece of identity evidence provided to support the claimed identity. Biometric comparison performed remotely SHALL adhere to all requirements as specified in *SP 800-63B,* Section 5.2.3.

Digital Identity Guidelines

Strength	Identity Verification Methods
Unacceptable	Evidence verification was not performed or verification of the evidence failed. Unable to confirm that the applicant is the owner of the claimed identity.
Superior	The applicant's ownership of the claimed identity has been confirmed by biometric comparison of the applicant to the strongest piece of identity evidence provided to support the claimed identity, using appropriate technologies. Biometric comparison performed remotely SHALL adhere to all requirements as specified in *SP 800-63B*, Section 5.2.3.

5.3.2. Knowledge-Based Verification Requirements

The following requirements apply to the identity verification steps for IAL2. There are no restrictions for the use of KBV for identity resolution.

1) The CSP SHALL NOT use KBV to verify an applicant's identity against more than one piece of validated identity evidence.
2) The CSP SHALL only use information that is expected to be known only to the applicant and the authoritative source, to include any information needed to begin the KBV process. Information accessible freely, for a fee in the public domain, or via the black market SHALL NOT be used.
3) The CSP SHALL allow a resolved and validated identity to opt out of KBV and leverage another process for verification.
4) The CSP SHOULD perform KBV by verifying knowledge of recent transactional history in which the CSP is a participant. The CSP SHALL ensure that transaction information has at least 20 bits of entropy. For example, to reach minimum entropy requirements, the CSP could ask the applicant for verification of the amount(s) and transaction numbers(s) of a micro-deposit(s) to a valid bank account, so long as the total number of digits is seven or greater.
5) The CSP MAY perform KBV by asking the applicant questions to demonstrate they are the owner of the claimed information. However, the following requirements apply:
    a) KBV SHOULD be based on multiple authoritative sources.
    b) The CSP SHALL require a minimum of four KBV questions with each requiring a correct answer to successfully complete the KBV step.
    c) The CSP SHOULD require free-form response KBV questions. The CSP MAY allow multiple choice questions, however, if

multiple choice questions are provided, the CSP SHALL require a minimum of four answer options per question.

d) The CSP SHOULD allow two attempts for an applicant to complete the KBV. A CSP SHALL NOT allow more than three attempts to complete the KBV.
e) The CSP SHALL time out KBV sessions after two minutes of inactivity per question. In cases of session timeout, the CSP SHALL restart the entire KBV process and consider this a failed attempt.
f) The CSP SHALL NOT present a majority of diversionary KBV questions (i.e., those where "none of the above" is the correct answer).
g) The CSP SHOULD NOT ask the same KBV questions in subsequent attempts.
h) The CSP SHALL NOT ask a KBV question that provides information that could assist in answering any future KBV question in a single session or a subsequent session after a failed attempt.
i) The CSP SHALL NOT use KBV questions for which the answers do not change (e.g., "What was your first car?").
j) The CSP SHALL ensure that any KBV question does not reveal PII that the applicant has not already provided, nor personal information that, when combined with other information in a KBV session, could result in unique identification.

5.3.3. In-Person Proofing Requirements
In-person proofing at IAL3 can be satisfied in either of two ways:

- A physical interaction with the applicant, supervised by an operator.
- A remote interaction with the applicant, supervised by an operator, based on the specific requirements Section 5.3.3.2.

5.3.3.1. General Requirements

1) The CSP SHALL have the operator view the biometric source (e.g., fingers, face) for presence of non-natural materials and perform such inspections as part of the proofing process.

Digital Identity Guidelines

2) The CSP SHALL collect biometrics in such a way that ensures that the biometric is collected from the applicant, and not another subject. All biometric performance requirements in *SP 800-63B,* Section 5.2.3 apply.

5.3.3.2. Requirements for Supervised Remote In-Person Proofing

CSPs can employ remote proofing processes to achieve comparable levels of confidence and security to in-person events. The following requirements establish comparability between in- person transactions where the applicant is in the same physical location as the CSP to those where the applicant is remote.

Supervised remote identity proofing and enrollment transactions SHALL meet the following requirements, in addition to the IAL3 validation and verification requirements specified in Section 4.6:

1) The CSP SHALL monitor the entire identity proofing session, from which the applicant SHALL NOT depart — for example, by a continuous high-resolution video transmission of the applicant.
2) The CSP SHALL have a live operator participate remotely with the applicant for the entirety of the identity proofing session.
3) The CSP SHALL require all actions taken by the applicant during the identity proofing session to be clearly visible to the remote operator.
4) The CSP SHALL require that all digital verification of evidence (e.g., via chip or wireless technologies) be performed by integrated scanners and sensors.
5) The CSP SHALL require operators to have undergone a training program to detect potential fraud and to properly perform a supervised remote proofing session.
6) The CSP SHALL employ physical tamper detection and resistance features appropriate for the environment in which it is located. For example, a kiosk located in a restricted area or one where it is monitored by a trusted individual requires less tamper detection than one that is located in a semi-public area such as a shopping mall concourse.
7) The CSP SHALL ensure that all communications occur over a mutually authenticated protected channel.

5.3.4. Trusted Referee Requirements

1) The CSP MAY use trusted referees — such as notaries, legal guardians, medical professionals, conservators, persons with power of attorney, or some other form of trained and approved or certified individuals — that can vouch for or act on behalf of the applicant in accordance with applicable laws, regulations, or agency policy. The CSP MAY use a trusted referee for both remote and in-person processes.
2) The CSP SHALL establish written policy and procedures as to how a trusted referee is determined and the lifecycle by which the trusted referee retains their status as a valid referee, to include any restrictions, as well as any revocation and suspension requirements.
3) The CSP SHALL proof the trusted referee at the same IAL as the applicant proofing. In addition, the CSP SHALL determine the minimum evidence required to bind the relationship between the trusted referee and the applicant.
4) The CSP SHOULD perform re-proofing of the subscriber at regular intervals defined in the written policy specified in item 1 above, with the goal of satisfying the requirements of Section 4.4.1.

5.3.4.1. Additional Requirements for Minors

1) The CSP SHALL give special consideration to the legal restrictions of interacting with minors unable to meet the evidence requirements of identity proofing to ensure compliance with the Children's Online Privacy Protection Act of 1998 (COPPA) [COPPA], and other laws, as applicable.
2) Minors under age 13 require additional special considerations under COPPA [COPPA], and other laws, to which the CSP SHALL ensure compliance, as applicable.
3) The CSP SHOULD involve a parent or legal adult guardian as a trusted referee for an applicant that is a minor, as described elsewhere in this section.

5.4. Binding Requirements

See *SP 800-63B,* Section 6.1 Authenticator Binding for instructions on binding authenticators to subscribers.

6. Derived Credentials

Deriving credentials is based on the process of an individual proving to a CSP that they are the rightful subject of an identity record (i.e., a credential) that is bound to one or more authenticators they possess. This process is made available by a CSP that wants individuals to have an opportunity to obtain new authenticators bound to the existing, identity proofed record, or credential. As minimizing the number of times the identity proofing process is repeated benefits the individual and CSP, deriving identity is accomplished by proving possession and successful authentication of an authenticator that is already bound to the original, proofed digital identity.

The definition of derived in this section does *not* imply that an authenticator is cryptographically tied to a primary authenticator, for example deriving a key from another key. Rather, an authenticator can be derived by simply issuing on the basis of successful authentication with an authenticator that is already bound to a proofed identity, rather than unnecessarily repeating an identity proofing process.

There are two specific use cases for deriving identity:

1) A claimant seeks to obtain a derived PIV, bound to their identity record, for use only within the limits and authorizations of having a PIV smartcard. This use case is covered in SP 800-157, Guidelines for Derived Personal Identity Verification (PIV) Credentials.
2) An applicant seeks to establish a credential with a CSP with which the individual does not have a pre-existing relationship. For example, an applicant wants to switch from one CSP to another, or have a separate authenticator from a new CSP for other uses (e.g., basic browsing vs. financial). This use case is covered by allowable identity evidence in Section 5.2.

As stated above, all requirements for PIV-derived credentials can be found in *SP 800-157*. For the second use case described above, this guideline does not differentiate between physical and digital identity evidence. Therefore it is acceptable, if the authenticator or an assertion generated by the primary CSP meet the requirements of *Section 5*, for them to be used at identity evidence for IAL2 and IAL3. In addition, any authenticators issued as a result of providing digital identity evidence are subject to the requirements of *SP 800-63B*.

7. Threats and Security Considerations

There are two general categories of threats to the enrollment process: impersonation, and either compromise or malfeasance of the infrastructure provider. This section focuses on impersonation threats, as infrastructure threats are addressed by traditional computer security controls (e.g., intrusion protection, record keeping, independent audits) and are outside the scope of this document. For more information on security controls, see *SP 800-53, Recommended Security and Privacy Controls for Federal Information Systems and Organizations*.

Threats to the enrollment process include impersonation attacks and threats to the transport mechanisms for identity proofing, authenticator binding, and credential issuance. Table 7-1 lists the threats related to enrollment and identity proofing.

Table 7-1. Enrollment and identity proofing threats

Activity	Threat/Attack	Example
Enrollment	Falsified identity proofing evidence	An applicant claims an incorrect identity by using a forged driver's license.
	Fraudulent use of another's identity	An applicant uses a passport associated with a different individual.
	Enrollment repudiation	A subscriber denies enrollment, claiming that they did not enroll with the CSP.

7.1. Threat Mitigation Strategies

Enrollment threats can be deterred by making impersonation more difficult to accomplish or by increasing the likelihood of detection. This recommendation deals primarily with methods for making impersonation more difficult; however, it does prescribe certain methods and procedures that may help prove who perpetrated an impersonation. At each level, methods are employed to determine that a person with the claimed identity exists, that the applicant is the person entitled to the claimed identity, and that the applicant cannot later repudiate the enrollment. As the level of assurance increases, the methods employed provide increasing resistance to casual, systematic, and insider impersonation. Table 7-2 lists strategies for mitigating threats to the enrollment and issuance processes.

Table 7-2. Enrollment and issuance threat mitigation strategies

Activity	Threat/Attack	Mitigation Strategy	Normative Reference(s)
Enrollment	Falsified identity proofing evidence	CSP validates physical security features of presented evidence.	4.4.1.3, 4.5.3, 5.2.2
		CSP validates personal details in the evidence with the issuer or other authoritative source.	4.4.1.3, 4.5.3, 4.5.6, 5.2.2.
	Fraudulent use of another's identity	CSP verifies identity evidence and biometric of applicant against information obtained from issuer or other authoritative source.	4.4.1.7, 4.5.7, 5.3
		Verify applicant-provided non-government-issued documentation (e.g., electricity bills in the name of the applicant with the current address of the applicant printed on the bill, or a credit card bill) to help achieve a higher level of confidence in the applicant's identity.	4.4.1.7, 4.5.7, 5.3
	Enrollment repudiation	CSP saves a subscriber's biometric.	4.4.1.7, 4.5.7

8. Privacy Considerations

These privacy considerations provide information regarding the General Requirements set forth in *Section 4.2*.

8.1. Collection and Data Minimization

Section 4.2 requirement 2 permits the collection of only the PII necessary to validate the existence of the claimed identity and associate the claimed identity to the applicant, based on best available practices for appropriate identity resolution, validation, and verification.

Collecting unnecessary PII can create confusion regarding why information not being used for the identity proofing service is being collected. This leads to invasiveness or overreach concerns, which can lead to loss of applicant trust. Furthermore, PII retention can become vulnerable to unauthorized access or use. Data minimization reduces the amount of PII vulnerable to unauthorized access or use, and encourages trust in the identity proofing process.

8.1.1. Social Security Numbers
Section 4.2 requirement 13 does not permit the CSP to collect the SSN unless it is necessary for performing identity resolution, when resolution cannot be accomplished by collection of another attribute or combination of attributes. Overreliance on the SSN can contribute to misuse and place the applicant at risk of harm, such as through identity theft. Nonetheless, the SSN may achieve identity resolution for RPs in particular federal agencies that use SSNs to correlate a subscriber to existing records. Thus, this document recognizes the role of the SSN as an identifier and makes appropriate allowance for its use.

Note: Evidence requirements at the higher IALs preclude using the SSN or the Social Security Card as acceptable identity evidence.

Prior to collecting the SSN for identity proofing, organizations need to consider any legal obligation to collect the SSN, the necessity of using the SSN for interoperability with third party processes and systems, or operational requirements. Operational requirements can be demonstrated by an inability to alter systems, processes, or forms due to cost or unacceptable levels of risk.

Operational necessity is not justified by ease of use or unwillingness to change.

For federal agencies, the initial requirement in *Executive Order (EO) 9397* to use the SSN as a primary means of identification for individuals working for, with, or conducting business with their agency, has since been eliminated. Accordingly, EO 9397 cannot be referenced as the sole authority establishing the collection of the SSN as necessary.

Federal agencies need to review any decision to collect the SSN relative to their obligation to reduce the collection and unnecessary use of SSNs under Office of Management and Budget policy.

8.2. Notice and Consent

Section 4.2 requirement 3 requires the CSP provide explicit notice to the applicant at the time of collection regarding the purpose for collecting and maintaining a record of the attributes necessary for identity proofing, including whether such attributes are voluntary or mandatory in order to complete the identity proofing transactions, and the consequences for not providing the attributes.

An effective notice will take into account user experience design standards and research, and an assessment of privacy risks that may arise from the collection. Various factors should be considered, including incorrectly inferring that applicants understand why attributes are collected, that collected information may be combined with other data sources, etc. An effective notice is never only a pointer leading to a complex, legalistic privacy policy or general terms and conditions that applicants are unlikely to read or understand.

8.3. Processing Limitation

Section 4.2 requirement 4 requires CSPs to use measures to maintain the objectives of predictability (enabling reliable assumptions by individuals, owners, and operators about PII and its processing by an information system) and manageability (providing the capability for granular administration of PII, including alteration, deletion, and selective disclosure) commensurate with privacy risks that can arise from the processing of attributes for purposes other than identity proofing, authentication, authorization, or attribute assertion, related fraud mitigation, or to comply with law or legal process [NISTIR8062].

CSPs may have various business purposes for processing attributes, including providing non- identity services to subscribers. However, processing attributes for purposes other than the identity service can create privacy risks when individuals are not expecting or comfortable with the additional processing. CSPs can determine appropriate measures commensurate with the privacy risk arising from the additional processing. For example, absent applicable law, regulation or policy, it may not be necessary to get explicit consent when processing attributes to provide non-identity services requested by subscribers, although notices may help subscribers maintain reliable assumptions about the processing (predictability). Other processing of attributes may carry different privacy risks that call for obtaining explicit consent or allowing subscribers more control over the use or disclosure of specific attributes (manageability).

Subscriber consent needs to be meaningful; therefore, when CSPs do use consent measures, they cannot make acceptance by the subscriber of additional uses a condition of providing the identity service.

Consult your SAOP if there are questions about whether the proposed processing falls outside the scope of the permitted processing or the appropriate privacy risk mitigation measures.

8.4. Redress

Section 4.2 requirement 5 requires the CSP to provide effective mechanisms for redressing applicant complaints or problems arising from the identity proofing and make the mechanisms easy for applicants to find and access.

The Privacy Act requires federal CSPs that maintain a system of records to follow procedures to enable applicants to access and, if incorrect, amend their records. Any Privacy Act Statement should include a reference to the applicable SORN(s), which provide the applicant with instructions on how to make a request for access or correction. Non-federal CSPs should have comparable procedures, including contact information for any third parties if they are the source of the information.

CSPs should make the availability of alternative methods for completing the process clear to users (e.g., in person at a customer service center, if available) in the event an applicant is unable to establish their identity and complete the registration process online.

Note: If the ID proofing process is not successful, CSPs should inform the applicant of the procedures to address the issue but should not inform the applicant of the specifics of why the registration failed (e.g., do not inform the applicant, "Your SSN did not match the one that we have on record for you"), as doing so could allow fraudulent applicants to gain more knowledge about the accuracy of the PII.

8.5. Privacy Risk Assessment

Section 4.2 requirement 7 and 10 require the CSP to conduct a privacy risk assessment.

In conducting a privacy risk assessment, CSPs should consider:

1) The likelihood that the action it takes (e.g., additional verification steps or records retention) could create a problem for the applicant, such as invasiveness or unauthorized access to the information; and
2) The impact if a problem did occur. CSPs should be able to justify any response it takes to identified privacy risks, including accepting the risk, mitigating the risk, and sharing the risk. The use of applicant consent should be considered a form of sharing the risk, and therefore should only be used when an applicant could reasonably be expected to have the capacity to assess and accept the shared risk.

8.6. Agency Specific Privacy Compliance

Section 4.2 requirement 12 covers specific compliance obligations for federal CSPs. It is critical to involve your agency's SAOP in the earliest stages of digital authentication system development to assess and mitigate privacy risks and advise the agency on compliance requirements, such as whether or not the PII collection to conduct identity proofing triggers the Privacy Act of 1974 [Privacy Act] or the E-Government Act of 2002 [E-Gov] requirement to conduct a Privacy Impact Assessment. For example, with respect to identity proofing, it is likely that the Privacy Act requirements will be triggered and require coverage by either a new or existing Privacy Act system of records due to the collection and maintenance of PII or other attributes necessary to conduct identity proofing.

The SAOP can similarly assist the agency in determining whether a PIA is required. These considerations should not be read as a requirement to develop a Privacy Act SORN or PIA for identity proofing alone; in many cases it will make the most sense to draft a PIA and SORN that encompasses the entire digital authentication process or include the digital authentication process as part of a larger programmatic PIA that discusses the program or benefit the agency is establishing online access to.

Due to the many components of digital authentication, it is important for the SAOP to have an awareness and understanding of each individual component. For example, other privacy artifacts may be applicable to an agency offering or using proofing services such as Data Use Agreements, Computer Matching Agreements, etc. The SAOP can assist the agency in determining what additional requirements apply. Moreover, a thorough understanding of the individual components of digital authentication will enable the SAOP to thoroughly assess and mitigate privacy risks either through compliance processes or by other means.

9. Usability Considerations

This section is intended to raise implementers' awareness of the usability considerations associated with enrollment and identity proofing (for usability considerations for typical authenticator usage and intermittent events, see SP 800-63B, Section 10.

ISO/IEC 9241-11 defines usability as the "extent to which a product can be used by specified users to achieve specified goals with effectiveness, efficiency and satisfaction in a specified context of use." This definition focuses on users, goals, and context of use as the necessary elements for achieving effectiveness, efficiency, and satisfaction. A holistic approach considering these key elements is necessary to achieve usability.

The overarching goal of usability for enrollment and identity proofing is to promote a smooth, positive enrollment process for users by minimizing user burden (e.g., time and frustration) and enrollment friction (e.g., the number of steps to complete and amount of information to track). To achieve this goal, organizations have to first familiarize themselves with their users.

The enrollment and identity proofing process sets the stage for a user's interactions with a given CSP and the online services that the user will access; as negative first impressions can influence user perception of subsequent interactions, organizations need to promote a positive user experience throughout the process.

Usability cannot be achieved in a piecemeal manner. Performing a usability evaluation on the enrollment and identity proofing process is critical. It is important to conduct usability evaluation with representative users, realistic goals and tasks, and appropriate contexts of use. The enrollment and identity proofing process should be designed and implemented so it is easy for users to do the right thing, hard to do the wrong thing, and easy to recover when the wrong thing happens.

From the user's perspective, the three main steps of enrollment and identity proofing are pre- enrollment preparation, the enrollment and proofing session, and post-enrollment actions. These steps may occur in a single session or there could be significant time elapsed between each one (e.g., days or weeks).

General and step-specific usability considerations are described in sub-sections below.

Assumptions

In this section, the term "users" means "applicants" or "subscribers." Guidelines and considerations are described from the users' perspective.

Accessibility differs from usability and is out of scope for this document. *Section 508* was enacted to eliminate barriers in information technology and require federal agencies to make their electronic and information technology public content accessible to people with disabilities. Refer to Section 508 law and standards for accessibility guidance.

9.1. General User Experience Considerations During Enrollment and Identity Proofing

This sub-section provides usability considerations that are applicable across all steps of the enrollment process. Usability considerations specific to each step are detailed in Sections *9.2* to *9.4*.

- To avoid user frustration, streamline the process required for enrollment to make each step as clear and easy as possible.

- Clearly communicate how and where to acquire technical assistance. For example, provide helpful information such as a link to online self-service feature, chat sessions, and a phone number for help desk support. Ideally, sufficient information should be provided to enable users to answer their own enrollment preparation questions without outside intervention.
- Clearly explain who is collecting their data and why. Also indicate the path their data will take, in particular where the data is being stored.
- Ensure all information presented is usable.
  - Follow good information design practice for all user-facing materials (e.g., data collection notices and fillable forms).
  - Write materials in plain language, typically at a 6th to 8th grade literacy level, and avoid technical jargon. Use active voice and conversational style, logically sequence main points, use the same word consistently rather than synonyms to avoid confusion, and use bullets, numbers, and formatting where appropriate to aid readability.
  - Consider text legibility, such as font style, size, color, and contrast with surrounding background. The highest contrast is black on white. Text legibility is important because users have different levels of visual acuity. Illegible text will contribute to user comprehension errors or user entry errors (e.g., when completing fillable forms).
  - Use sans serif font styles for electronic materials and serif fonts for paper materials.
  - When possible, avoid fonts that do not clearly distinguish between easily confusable characters (such as the letter "O" and the number "0"). This is especially important for enrollment codes.
  - Use a minimum font size of 12 points, as long as the text fits the display.
- Perform a usability evaluation for each step with representative users. Establish realistic goals and tasks, and appropriate contexts of use for the usability evaluation.

9.2. Pre-Enrollment Preparation

This section describes an effective approach to facilitate sufficient pre-enrollment preparation so users can avoid challenging, frustrating enrollment sessions. Ensuring users are as prepared as possible for their enrollment sessions is critical to the overall success and usability of the enrollment and identity proofing process.

Such preparation is only possible if users receive the necessary information (e.g., required documentation) in a usable format in an appropriate timeframe. This includes making users aware of exactly what identity evidence will be required. Users do not need to know anything about IALs or whether the identity evidence required is scored as "fair," "strong," or "superior," whereas organizations need to know what IAL is required for access to a particular system.

To ensure users are equipped to make informed decisions about whether to proceed with the enrollment process, and what will be needed for their session, provide users:

- Information about the entire process, such as what to expect in each step
  o Clear explanations of the expected timeframes to allow users to plan accordingly.
- Explanation of the need for — and benefits of — identity proofing to allow users to understand the value proposition.
- Information on the monetary amount and acceptable forms of payment, and if there is an enrollment fee. Offering a larger variety of acceptable forms of payment allows users to choose their preferred payment operation.
- Information on whether the user's enrollment session will be in-person or in-person over remote channels, and whether a user can choose. Only provide information relevant to the allowable session option(s).
  o Information on the location(s), whether a user can choose their preferred location, and necessary logistical information for in-person or in-person over remote channels session. Note that users may be reluctant to bring identity evidence to certain public places (bank versus supermarket), as they perceive that it increases exposure to loss or theft.
  o Information on the technical requirements (e.g., requirements for internet access) for remote sessions.
  o An option to set an appointment for in-person or in-person over remote channels identity proofing sessions to minimize wait

times. If walk-ins are allowed, make it clear to users that their wait times may be greater without an appointment.
- Provide clear instructions for setting up an enrollment session appointment, reminders, and how to reschedule existing appointments.
- Offer appointment reminders and allow users to specify their preferred appointment reminder format(s) (e.g., postal mail, voicemail, email, text message). Users need information such as date, time, location, and a description of required identity evidence.

- Information on the allowed and required identity evidence and attributes, whether each piece is voluntary or mandatory, and the consequences for not providing the complete set of identity evidence. Users need to know the specific combinations of identity evidence, including requirements specific to a piece of identity evidence (e.g., a raised seal on a birth certificate). This is especially important due to potential difficulties procuring the necessary identity evidence.
  o Where possible, implement tools to make it easier to obtain the necessary identity evidence.
  o Inform users of any special requirements for minors and people with unique needs. For example, provide users with the information necessary to use trusted referees, such as a notary, legal guardian, or some other form of certified individual that can legally vouch for or act on behalf of the individual (see Section 5.3.4).
  o If forms are required:
    - Provide fillable forms before and at the enrollment session. Do not require users to have access to a printer.
    - Minimize the amount of information users must enter on a form, as users are easily frustrated and more error-prone with longer forms. Where possible, pre-populate forms.

9.3. Enrollment Proofing Session

Usability considerations specific to the enrollment session include:

- Remind users at the start of the enrollment session of the enrollment session procedure, without expecting them to remember from the pre-enrollment preparation step. If the enrollment session does not

Digital Identity Guidelines

immediately follow pre-enrollment preparation, it is especially important to clearly remind users of the typical timeframe to complete the proofing and enrollment phase.

- o Provide rescheduling options for in-person or in-person over remote channels.
- o Provide a checklist with the allowed and required identity evidence to ensure users have the requisite identity evidence to proceed with the enrollment session, including enrollment codes, if applicable. If users do not have the complete set of identity evidence, they must be informed regarding whether they can complete a partial identity proofing session.
- o Notify users regarding what information will be destroyed, what, if any, information will be retained for future follow-up sessions, and what identity evidence they will need to bring to complete a future session. Ideally, users can choose whether they would like to complete a partial identity proofing session.
- o Set user expectations regarding the outcome of the enrollment session as prior identity verification experiences may drive their expectations (e.g., receiving a driver's license in person, receiving a passport in the mail).
- o Clearly indicate whether users will receive an authenticator immediately at the end of a successful enrollment session, if users have to schedule an appointment to pick it up in person, or if users will receive it in the mail and when they can expect to receive it.

- During the enrollment session, there are several requirements to provide users with explicit notice at the time of identity proofing, such as what data will be retained on record by the CSP (see Section 4.2 and Section 8. for detailed requirements on notices). If CSPs seek consent from a user for additional attributes or uses of their attributes for any purpose other than identity proofing, authentication, authorization or attribute assertions, per 4.2 requirement (5), make CSPs aware that requesting additional attributes or uses may be unexpected or may make users uncomfortable. If users do not perceive benefit(s) to the additional collection or uses, but perceive extra risk, they may be unwilling or hesitant to provide consent or continue the process. Provide users with explicit notice of the additional requirements.
- Avoid using KBV since it is extremely problematic from a usability perspective. KBV tends to be error-prone and frustrating for users

given the limitations of human memory. If KBV is used, address the following usability considerations.
- o KBV questions should have relevance and context to users for them to be able to answer correctly.
- o Phrase KBV questions clearly, as ambiguity can lead to user errors. For example, when asking about a user's social security balance, clearly specify which time period as social security accounts fluctuate.
- o Prior to being asked KBV questions, users must be informed of:
  - The number of allowed attempts and remaining attempt(s).
  - The fact that KBV questions will change on subsequent attempts.
  - During the KBV session, provide timeout inactivity warnings prior to timeout.
- If an enrollment code is issued:
  - o Notify users in advance that they will receive an enrollment code, when to expect it, the length of time for which the code is valid, and how it will arrive (e.g., physical mail, SMS, landline telephone, email, or physical mailing address).
  - o When an enrollment code is delivered to a user, include instructions on how to use the code, and the length of time for which the code is valid. This is especially important given the short validity timeframes specified in Section 4.4.1.6.
  - o If issuing a machine-readable optical label, such as a QR Code (see Section 4.6), provide users with information on how to obtain QR code scanning capabilities (e.g., acceptable QR code applications).
  - o Inform users that they will be required to repeat the enrollment process if enrollment codes expire or are lost before use.
  - o Provide users with alternative options as not all users are able to use this level of technology. For example, users may not have the technology needed for this approach to be feasible.
- At the end of the enrollment session,
  - o If enrollment is successful, send users confirmation regarding the successful enrollment and information on next steps (e.g., when and where to pick up their authenticator, when it will arrive in the mail).

- If enrollment is partially complete (due to users not having the complete set of identity evidence, users choosing to stop the process, or session timeouts), communicate to users:
    - What information will be destroyed;
    - What, if any, information will be retained for future follow-up sessions;
    - How long the information will be retained; and
    - What identity evidence they will need to bring to a future session.
  - If enrollment is unsuccessful, provide users with clear instructions for alternative enrollment session types, for example, offering in-person proofing for users that can not complete remote proofing.
- If users receive the authenticator during the enrollment session, provide users information on the use and maintenance of the authenticator. For example, information could include instructions for use (especially if there are different requirements for first-time use or initialization), information on authenticator expiration, how to protect the authenticator, and what to do if the authenticator is lost or stolen.
- For both in-person and in-person proofing performed over remote channels enrollment sessions, additional usability considerations apply:
  - At the start of the enrollment session, operators or attendants need to explain their role to users (e.g., whether operators or attendants will walk users through the enrollment session or observe silently and only interact as needed).
  - At the start of the enrollment session, inform users that they must not depart during the session, and that their actions must be visible throughout the session.
  - When biometrics are collected during the enrollment session, provide users clear instructions on how to complete the collection process. The instructions are best given just prior to the process. Verbal instructions with corrective feedback from a live operator are the most effective (e.g., instruct users where the biometric sensor is, when to start, how to interact with the sensor, and when the biometric collection is completed).
- Since remote identity proofing is conducted online, follow general web usability principles. For example:

- Design the user interface to walk users through the enrollment process.
- Reduce users' memory load.
- Make the interface consistent.
- Clearly label sequential steps.
- Make the starting point clear.
- Design to support multiple platforms and device sizes.
- Make the navigation consistent, easy to find, and easy to follow.

9.4. Post-Enrollment

Post-enrollment refers to the step immediately after enrollment but prior to typical usage of an authenticator (for usability considerations for typical authenticator usage and intermittent events, see SP800-63B, Section 10.1-10.3. As described above, users have already been informed at the end of their enrollment session regarding the expected delivery (or pick-up) mechanism by which they will receive their authenticator.

Usability considerations for post-enrollment include:

- Minimize the amount of time that users wait for their authenticator to arrive. Shorter wait times will allow users to access information systems and services more quickly.
- Inform users whether they need to go to a physical location to pick up their authenticators. The previously identified usability considerations for appointments and reminders still apply.

Along with the authenticator, give users information relevant to the use and maintenance of the authenticator; this may include instructions for use, especially if there are different requirements for first-time use or initialization, information on authenticator expiration, and what to do if the authenticator is lost or stolen.

References

General References

[A-130] OMB Circular A-130, *Managing Federal Information as a Strategic Resource*, July 28, 2016, available at: https://obamawhitehouse.archives.gov/sites/default/files/omb/assets/OMB/circulars/a130/a13 0revised.pdf.

[COPPA] *Children's Online Privacy Protection Act of 1998 ("COPPA")*, 15 U.S.C. 6501-6505, 16 CFR Part 312, available at: https://www.law.cornell.edu/uscode/text/15/chapter-91.

[DMF] National Technical Information Service, *Social Security Death Master File*, available at: https://www.ssdmf.com/Library/InfoManage/Guide.asp?FolderID=1.

[E-Gov] *E-Government Act of 2002* (includes FISMA) (P.L. 107-347), December 2002, available at: http://www.gpo.gov/fdsys/pkg/PLAW-107publ347/pdf/PLAW-107publ347.pdf.

[EO 9397] Executive Order 9397, *Numbering System for Federal Accounts Relating to Individual Persons*, November 22, 1943, available at: https://www.ssa.gov/foia/html/EO9397.htm.

[FBCACP] *X.509 Certificate Policy For The Federal Bridge Certification Authority (FBCA)*, Version 2.30, October 5, 2016, available at: https://www.Idmanagement.gov/wp-content/uploads/sites/1171/uploads/FBCA_CP.pdf.

[FBCASUP] *FBCA Supplementary Antecedent, In-Person Definition*, July 16, 2009.

[FEDRAMP] General Services Administration, *Federal Risk and Authorization Management Program*, available at: https://www.fedramp.gov/.

[GPG 45] UK Cabinet Office, Good Practice Guide 45, *Identity proofing and verification of an individual*, November 3, 2014, available at: https://www.gov.uk/government/publications/identity-proofing-and-verification-of-an- individual.

[M-03-22] OMB Memorandum M-03-22, *OMB Guidance for Implementing the Privacy Provisions of the E-Government Act of 2002*, September 26, 2003, available at: https://georgewbush-whitehouse.archives.gov/omb/memoranda/m03-22.html.

[M-04-04] OMB Memorandum M-04-04, *E-Authentication Guidance for Federal Agencies*, December 16, 2003, available at: https://georgewbush- whitehouse.archives.gov/omb/memoranda/fy04/m04-04.pdf.

[NISTIR8062] NIST Internal Report 8062, *An Introduction to Privacy Engineering and Risk Management in Federal Systems*, January 2017, available at: http://nvlpubs.nist.gov/nistpubs/ir/2017/NIST.IR.8062.pdf.

[Privacy Act] *Privacy Act of 1974* (P.L. 93-579), December 1974, available at: https://www.justice.gov/opcl/privacy-act-1974.

[Red Flags Rule] 15 U.S.C. 1681m(e)(4), Pub. L. 111-319, 124 Stat. 3457, *Fair and Accurate Credit Transaction Act of 2003*, December 18, 2010, available at: https://www.ftc.gov/sites/default/files/documents/federal_register_notices/identity-theft-red- flags-and-address-discrepancies-under-fair-and-accurate-credit-transactions-act/071109redflags.pdf.

[Section 508] Section 508 Law and Related Laws and Policies (January 30, 2017), available at: https://www.section508.gov/content/learn/laws-and-policies.

Standards

[Canada] Government of Canada, *Guideline on Identity Assurance*, available at: http://www.tbs- sct.gc.ca/pol/doc-eng.aspx?id=30678&section=HTML.

[ISO 9241-11] International Standards Organization, ISO/IEC 9241-11 *Ergonomic requirements for office work with visual display terminals (VDTs) — Part 11: Guidance on usability*, March 1998, available at: https://www.iso.org/standard/16883.html.

NIST Special Publications

NIST 800 Series Special Publications are available at: http://csrc.nist.gov/publications/PubsSPs.html. The following publications may be of particular interest to those implementing systems of applications requiring e-authentication.

[SP 800-53] NIST Special Publication 800-53 Revision 4, Recommended Security and Privacy Controls for Federal Information Systems and Organizations, April 2013 (updated January 22, 2015), https://doi.org/10.6028/NIST.SP.800-53r4.

[SP 800-63-3] NIST Special Publication 800-63-3, Digital Identity Guidelines, June 2017, https://doi.org/10.6028/NIST.SP.800-63-3.

[SP 800-63B] NIST Special Publication 800-63B, Digital Identity Guidelines: Authentication and Lifecycle Management, June 2017, https://doi.org/10.6028/NIST.SP.800-63b.

[SP 800-63C] NIST Special Publication 800-63C, Digital Identity Guidelines: Assertions and Federation, June 2017, https://doi.org/10.6028/NIST.SP.800-63c.

[SP 800-157] NIST Special Publication 800-157, Guidelines for Derived Personal Identity Verification (PIV) Credentials, December 2014, http://doi.org/10.6028/NIS T.SP.800-157.

Index

A

access, vii, 2, 4, 5, 6, 15, 18, 22, 25, 27, 30, 33, 36, 41, 42, 53, 55, 56, 58, 59, 64, 65, 71, 74, 81, 112, 118, 154, 158, 163, 166, 171, 194, 199, 201, 214, 222, 224, 225, 226, 229, 230, 234
administrators, 7, 12, 81, 85
agencies, vii, 5, 6, 8, 15, 19, 31, 33, 42, 50, 65, 66, 74, 77, 193, 222, 223, 227
assessment, 7, 12, 17, 26, 27, 50, 55, 200, 223, 225
assets, 12, 18, 28, 234
attacker, 20, 21, 22, 53
audit, 25, 29, 31, 37, 200, 220
authentication, vii, 1, 2, 3, 4, 5, 6, 8, 12, 13, 14, 16, 18, 20, 21, 22, 24, 29, 32, 37, 40, 42, 43, 45, 47, 48, 50, 53, 54, 55, 56, 58, 59, 60, 63, 64, 65, 66, 67, 68, 69, 70, 71, 72, 73, 74, 75, 79, 83, 87, 88, 90, 91, 101, 103, 104, 112, 118, 119, 120, 179, 193, 194, 199, 204, 209, 219, 223, 225, 226, 231, 235, 236
authenticity, 26, 54, 63, 210, 211, 212
authority, 9, 16, 37, 50, 64, 77, 98, 117, 223

B

base, 5, 6, 29, 47
benefits, 7, 10, 40, 76, 199, 219, 229

C

certificate, 8, 9, 13, 16, 19, 20, 29, 31, 32, 37, 41, 42, 43, 45, 47, 48, 50, 53, 54, 58, 64, 67, 68, 69, 70, 71, 77, 87, 88, 89, 90, 91, 98, 103, 104, 115, 117, 118, 119, 121, 123, 139, 140, 141, 143, 230
certification, 16, 50, 64
challenges, 3, 8, 10, 23, 60, 61, 76, 194
commercial, 3, 4, 5, 6, 9, 11, 74, 76
communication, 17, 24, 62, 66, 70
compliance, 4, 42, 100, 189, 218, 225, 226
computer, 2, 5, 6, 8, 25, 42, 66, 73, 74, 77, 82, 89, 102, 124, 147, 152, 157, 163, 165, 170, 220, 226
computing, 2, 5, 9, 12, 17, 66, 74
confidentiality, 18, 26, 57, 200
configuration, 11, 30, 40, 50, 55, 56, 76, 80, 81, 87, 88, 110, 113, 117, 121
consent, 22, 199, 224, 225, 231
containers, 8, 37, 50, 60
cost, 4, 209, 222
Credential Service Providers (CSPs), 20, 193, 194, 196, 197, 199, 200, 217, 223, 224, 225, 231
credentials, 2, 3, 4, 5, 6, 8, 9, 10, 13, 16, 19, 20, 27, 29, 30, 31, 33, 54, 65, 66, 72, 74, 76, 77, 194, 219
cybersecurity, 2, 5, 6, 7, 9, 10, 11, 14, 18, 19, 27, 28, 32, 55, 62, 72, 73, 74, 75, 76, 77

D

database, 16, 26, 30, 34, 37, 53, 54, 112
decision makers, 7, 10, 75
Department of Homeland Security, vii, 2, 5, 18, 61, 62, 64, 72, 73
Derived PIV Credential (DPC), 2, 3, 4, 5, 6, 7, 8, 9, 10, 11, 12, 13, 14, 15, 16, 17,

18, 19, 20, 21, 22, 25, 26, 27, 28, 29, 30, 32, 33, 34, 35, 36, 37, 38, 39, 40, 41, 42, 44, 45, 47, 48, 50, 51, 52, 53, 54, 55, 56, 57, 58, 60, 61, 63, 64, 65, 67, 68, 69, 70, 71, 72, 74, 75, 76, 77, 79, 80, 81, 82, 83, 84, 85, 86, 87, 88, 89, 93, 101, 102, 103, 109, 110, 111, 112, 114, 115, 117, 118, 119, 120, 121, 122, 123, 181, 182, 183, 185, 186, 187, 189, 190
desktop, 2, 5, 6, 8, 25, 36, 48, 50, 54, 74, 77, 113, 114, 118, 119, 121, 122, 174, 181
detection, 21, 22, 209, 217, 220
digital authentication, 3, 193, 194, 225, 226
disclosure, 58, 199, 223, 224

E

ecosystem, 3, 12, 23, 25
E-Government Act, 201, 225, 235
employees, 5, 6, 33, 74
encryption, 16, 22, 31, 60, 63
enrollment, vii, 16, 20, 26, 36, 37, 40, 48, 54, 88, 121, 187, 193, 194, 196, 197, 198, 199, 200, 203, 204, 206, 207, 208, 217, 220, 226, 227, 228, 229, 230, 231, 232, 233, 234
Enterprise Mobility Management (EMM), 4, 5, 8, 9, 10, 12, 13, 16, 20, 21, 23, 24, 30, 31, 32, 33, 34, 35, 36, 37, 56, 57, 61, 75, 79, 190
environment, 2, 3, 6, 8, 9, 11, 15, 28, 41, 75, 76, 77, 80, 83, 84, 104, 112, 117, 196, 217
evidence, vii, 19, 193, 194, 195, 196, 197, 199, 200, 202, 203, 204, 205, 206, 208, 209, 210, 211, 212, 213, 214, 215, 217, 218, 219, 220, 221, 222, 229, 230, 231, 233
Executive Order, 19, 73, 223, 235

F

federal government, 2, 5, 9, 15, 74
Federal Register, 11, 62, 72
federation, 13, 190, 194, 236

force, 21, 53, 56
fraud, 199, 200, 205, 209, 217, 224

G

General Services Administration (GSA), 31, 33, 62, 73, 235
Google, 29, 37, 121
GPS, 24
guidance, 2, 9, 18, 23, 50, 56, 227
guidelines, 3, 4, 5, 8, 9, 11, 14, 16, 18, 27, 50, 66, 74, 76, 193, 204, 211, 213

H

host, 87, 118, 121, 123
hybrid, 5, 17, 29, 36, 37, 38, 39, 40, 55, 58, 74, 111

I

identity, v, vii, 1, 2, 3, 4, 5, 6, 7, 9, 12, 14, 15, 17, 18, 19, 20, 24, 27, 29, 30, 31, 32, 36, 37, 40, 41, 45, 48, 50, 51, 54, 55, 56, 57, 58, 60, 62, 63, 64, 65, 66, 67, 69, 72, 74, 75, 77, 79, 80, 96, 105, 112, 115, 119, 120, 121, 182, 183, 185, 189, 190, 191, 193, 194, 195, 196, 197, 198, 199, 200, 201, 202, 203, 205, 206, 207, 208, 209, 210, 211, 212, 213, 214, 215, 217, 218, 219, 220, 221, 222, 223, 224, 225, 226, 227, 229, 230, 231, 233, 235, 236
Identity Assurance Level (IAL), vii, 13, 62, 194, 195, 196, 197, 201, 205, 208, 218, 229
identity, credential, and access management (ICAM), 15, 33, 34, 62
identification, 6, 20, 66, 193, 198, 216, 223
identity proofing, vii, 2, 3, 5, 6, 19, 65, 69, 74, 77, 193, 194, 196, 197, 198, 199, 200, 201, 202, 203, 205, 206, 207, 209, 210, 217, 218, 219, 220, 222, 223, 224, 225, 226, 227, 229, 231, 233, 235
image, 17, 42, 50, 198, 200, 207
individuals, 5, 18, 55, 74, 209, 218, 219, 223, 224

Index

industry, 7, 18, 194, 204, 207, 208
information technology, 3, 6, 65, 75, 227
infrastructure, vii, 4, 6, 8, 11, 15, 16, 23, 25, 30, 40, 41, 42, 54, 67, 76, 79, 112, 220
integration, 4, 8, 9, 10, 11, 16, 30, 34, 35, 36, 56, 76, 80, 112
integrity, 18, 26, 54, 57, 70, 200, 210, 211, 212, 213
interface, 47, 53, 67, 68, 234
issues, 16, 29, 31, 32, 64, 77
IT professionals, 3, 4, 6, 7, 9, 11, 12, 14, 29, 30, 31, 62, 75, 76, 190

J

Java, 54, 113, 190

L

laptop, 2, 5, 6, 8, 17, 36, 74, 77, 89, 102, 121, 122, 197
laws, 200, 218, 235
life cycle, 2, 5, 8, 40, 64, 74

M

malware, 20, 21, 22, 53
management, 5, 6, 8, 10, 13, 14, 15, 16, 18, 19, 25, 27, 29, 30, 32, 33, 34, 35, 36, 37, 38, 39, 42, 45, 47, 50, 54, 55, 60, 61, 64, 65, 68, 71, 74, 75, 77, 80, 99, 110, 111, 112, 200
mapping, 28, 31, 58, 59
memory, 26, 232, 234
Microsoft, 13, 30, 53, 112, 113, 115, 117, 139, 140
mobile device, 2, 3, 5, 6, 7, 8, 9, 10, 12, 13, 14, 15, 16, 17, 18, 20, 21, 22, 23, 25, 26, 30, 32, 33, 34, 36, 37, 38, 40, 41, 42, 47, 48, 50, 54, 55, 56, 57, 58, 60, 65, 66, 74, 75, 76, 77, 81, 85, 89, 93, 101, 106, 107, 110, 111, 112, 118, 120, 182, 183
mobile threat, 5, 23, 24, 75
multifactor authentication, 2, 3, 5, 6, 18, 20, 21, 22, 29, 42, 66, 74, 75

N

National Cybersecurity Center of Excellence (NCCoE), 2, 3, 4, 5, 6, 8, 9, 10, 11, 13, 14, 18, 56, 61, 62, 74, 76, 77, 80, 112, 117, 190
National Institute of Standards and Technology (NIST), 1, 2, 5, 7, 8, 9, 10, 11, 12, 13, 14, 16, 17, 18, 19, 20, 22, 23, 25, 26, 27, 28, 29, 32, 40, 41, 42, 50, 56, 57, 58, 59, 60, 61, 62, 63, 65, 66, 67, 68, 69, 70, 72, 73, 74, 75, 76, 77, 101, 190, 193, 235, 236
network, 9, 14, 19, 23, 24, 25, 26, 30, 34, 36, 37, 40, 41, 47, 57, 63, 64, 73, 77, 78, 117, 145, 156, 191

O

Office of Management and Budget (OMB), 65, 66, 223, 234, 235
operating system, 8, 17, 25, 26, 29, 30, 36, 60
operations, 3, 14, 16, 17, 29, 41, 54, 63
ownership, 48, 210, 214, 215

P

passwords, vii, 1, 17, 18, 20, 21, 22, 42, 43, 45, 58, 59, 62, 66, 69, 71, 80, 88, 101, 102, 104, 107, 113, 114, 127, 154, 158, 163, 166, 171
personal identity, 5, 66, 67, 75
personal identity verification, 5, 66, 67, 75
Personal Identity Verification (PIV) Cards, v, vii, 1, 2, 3, 4, 5, 6, 7, 8, 12, 13, 14, 16, 17, 19, 20, 21, 27, 29, 30, 32, 33, 34, 35, 36, 37, 38, 39, 40, 41, 42, 43, 44, 45, 46, 47, 48, 49, 50, 53, 54, 55, 56, 57, 58, 59, 60, 61, 62, 63, 64, 65, 66, 67, 68, 69, 70, 71, 72, 73, 74, 75, 77, 79, 87, 88, 89, 90, 91, 101, 102, 103, 104, 106, 107, 108, 109, 110, 111, 114, 115, 118, 119, 120, 122, 182, 183, 185, 186, 189, 191, 219, 236
platform, 3, 7, 13, 26, 29, 30, 31, 112

Index

policy, 3, 8, 9, 18, 29, 34, 37, 42, 56, 64, 70, 85, 88, 101, 115, 119, 189, 199, 209, 218, 223, 224
population, 37, 195, 197, 202, 209
predictability, 199, 223, 224
preparation, 227, 228, 229, 230
privacy, 13, 17, 19, 24, 25, 56, 72, 80, 95, 195, 197, 199, 200, 201, 218, 220, 222, 223, 224, 225, 226, 235, 236
private sector, 3, 5, 7, 74, 201
professionals, 7, 11, 25, 75, 76, 218
project, 5, 7, 11, 12, 13, 14, 15, 18, 29, 31, 33, 37, 40, 41, 50, 56, 60, 74, 77
protection, 50, 57, 59, 70, 201, 220

R

recovery, 34, 54, 110, 112
requirements, vii, 4, 8, 9, 12, 13, 20, 31, 32, 33, 34, 36, 40, 41, 42, 45, 53, 56, 58, 59, 64, 66, 70, 77, 112, 193, 194, 195, 196, 197, 199, 200, 201, 202, 205, 207, 208, 209, 210, 213, 214, 215, 216, 217, 218, 219, 222, 223, 224, 225, 226, 229, 230, 231, 233, 234, 236
resolution, 199, 201, 202, 205, 208, 209, 215, 217, 222
resources, vii, 4, 12, 18, 26, 36, 58, 117, 154, 158, 163, 166, 171, 194, 209
response, 6, 11, 19, 22, 26, 28, 37, 67, 211, 215, 225
restrictions, 16, 56, 215, 218
risk, 7, 10, 11, 12, 13, 17, 18, 19, 21, 26, 27, 28, 50, 56, 62, 72, 76, 194, 199, 200, 222, 223, 224, 225, 226, 231, 235
risk assessment, 7, 12, 17, 26, 27, 200, 225
risk management, 13, 18, 19, 27, 50, 200
root, 87, 98, 115

S

scope, 7, 12, 13, 23, 25, 56, 60, 75, 220, 224, 227
security, vii, 2, 3, 4, 5, 6, 7, 8, 9, 10, 11, 12, 13, 14, 15, 16, 18, 19, 20, 21, 22, 23, 25, 30, 31, 32, 33, 34, 40, 50, 53, 55, 56, 68, 70, 72, 74, 75, 76, 80, 82, 83, 85, 198, 200, 202, 204, 207, 210, 211, 212, 213, 217, 220, 221, 232
sensors, 17, 66, 217, 233
servers, 9, 26, 77
service provider, 8, 9, 16, 20, 33, 60, 193, 194, 198
services, 3, 5, 7, 9, 10, 12, 14, 16, 18, 23, 29, 31, 32, 33, 34, 36, 37, 50, 57, 72, 73, 74, 79, 193, 199, 224, 226, 234
smart card, 2, 5, 6, 17, 29, 31, 40, 74, 75, 77
Social Security, 201, 222, 232, 235
software, 5, 8, 9, 13, 15, 16, 20, 21, 22, 23, 25, 30, 36, 37, 40, 42, 47, 50, 54, 58, 59, 60, 69, 74, 111, 112, 121, 122, 183
software as a service (SaaS), 9, 32, 62
solution, 4, 5, 7, 9, 10, 11, 12, 14, 16, 18, 26, 28, 29, 30, 31, 33, 34, 36, 40, 41, 48, 56, 74, 75, 76, 112, 121
state, 17, 63, 194, 204
storage, 8, 17, 22, 25, 30, 58, 66, 67
subscribers, 56, 218, 224, 227

T

target, 42, 54, 89, 93, 101, 106, 107, 112, 182, 183, 189
Task Force, 7, 62, 72, 73
techniques, 7, 21, 201
technology, 2, 3, 5, 6, 7, 9, 10, 11, 12, 29, 30, 31, 32, 33, 59, 60, 62, 65, 66, 74, 75, 76, 190, 198, 211, 212, 213, 214, 215, 217, 227, 232
testing, 15, 41, 88, 209
theft, 222, 229, 235
threats, 7, 13, 18, 19, 20, 21, 22, 23, 24, 25, 26, 27, 55, 62, 72, 73, 195, 220, 221
transactions, 70, 194, 196, 200, 217, 223, 235
transport, 20, 48, 220

U

United States (USA), 63, 194, 204, 211

V

validation, vii, 20, 55, 57, 65, 194, 197, 199, 202, 203, 206, 208, 209, 212, 213, 217, 222

Verizon, 31, 32, 37, 50, 54, 113, 114, 115

vulnerability, 18, 25, 26

W

web, 9, 26, 29, 30, 37, 40, 77, 87, 89, 103, 112, 113, 118, 233

web service, 37, 40, 113, 118

websites, 2, 4, 6

workflow, 34, 41, 42, 47, 48, 49, 54, 93, 106, 109, 118, 189